WORLD'S GREATEST CITIES

A FAMILY REFERENCE GUIDE
WORLD'S GREATEST CITIES
A JOURNEY THROUGH THE MOST FASCINATING CITIES AROUND THE WORLD

Bath · New York · Singapore · Hong Kong · Cologne · Delhi
Melbourne · Amsterdam · Johannesburg · Shenzhen

Based on an idea by Joan Ricart
Editorial coordination Marta de la Serna
Design Clara Miralles
Editing Alberto Hernández
Copy (supplied by) Ricard Regàs
Graphic editing Alberto Hernández
Layout Paola Fornasaro, Clara Miralles
Copy Editor Stuart Franklin
Infographics Sol90Images

CONTENTS

Introduction

For thousands of years, cities built by humans have reflected their beliefs, their power, their needs and their desires. Palaces and prisons, churches and mosques, skyscrapers and suspension bridges are the tracks which history, sometimes glorious, often violent, imprints on these cities. But these cities are also the men and women who inhabit them and who stamp a unique character onto each of them. The spirit of each city resides in the centennial stones which surprise us with their beauty, but it is also etched in the daily coming and going of the streets, the hustle and bustle of the markets and in the unhurried discussions of the café. Of all the cities in the world today, there are however, only a few that leave a strong impression on those who visit them. These are the ones which have a rich architectural heritage or a spectacular natural environment. But above all, they have a vitality which makes them unique. They are cities which know how to grow, transform and reinvent themselves without losing their essence.

SAN FRANCISCO

The spirit of California

Located in northern California, bordering the Pacific Ocean, San Francisco is one of the most historic cities in the United States.

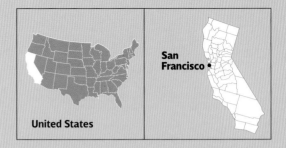

United States

San Francisco

ST. MARY'S CATHEDRAL

ROYAL PRESIDIO

PALACE OF THE LEGION OF HONOR

Lincoln Park

Situated at the extreme northeast of the San Francisco Peninsula, this park is dedicated to President Lincoln, who abolished slavery in 1862. It also houses the Legion of Honor Palace—today an art museum with a golf course (created in 1907). It marks the end of the Lincoln Highway which opened in 1913 and was the first road to cross the United States from east to west.

🌐 KEY FACTS ABOUT SAN FRANCISCO

LIVING ON THE FAULT
San Francisco was founded on the San Andreas Fault which caused the earthquake of 1906 and is also responsible for other significant temblors in the region.

LOCATION
Latitude 37° 46' 45" N
Longitude 122° 25' 9" W
Altitude 52.49 ft (16 m) above sea level

IN FIGURES
Surface area 46.72 mi² (121 km²)
Population 805,000
Population density 17,230/mi² (6,652/km²)
FOUNDATION
Foundation date 1776

Founders
Spanish army and Spanish Franciscan Mission.
Military and religious colony
San Francisco's origin stems from the double Spanish colonization of Alta California during the second half of the 18th century. The army first installed itself in a strategic location on the edge of the peninsula and a few months later, in collaboration with the indigenous Yelamu tribe, they built the Mission San Francisco de Asís, otherwise known as the Mission Dolores.

Extended area

SAN FRANCISCO

N

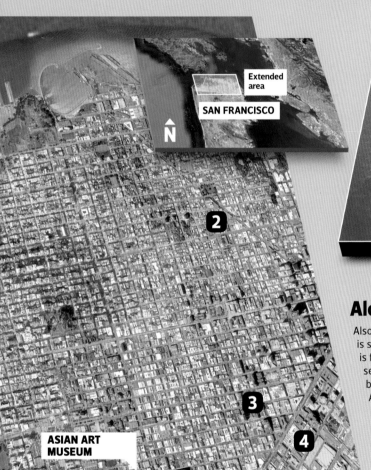

2

3

4

ASIAN ART MUSEUM

Alcatraz Island

Also known as The Rock, this island is situated in San Francisco Bay. It is famous for housing the high-security federal prison, in operation between 1934 and 1963, in which Al Capone was held and from which it is said that no prisoner could escape. The island is also home to the oldest lighthouse on the West Coast and has been open to visitors as a national park since 1972.

1
Golden Gate Bridge
This suspension bridge, built between 1933 and 1937, links the peninsula with the north coast of California over a 0.81-mi (1.3-km) strait. The bridge received its name from its similarity to the Golden Gate of Istanbul (Turkey).

2
Chinatown
San Francisco has the oldest and one of the most populated Chinatowns in North America. Created in 1840 thanks to the first large Asian immigration, today it is an influential tourist attraction.

3
Union Square
This square and the surrounding area, filled with boutiques, hotels and theaters is one of the most elegant commercial zones in the world. The first underground parking lot in the world was built underneath the square in 1939.

4
SF MOMA
The Modern Art Museum opened in 1935 as the first art gallery dedicated exclusively to 20th-century art. In 1995 it was moved to its current headquarters under the guidance of Swiss architect Mario Botta.

An air of freedom

Enterprising and modern, San Francisco retains the nonconformist and liberal nature that has characterized the city throughout its history.

"If you're going to San Francisco, be sure to wear some flowers in your hair". The ingenuity of the Scott McKenzie song, the anthem for the Summer of Love of 1967, contrasts with the hallucinogenic excursions of local idols Grateful Dead, Jefferson Airplane and Santana who played at the legendary Fillmore Auditorium, considered the Mecca for psychedelic music and the counterculture of the sixties. These are two faces of a movement which gathered force in the central district of Haight–Ashbury and which are a sample of the unorthodox vocation of San Francisco, the capital of social liberalism in the United States of America. A half century later, Haight–Ashbury still retains elements of the Bohemian lifestyle of that period, but today is focused on tourism, viewed as a new El Dorado for a young city which has lived through more in its two centuries of history than many cities do in two millennia.

From village to city

It is the fourth most populated city in California and the twelfth in the United States. The City grew up around El Presidio Real and the San Francisco de Asís Mission, founded by the Spanish in 1776. In 1821, it passed into the hands of Mexico and, following the Mexican–American war of 1846, it returned to the United States. Two years later the Gold Rush exploded. This phenomenon changed the face of the village forever. The discovery of gold in the areas surrounding the city caused a massive influx of fortune hunters from around the world. In barely a year, San Francisco grew from a population of 1,000 to 25,000 inhabitants. The development of the railroad in 1869 opened up the city to east coast trade and signaled the arrival of tens of thousands of Asian immigrants who settled in Chinatown. At the end of the 19th century, the city was one of the most dynamic capitals in America; its Nob Hill shows, hotels and mansions acquired worldwide

fame, while press magnate William Randolph Hearst operated the American political strings from the *San Francisco Examiner* and other daily newspapers.

Not even the great earthquake of 1906 halted that epoch of splendor. The shift in the San Andreas Fault, which crosses the city, caused more than 3,000 deaths. With 500 blocks in ruins, around 300,000 people were left homeless. However, the reconstruction was so spectacular that in 1915, barely nine years later, San Francisco successfully hosted the International Exposition, and during the thirties it was one of the few financial centers to resist the Great Depression. This economic security paved the way for the opening in 1936 and 1937 of the two bridges over the bay which had previously made communications difficult. During the same period, the famous prison was established on Alcatraz Island.

After World War II, the city accentuated its liberal profile with the arrival of several representatives from the Beat Generation, attracted by the activity of the bookshop City Lights, in the North Beach district. In 1956, the owner of the bookshop, the poet Lawrence Ferlinghetti, was charged with obscenity after publishing, *Howl and Other Poems* by Allen Ginsberg, one of the pillars of a generation of writers who rejected traditional North

←**Alamo Square**
The Victorian houses of this neighborhood contrast with the skyscrapers and the Transamerica Pyramid constructed on the San Andreas Fault.

↓**The sea lions at Pier 39**
This wharf is one of the main tourist and business areas made famous by the sea lions that come here to rest.

↓↓**Haight-Ashbury**
The psychedelic aesthetics of the seventies mark the personality of this legendary district.

American values. The distance separating these two ideologies of the world increased with the emergence of the hippie movement in the sixties. The liberal nature of the city led to an increase in the gay community and a few years later, activist Harvey Milk initiated the fight for homosexual rights, and became the first openly gay candidate to be elected for public office. However, at the end of 1978 he was assassinated by a political rival. Since then, his camera shop in Castro Street has become a center for gay pilgrimage.

In 1989, the city suffered another earthquake which necessitated the demolition of various highway viaducts leading into the heart of the city. This led to the restoration of the east side, including two of San Francisco's main tourist attractions; the area around Fisherman's Wharf and the popular Pier 39. This period also saw the rise of the ".com" companies, many of which were based in Silicon Valley, to the south of the Bay. The city experienced a profound demographic change with the departure of much of the white population from the historic center, which was substituted by Latin American and Asian immigrants. None of this has affected the magic of this young and nonconformist city which still tolerates the persistent spring fog and the steep slopes of its streets from the 50 or so hills that dot the peninsula.

Golden Gate Bridge

At 1.7 miles (2,737 m) long– 0.8 mile (1,280 m) suspended– and some 220 ft (67 m) high, the Golden Gate Bridge was a landmark feat of engineering when it was completed in 1937.

Bridge deck The road measures 89 ft (27 m) wide and has six lanes over which around 100,000 vehicles pass every day, as well as the pedestrian and cycle lane traffic.

Main cables Two steel cables, each weighing 24.25 million lb (11,000 tonnes) and made from 27,000 galvanized steel fibers, support the deck and distribute a weight of 34.8 million lb (56 million kilograms) over each tower.

Land anchorage Almost a third of the total length of the bridge is firmly anchored into the ground.

Towers Two steel towers extend 754 ft (230 m) above the sea and support the entire structure.

Secondary cables Support the deck from the main cables.

Foundations and concrete The tower anchorages are made of concrete and are set 85 ft (26 m) into the ground.

Proportions For 27 years the Golden Gate Bridge was the largest suspension bridge in the world. This type of structure allows very light bridges of enormous proportions to be constructed. The distance from the top of the towers to the road measures 497 ft (152 m).

NEW YORK

Manhattan

Situated between the Hudson River and the East River, the island of Manhattan is the original nucleus of New York and houses some of its most famous buildings.

United States

New York

Manhattan

Central Park

In the middle of the 19th century, local authorities saw that the rapid urbanization of Manhattan compromised its habitability as there were no green areas. An area of 2.49 mi (4 km) by 0.5 mi (800 m) in the center of the island was reserved and lakes and green areas were created as part of the 1857 project.

The Big Apple

The high population density is an indication of the daily activity in this central district, which is characterized by skyscrapers, wide avenues forming its street grid system and traffic based almost exclusively on public transportation.

NEW YORK

Extended area

EAST RIVER

MANHATTAN

N

DOWNTOWN

South Street Seaport

The historic heart of the port of New York, this area was renovated for tourism and is home to the city's restored early 19th century commercial buildings.

Brooklyn Bridge

Opened in 1883, Brooklyn Bridge spans the East River and connects Manhattan and Brooklyn. It was the largest suspension bridge of its time and the first to be constructed from steel.

The Civic Center

Situated around the New York City Hall, the Civic Center area is bordered by the Financial District and houses several official buildings such as the Police Department and the Manhattan Municipal Building, a beautiful 40 story skyscraper based on the Beaux-Arts design principals and opened in 1914.

1

Times Square

The most famous and central square of Manhattan is found on the corner of Broadway and Seventh Avenue. It owes its name to the offices of the New York Times newspaper.

⊕ KEY FACTS ABOUT NEW YORK

THE LARGEST CITY IN THE UNITED STATES OF AMERICA
Despite not actually being the capital of its own state (which is actually Albany and has been since 1797), New York is the largest city in America.

LOCATION
Latitude 40° 43' 0" N
Longitude 74° 0' 0" W
Altitude
33 ft (10 m) above sea level

IN FIGURES
Surface area 469 mi² (1,214 km²)
Population 8,215,000 (22 million in the metropolitan area)
Population density 17,526/mi² (6,767/km²)

FOUNDATION
Foundation date
1624
From Amsterdam to York
Manhattan Island was already inhabited by the Algonquin indigenous population before the arrival of Europeans. Dutch immigrants who arrived at the island at the beginning of the 17th century founded a colony and called it New Amsterdam. In 1664, the English conquered the settlement and renamed it New York.

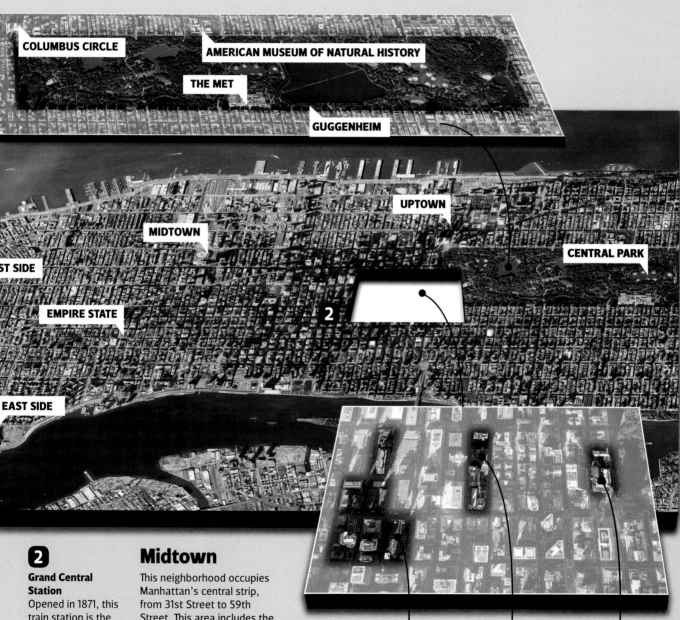

COLUMBUS CIRCLE

AMERICAN MUSEUM OF NATURAL HISTORY

THE MET

GUGGENHEIM

UPTOWN

MIDTOWN

CENTRAL PARK

EST SIDE

EMPIRE STATE

2

EAST SIDE

2

Midtown

Grand Central Station
Opened in 1871, this train station is the largest in the world in terms of the number of tracks and platforms. Its main hall houses a clock with four faces which is the emblem for the station.

This neighborhood occupies Manhattan's central strip, from 31st Street to 59th Street. This area includes the majority of the most famous skyscrapers of the city such as the Empire State Building and the Chrysler Building as well as Times Square, St. Patrick's Cathedral, Grand Central Station and the Rockefeller Center.

St. Patrick's Cathedral
Constructed in neo-Gothic style between 1858 and 1865, St. Patrick's Cathedral is the primary Catholic center of the city.

MOMA
The Museum of Modern Art is home to one of the main art collections in the world and includes works from Picasso, van Gough, and Matisse.

Hotel Plaza
Located across from Central Park, this famous luxury hotel occupies a 1907 neo-Renaissance building.

The city of skyscrapers

A symbol of the power of capitalism, New York grew at an astonishing rate during the 19th and 20th centuries to become the capital of the Western world.

From Harlem to Little Italy; from Broadway to Wall Street and Fifth Avenue; from the Empire State Building to the Statue of Liberty; from Madison Square Garden to yellow taxis... Who hasn't heard of these icons? No other city in the world has such universally known iconic places. New York is not the capital of the United States, nor is it the capital of its own state. However, no one doubts that it is the capital of the Western world and a model of all that is good–dynamism, vitality, initiative, wealth–and all that is bad–consumerism, inequality, excess–which takes the models of liberalism and capitalism to the extreme.

Unlike the vast majority of large cities, all the power this city has amassed stems not from the political or military authority of its governors, but from its economic strength. Although founded in 1624 by Dutch settlers on Manhattan and conquered 40 years later by the English, New York was the capital of the United States for just five years between 1785 and 1790. Since then, it has done nothing but grow thanks to the feverish commercial activity concentrated in its extraordinary natural port on the Hudson River estuary and a noble and enterprising immigration policy. This is evident even today, reflected in the millions of workaholics who run through its streets gesticulating, cell phone to their ear, trying to find ten minutes out of their day to eat a bagel in a small park across from their office.

Hometown to tycoons of the past such as John Jacob Astor, Andrew Carnegie and John Rockefeller, and of the present, such as Donald Trump and Michael Bloomberg, the Big Apple today generates a GDP that, if it were an independent state, would place it among the top 15 economies in the world. This privileged position

📷
←Toward the skies
Manhattan grew upward, accumulating a large number of skyscrapers that today are emblematic of New York.

↙Central Park
This great green space of Manhattan is a favorite place for recreation and relaxation for New Yorkers.

↓Ground Zero
This memorial to the victims of 9/11 occupies the place where the World Trade Center, destroyed by a terrorist attack in 2001, once stood.

is due in large part to its vigorous demographic growth. In barely 50 years, between 1800 and 1850, the city's population multiplied tenfold, from 70,000 to 700,000 and from 1850 to 1950 again to almost eight million in the center alone. Today it is the most populated city of the United States with 22 million residents in an area which covers the five municipal districts of Manhattan, the Bronx, Brooklyn, Queens and Staten Island, in addition to the various neighboring populations of Long Island and New Jersey.

Land of dreams

Ever since its foundation, New York has been a city of immigrants, and its people saw the arrival of new generations from all corners of the world seeking the American dream as a natural occurrence. In 1811, local authorities were obliged to plan the urbanization of Manhattan by means of the famous grid system comprising 16 large avenues from north to south, named with ordinal numbers and 155 streets running east to west named also with ordinal numbers. Throughout the 19th century, millions of Irish and Germans began to inhabit these new districts, followed in 1890 by the Italians and Eastern Europeans who flooded Ellis Island, a small island in the Bay set up as a customs office to control immigration. During the first decades of the 20th century, New York also became one of the principal destinations for what was called the Great Migration. This was the displacement of hundreds of thousands of African-Americans from the former slavery states of the south to the industrialized areas of the east as well as hundreds of thousands of Puerto Ricans who took advantage of their new status as American citizens from 1917.

This migratory phenomenon transformed the Big Apple into a model of diversity and a society with an independent dynamism little related to the rest of the United States both in material and ideological terms. Currently, six out of every ten residents have descendants from multiple countries from all corners of Europe, with 16 percent having African-American roots, 15 percent Hispanic and the remainder mainly Asian.

→ **The Statue of Liberty**
Since its opening in 1886 it has remained the single most iconic image of New York.

1. Ellis Island
This small island where immigrants disembarked on arrival at New York houses the History of Immigration Museum which tells the story of those who came to the land of opportunity in search of a new life.

2. New York taxis
The classic yellow taxis circulating around Seventh Avenue. The city has more than 13,000 of them.

3. Broadway
This Manhattan street is famous for the musical extravaganzas in its theaters.

4. Fifth Avenue
This is one of the most exclusive areas in the world, filled with luxury apartments, mansions and expensive stores.

This constant shift generated an incessant need for space which quickly overflowed Manhattan's capacity and caused a gradual rise in the price of land which obliged builders to build upward.

Growing up...

In just a few decades, and despite the Great Depression, Manhattan was raised to new heights. The skyscrapers became the principal symbol of the city's identity. These enormous structures adorned with art in the style of the admired European aesthetic fashions, represented huge engineering challenges; the Woolworth building (1913) was created in a neo-Gothic style in the manner of the great Medieval cathedrals; the Chrysler building (1930), with its silvery crown and spectacular lobby became a paradigm of Art Deco. In 1931, the Empire State Building became the tallest building on the planet, a title it held for more than 40 years. It became a universal icon thanks to the gorilla King Kong in the 1933 film. It served as one example of cultural ideas exported by New York to the rest of the world, based on originality, professionalism, and popularization. It was expressed in forms as distinct as Broadway musicals, the films of Woody Allen, the literature of Truman Capote, Tom Wolfe and Paul Auster, the music of Gershwin, Charlie Parker, Pete Seeger and Lou Reed, and the art of Andy Warhol and Roy Lichtenstein, interpreted or exhibited in contemporary cultural venues such as the Lincoln Center, Carnegie Hall, the MOMA and the Metropolitan Museum.

The Empire State Building

Standing 1,250 ft (381 m) high and with 102 floors, it was the tallest building in the world from its construction in 1931 until 1973.

Mast and antenna The antenna— 203 ft (62 m)— was conceived as a mooring mast for airships. Now it is used for TV transmissions.

86th floor observatory Located at 1,050 ft (320 m) high, the observatory is a glass-enclosed area where visitors are treated to spectacular views of the city.

The marathon Each year a race to the top of the building, which has 1,860 steps, is held. The Empire State Building has 73 elevators, eight of which are high-speed (they take 45 seconds to get to the 80th floor).

Foundations The building is supported on a base of almost 2.5 acres (1 ha), which reaches to the fourth floor. From there it is staggered.

Entrance It has five entrances which open onto Fifth Avenue, the main street, 33rd Street and 34th Street.

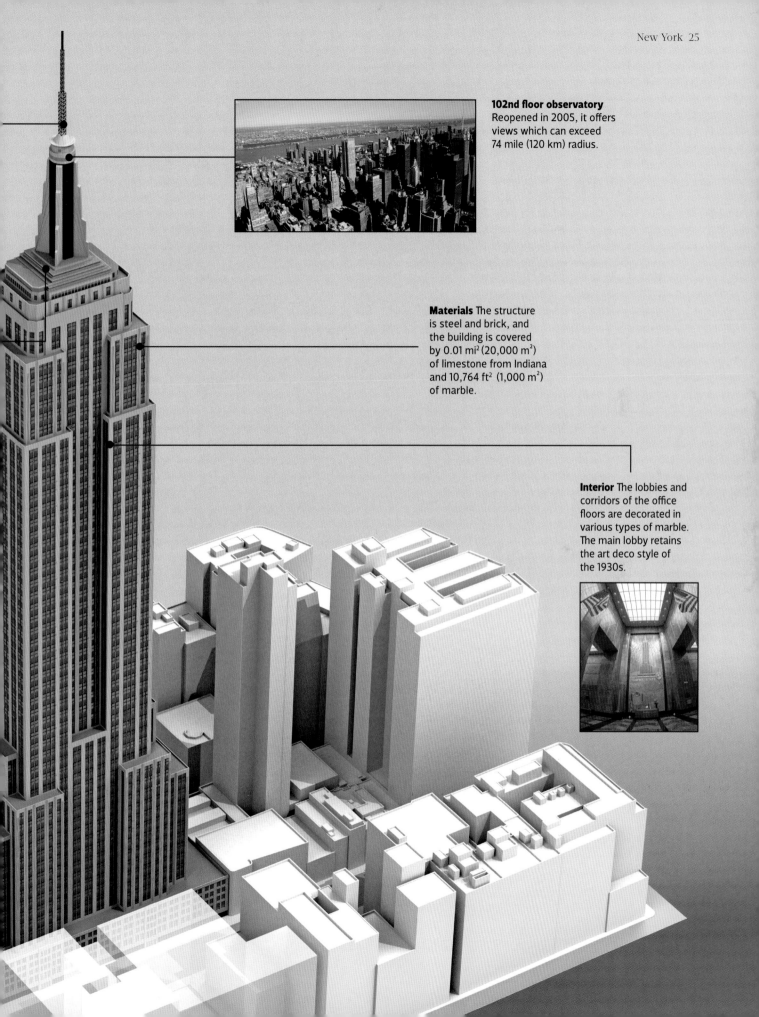

102nd floor observatory
Reopened in 2005, it offers
views which can exceed
74 mile (120 km) radius.

Materials The structure
is steel and brick, and
the building is covered
by 0.01 mi^2 (20,000 m^2)
of limestone from Indiana
and 10,764 ft^2 (1,000 m^2)
of marble.

Interior The lobbies and
corridors of the office
floors are decorated in
various types of marble.
The main lobby retains
the art deco style of
the 1930s.

TORONTO

The driving force of Canada

Although the capital of Canada is Ottawa, Toronto is the largest city and the economic and financial hub of the country.

Canada

Toronto

Vast immigration

The high living standards and the low crime rate are two of the factors which have made Toronto one of the most cosmopolitan cities in the world. Almost half of its residents were born outside of Canada.

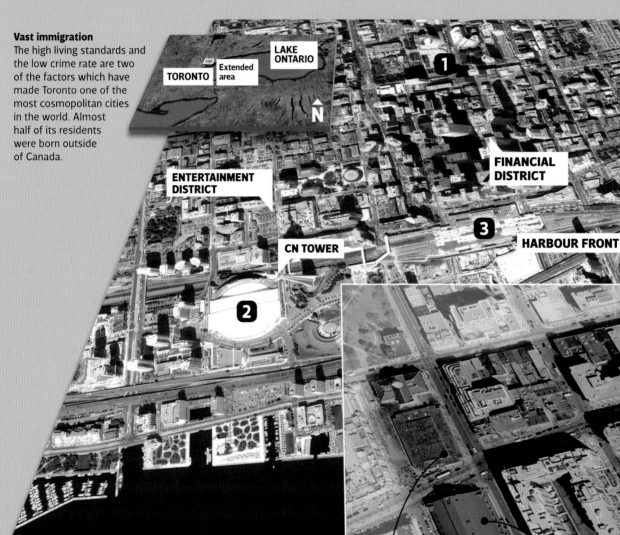

LAKE ONTARIO

TORONTO | Extended area

N

ENTERTAINMENT DISTRICT

FINANCIAL DISTRICT

CN TOWER

HARBOUR FRONT

1

2

3

Old Toronto

The old town is the most densely populated area of Toronto and occupies downtown and the center of the city. At one end of this neighborhood is the Financial District with the largest concentration of skyscrapers in Canada, several elite residential areas such as The Annex, Rosedale, Lytton Park and Yorkville, suburbs for working–class families and immigrants such as Little Italy, Chinatown, Little India, Portugal Village and the Greek community, and neighbourhoods such as Kensington Market, Riverdale and Cabbagetown, today inhabited by artists and liberal professionals.

North market On Saturdays this venue hosts the farmers' market and on Sundays the antique market.

South market Occupies a building constructed in 1845 and houses restaurants, an exhibition center and delicatessens.

KEY FACTS ABOUT TORONTO

CAPITAL OF ONTARIO
Toronto is the capital of the province of Ontario and the largest city of the Golden Horseshoe, the arc which forms the banks of Lake Ontario.

LOCATION
Latitude 43° 40' 0" N
Longitude 79° 25' 0" W
Altitude 249 ft (76 m) above sea level
IN FIGURES
Surface area 243 mi^2 (630 km^2)

Population
2,504,000
Population density
10,294/mi^2 (3,975/km^2)
FOUNDATION
Foundation date
March 6, 1834

First Mayor
William L. Mackenzie
From York to Toronto
In 1793, the settlement of York, chosen for its easily defendable position, was founded on the northern shore of Lake Ontario. On March 6, 1834 York was incorporated into the city of Toronto, ("meeting place" in native), which at this point had grown into a military fort and harbor on the lake reaching a population of 9,000 inhabitants, not including the African-American people who had escaped as slaves.

Fort York

Integral to the origins of Canada, Fort York is a collection of fortifications built at the end of the 18th century by Canadian militia and the British Navy to defend the region from attacks by the Army of the recently constituted United States. The majority of these buildings were destroyed in the Battle of York (1813) which concluded with a convincing victory by the American forces.

1

Nathan Phillips Square
This square, dominated by the old town hall known as Old City Hall, was built between 1889 and 1899. In 1965 the square was remodeled to house the new town hall—Toronto City Hall—culminating in two skyscrapers in the shape of a pair of parentheses.

2

Rogers Center
With a capacity for 50,000 spectators, this stadium hosts numerous sporting events, concerts and conventions. It was built in 1989, originally called SkyDome, and it was the first building in the world to have a retractable roof.

Union Station
The largest railroad and subway station in Toronto was created by Canadians Ross and Macdonald Beaux-Arts style. It was built between 1914 and 1920 and is 754 ft (230 m) long.

Saint Lawrence Market
Considered by the National Geographic Society to be the best food market in the world.

Land of plenty

With first rate economic activity and a peaceful quality of life, Toronto stands out due to its enormous cultural diversity.

Because of the harshness of the Canadian winter, the majority of the country's most populated cities are found in the south, close to the border with the United States, where the Arctic winds are not so strong. The most southern of these capitals is Toronto, the great city of Lake Ontario. Until the European conquest, the territory was inhabited by the indigenous tribes of the Huron and the Iroquois who were few in number and lived a life of hunting, gathering and a primitive form of agriculture. French explorers, the first Europeans who dared to enter from the northern shores of the Great Lakes, arrived in the middle of the 18th century. A few decades later, a large group of British settlers who lost the US War of Independence took refuge in the area and founded the town of York, building a military fort and using the harbor as a naval base. This British settlement sowed the first seeds of Toronto, a word with indigenous origins meaning "meeting place."

During the following two centuries, up to the present day, the city took this name very seriously as it welcomed arrivals from all continents, from the Irish who emigrated because of the Great Famine of 1846, to the waves of Italians, Greeks and Portuguese who arrived to contribute to the great territorial expansion of the city after World War II. Today, in addition to being the capital of Canadian Anglophone culture, Toronto is an authentic focus of multiculturalism with half of its inhabitants born outside of Canada and a third speaking a language other than English at home.

However, this diversity doesn't prevent the city from having its own distinct personality. It has one that remains closely related to the development of Canada as a society with a lifestyle which lies halfway between that of North America and that of Europe. Torontonians boast about the low crime rate in the streets compared with that of cities on the other side of the border and brag about their calm quality of life while enjoying a magnificent natural environment. In the last half century, the city has also experienced a radical change from the dominant puritanism of the 1950s to the social liberalism which prevails today.

Financial force of Canada

Toronto is also the headquarters of the first Canadian stock exchange, the second in North America after New York, and has, since the 1970s, displaced French-speaking Montreal as the largest economic and financial center of the country thanks to, among other things, a vigorous automobile industry, the discovery in Ontario of raw material deposits and the opening in 1959 of the San Lorenzo Canal, which enabled merchant ships to sail from the Great Lakes to the Atlantic.

The economic strength has given rise to a dynamic downtown filled with contrasts, from the skyscrapers of the financial district, dominated by the needle of the 1,814 ft (553 m) high CN Tower to the upper-class residential districts of Rosedale, Cabbagetown, Wychwood Park, The Annex and Casa Loma, situated more inland, have tranquil streets filled with houses conserved in their original Victorian and Edwardian styles.

The nerve center of the city is, however, Nathan Phillips Square, located alongside the financial district and site of the impressive modern City Hall. Two blocks away is the Eaton Centre, the largest shopping

center in the city and its biggest tourist attraction. Most of the shopping centers, distributed throughout the various districts of the city, are underground, which ensures a comfortable temperature even on the coldest winter days.

Working-class area

Further away from the lake are the working class districts, with anonymous appartment blocks which in the last few years have been occupied by the latest wave of immigration. While on the waterfront, next to the city harbor, is the unique Distillery District which houses the finest examples of Victorian-era industrial architecture throughout the entire American continent. In their fondness for an outdoor lifestyle, Torontonians highly value the city promenade, ideal for escaping on foot or on bicycle, as well as enjoying its well-maintained city beaches, despite Lake Ontario freezing several months of the year and the contamination of its waters—as a result of the intense shipping—which are fast becoming a significant problem in the region.

↖ **Toronto's emblem**
From 1975 to 2010, the CN Tower held the honor of being the tallest building in the world with its 1,815.39 ft (553.33 m) offering enviable views.

↑↑ **Gooderham Building**
Built in 1892, this strange wedge shaped building is one of the city's main attractions in the financial district.

↑ **Eaton Centre**
It is the main shopping center of Toronto with more than 230 shops, restaurants and services. In fact it is one of the places most visited by tourists.

CN Tower

Opened in 1976, this telecommunications tower boasts spectacular observation platforms, restored areas and attractions which draw two million visitors each year.

Main observation floor Located at 1,122 ft (342 m), it has a glass floor capable of supporting the weight of 14 adult hippopotami. It also has an open air External Observation Platform.

Rogers Center The CN Tower is situated next to this multi-sports stadium which incorporates a hotel with rooms looking out over the playing field.

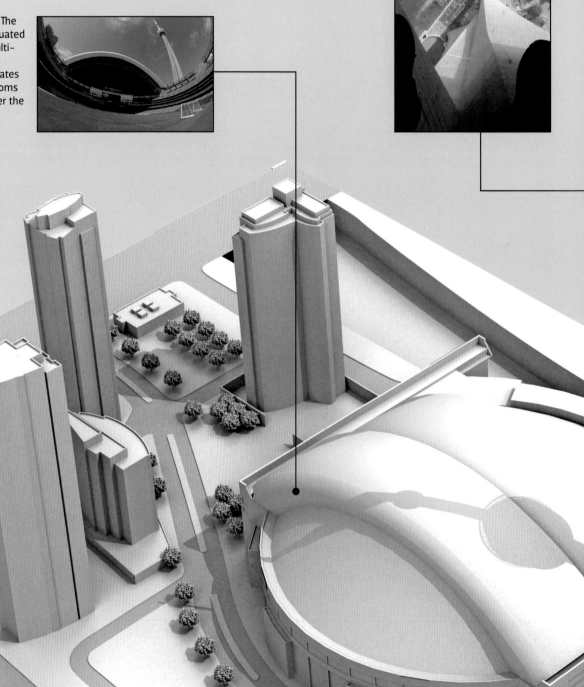

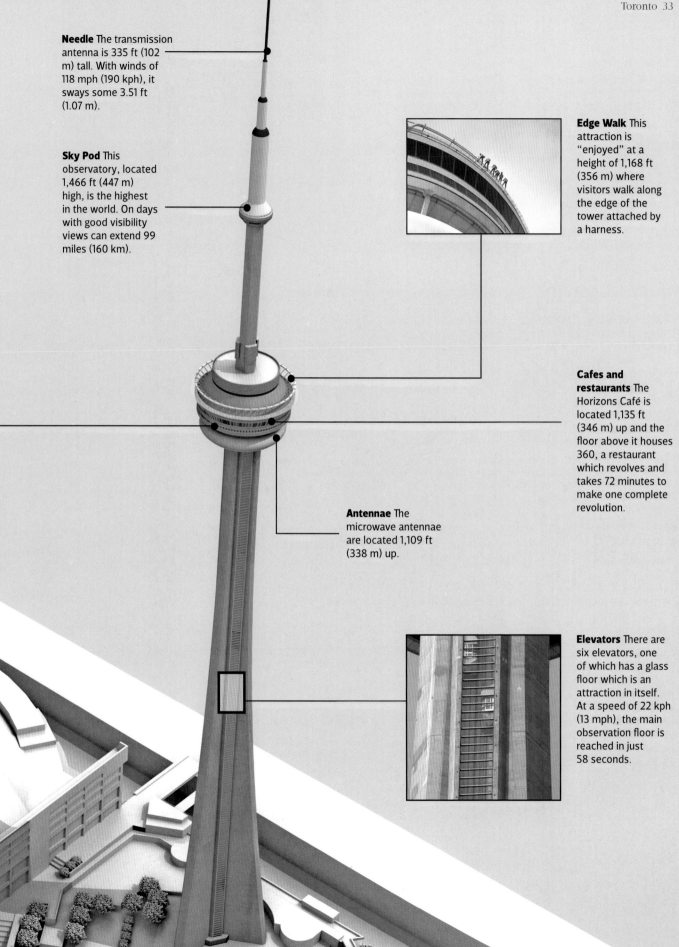

Needle The transmission antenna is 335 ft (102 m) tall. With winds of 118 mph (190 kph), it sways some 3.51 ft (1.07 m).

Sky Pod This observatory, located 1,466 ft (447 m) high, is the highest in the world. On days with good visibility views can extend 99 miles (160 km).

Edge Walk This attraction is "enjoyed" at a height of 1,168 ft (356 m) where visitors walk along the edge of the tower attached by a harness.

Cafes and restaurants The Horizons Café is located 1,135 ft (346 m) up and the floor above it houses 360, a restaurant which revolves and takes 72 minutes to make one complete revolution.

Antennae The microwave antennae are located 1,109 ft (338 m) up.

Elevators There are six elevators, one of which has a glass floor which is an attraction in itself. At a speed of 22 kph (13 mph), the main observation floor is reached in just 58 seconds.

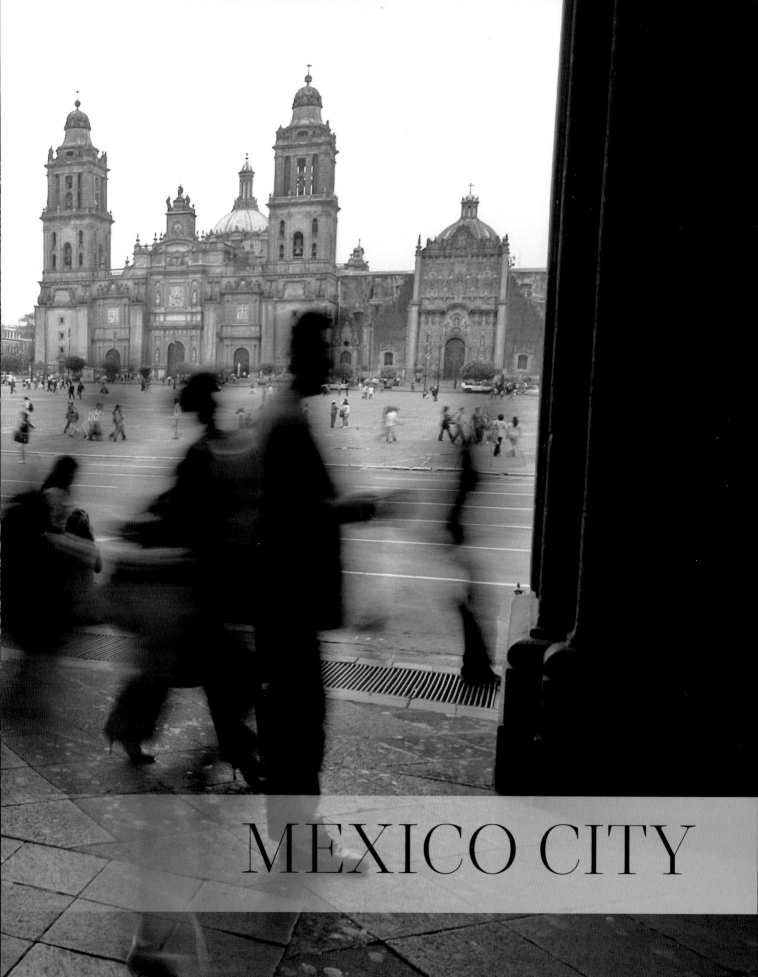

MEXICO CITY

The great Latin American city

Located on a high plateau over 6,562 ft (2,000 m) above sea level, Mexico City is one of the most influential cities in Latin America.

Mexico City

Mexico

Mythological origins

Mexico City was established around the old Tenochtitlán settlement. Founded on marshland, the area grew to house 500,000 residents at the height of the Aztec Empire. According to mythology, Huitzilopochtli, the Aztec god of war, ordered that a kingdom be established "where the eagle was devouring a snake." This vision was seen on the shores of Lake Texcoco, on a high plateau to the north of Tehuantepec Isthmus.

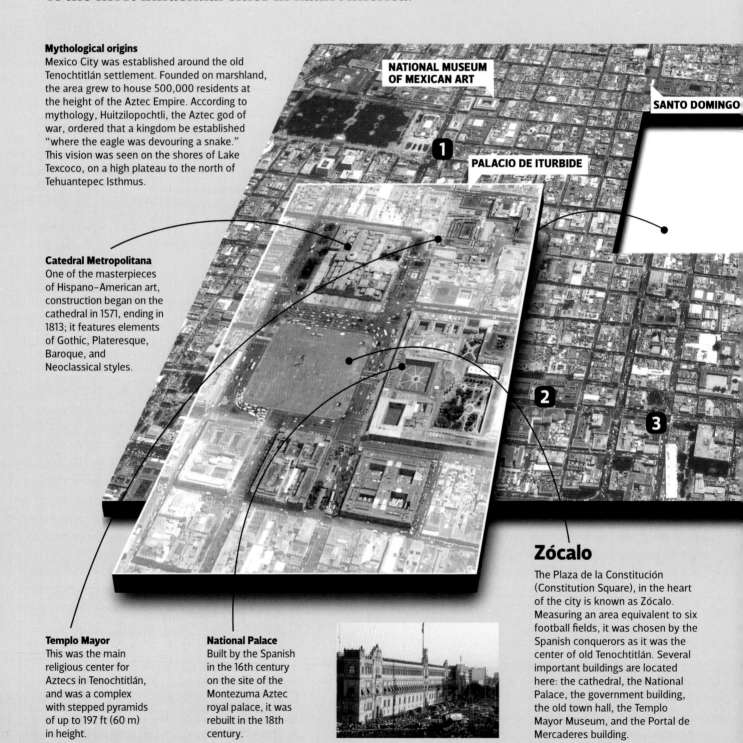

NATIONAL MUSEUM OF MEXICAN ART

SANTO DOMINGO

PALACIO DE ITURBIDE

Catedral Metropolitana

One of the masterpieces of Hispano–American art, construction began on the cathedral in 1571, ending in 1813; it features elements of Gothic, Plateresque, Baroque, and Neoclassical styles.

Templo Mayor

This was the main religious center for Aztecs in Tenochtitlán, and was a complex with stepped pyramids of up to 197 ft (60 m) in height.

National Palace

Built by the Spanish in the 16th century on the site of the Montezuma Aztec royal palace, it was rebuilt in the 18th century.

Zócalo

The Plaza de la Constitución (Constitution Square), in the heart of the city is known as Zócalo. Measuring an area equivalent to six football fields, it was chosen by the Spanish conquerors as it was the center of old Tenochtitlán. Several important buildings are located here: the cathedral, the National Palace, the government building, the old town hall, the Templo Mayor Museum, and the Portal de Mercaderes building.

🌐 KEY FACTS ABOUT MEXICO CITY

CAPITAL CITY
Mexico City occupies the Federal District, which is home to the federal capital and all branches of the Mexican federal government.

LOCATION
Latitude 19° 29' 52" N
Longitude 99° 07' 37" W
Altitude 7,349 ft (2,240 m) above sea level
IN FIGURES
Surface area
573 mi² (1,485 km²)

Population 8,860,000
Population density
15,453/mi²
(5,966/km²)
FOUNDATION
Foundation date
July 18, 1325
(according to legend)

Founders
Mexicas or Aztecs
Legend and reality
Several Mexica documents state 1325 as the date on which Tenochtitlán, where Mexico City now stands, was founded. According to these sources, a group of Nahua tribes from Aztlán founded the settlement on the shores of Lake Texcoco; however, archaeological excavations have suggested that the area was inhabited prior to the 14th century.

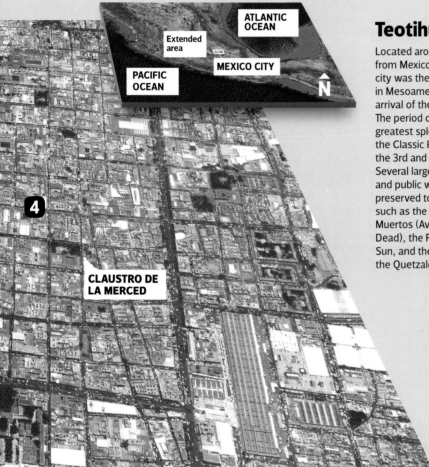

ATLANTIC OCEAN
Extended area
MEXICO CITY
PACIFIC OCEAN
N

4

CLAUSTRO DE LA MERCED

Teotihuacán

Located around 28 miles (45 km) from Mexico City, this ancient city was the largest urban center in Mesoamerica before the arrival of the Spanish forces. The period of the region's greatest splendor was during the Classic Period, between the 3rd and 7th centuries. Several large-scale buildings and public works have been preserved to this day, such as the Calzada de los Muertos (Avenue of the Dead), the Pyramids of the Sun, and the Moon and the Quetzalcóatl Temple.

1
Casa de los Azulejos
This palace was built in the 16th century and has a facade decorated with ceramic tiles from the state of Puebla. This baroque style appearance can be attributed to the refurbishment ordered by the fifth Countess of Orizaba in the 18th century.

2
Claustro de Sor Juana
Sister Juana Inés de la Cruz, a Mexican nun and writer, wrote the majority of her works here. Today, the cloister houses the university and San Jerónimo Convent, built in the 16th century and reformed in the 20th century.

3
Avenida Pino Suárez
The famous meeting between Hernán Cortés and Montezuma took place on the corner of this avenue with Calle la República del Salvador on November 8, 1519. The Spaniard's remains were found in the nearby Church of Jesus of Nazareth.

4
Academia San Carlos
Founded in 1781 under the influence of European enlightenment, this academy houses a large range of Mexican works dating from the 18th century to today. The current building benefits from reformation work in the 19th century.

Aztec and Colonial capital

Mexico City preserves evidence of its Aztec past and a rich architectural heritage which it inherited from the Colonial period.

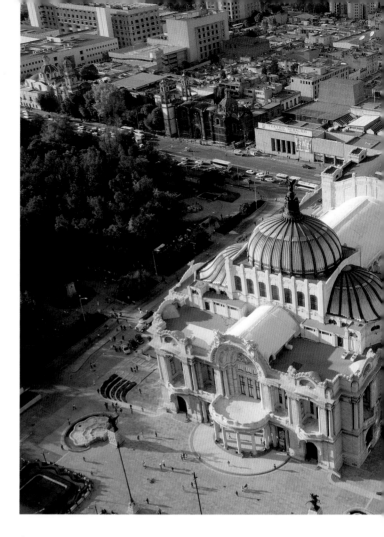

Uninformed travelers could visit the Mexican capital without realising what really defined the city until just a few hundred years ago: its foundation on an island surrounded by the waters of Lake Texcoco by the Aztecs at the start of the 14th century. This gave its founders the opportunity for growth without worrying about the enclave's security; today, stripped of its protective waters, it occupies the historic center of the city. Tenochtitlán, as the Aztec settlement was called, grew to become the capital of a vast empire in the 15th century. It controlled a territory with a larger area than Great Britain, with architecture and a level of social organisation that still surprises archaeologists to this day.

This was how the first European settlers found the Aztec populated region at the beginning of the 16th century. Deceived by the cunning diplomatic tactics of the Spanish and decimated by the smallpox brought to the New World by the Spanish Conquistadores, the Aztecs eventually surrendered and their vast territory became the Viceroyalty of New Spain. The capital of this new order was founded on the same island, that today is the heart of this great Mexican metropolis. Thus, the long Colonial period began, in which Mexico City was one of the largest strategic centers throughout the American continent.

Today, Constitution Square, the 12 acre (5 ha) esplanade known as the Zócalo, occupies the heart of the former island; however, the ancient waters have long since disappeared. Up to six significant floods devastated the city between the 16th and 18th centuries; this led the Colonial authorities to design ambitious plans to drain the lake. However, the definitive push to complete this task came after independence: the *Gran Canal de Desagüe* (Great Drainage Channel) was built between 1885 and 1900, resolving the flooding problems and changing the face of the city forever.

Demographic and urban boom

The drainage of the lake allowed the city to grow onto a previously submerged area; this territorial expansion that took just over a century and made the area the largest metropolitan area on the American continent, with 27 million residents, and second, behind Tokyo, worldwide. The period known as the "Mexican Miracle," during the 1950s and 1960s, was especially productive in this respect. In just 20 years, the capital's population doubled, absorbing numerous neighboring towns as it grew until it reached the geographical limits of the Federal District itself, founded in 1837. This concept was created as a political entity to house the seat of federal government after the country's emancipation from Spain.

The urban boom in the mid-20th century had a serious impact on the social, economic, and ecological balance of Mexico City. Today, there are significant differences between districts. Whereas the Benito Juarez delegation in the center of the city has a Human Development Index (HDI) comparable with the United States average,

the HDI of Milpa Alta, to the south of the city, is similar to the average of the Dominican Republic, which occupies 70th place on the global standard of living ranking. As a result, the area experiences problems with poverty, crime, and drug addiction. Furthermore, the erroneous urban planning of such neighborhoods brought overcrowding and excessive levels of traffic that, together with industry based in the region, contribute to one of the highest pollution levels on the planet.

Logically, the effects of development have not all been negative. Thanks to its demographic strength, its extensive history and its proximity to the United States, Mexico City contributes a third of the country's GDP and is the largest cultural and financial center in Latin America. It has a rich architectural and museum heritage that covers the majority of artistic styles originating in both Europe and the Americas: Gothic, Plateresque, baroque and Neoclassic styles imported by the Spanish (the Catedral Metropolitana is the best example from the Colonial period); this heritage includes Aztec ruins such as Templo Mayor, in Zócalo, the better-preserved ruins at Teotihuacan, just 28 miles (45 km) from the city; and the colonial style, art deco and art nouveau buildings that can be found throughout this lively and contrasting city.

1. Palace of Fine Arts
An aerial view of one of the most famous buildings in the historic center of the city.

2. Volkswagen Beetle
For years most taxi drivers have used this model, making it one of the city's main icons.

3. Muralism
This artistic movement started in Mexico at the start of the 20th century. This one at Ciudad Universitaria is by Siqueiros.

4. Basilica of Our Lady of Guadalupe
This is one of the best examples of Mexican baroque architecture and one of the most visited Catholic temples in the world.

5. Post Office Palace
The ornate steps of this architectural marvel that combines Gothic, Arabic, baroque and art deco styles.

6. Aztec ruins
Statue of Chac Mool in the Aztec ruins at Templo Mayor located in Zócalo.

Catedral Metropolitana

Construction on this monumental building in the baroque style began in 1573 under the initiative of Hernán Cortés and was completed in 1813.

The organ This dates back to 1735, measuring 46 ft (14 m) high, 33 ft (10 m) wide and 10 ft (3 m) deep. Positioned 20 ft (6 m) from the ground, it is six storeys high.

Altar del Perdón (Altar of Pardon) Located in the *trascoro* (behind the choir) across from the main entrance, this churrigueresque work was created by Jerónimo de Balbás.

The dome The work of Manuel Tolsá, the dome possesses an octagonal drum base, is positioned above the center of the cross and is topped by a small lantern.

The chapels There are fourteen chapels in total, seven on each side, created by brotherhoods, guilds or individuals to worship saints or the Virgin Mary.

Altar de los Reyes (Altar of the Kings) Created by Jerónimo de Balbás, this altar represents the peak of churrigueresque style. The focal painting is *La Adoración de los Reyes* (Adoration of the Kings) and the tabernacle was created by Juan Rodríguez Juárez. The altarpiece measures 82 ft (25 m) high and 43 ft (13 m) wide.

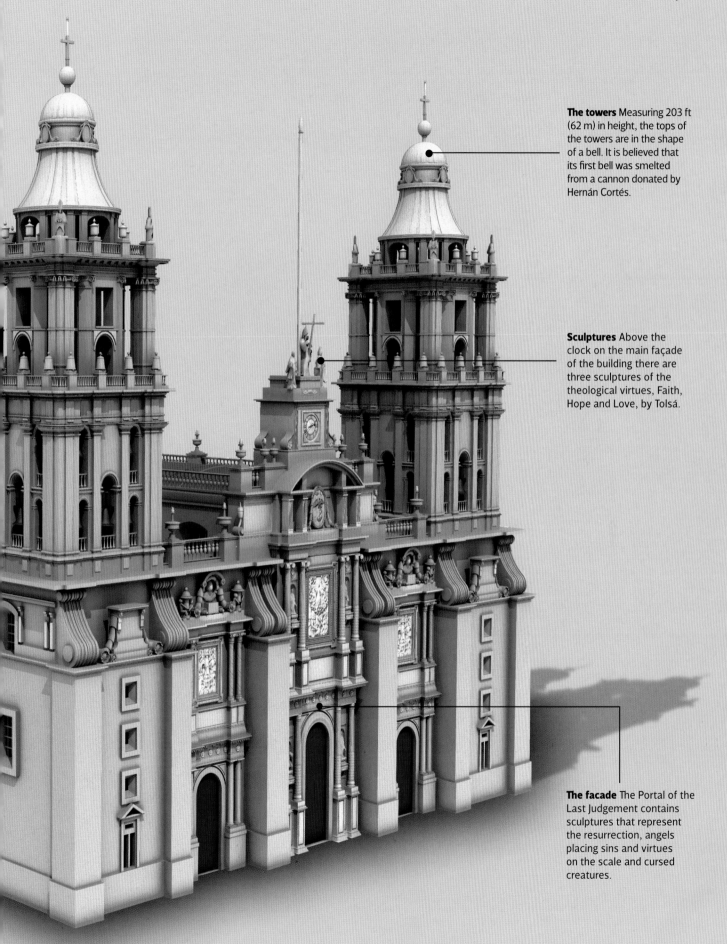

The towers Measuring 203 ft (62 m) in height, the tops of the towers are in the shape of a bell. It is believed that its first bell was smelted from a cannon donated by Hernán Cortés.

Sculptures Above the clock on the main façade of the building there are three sculptures of the theological virtues, Faith, Hope and Love, by Tolsá.

The facade The Portal of the Last Judgement contains sculptures that represent the resurrection, angels placing sins and virtues on the scale and cursed creatures.

BUENOS AIRES

The historic center

Plaza de Mayo, in the Montserrat neighborhood, is the historic center around which many of the city's main buildings are located.

Buenos
Aires

Argentina

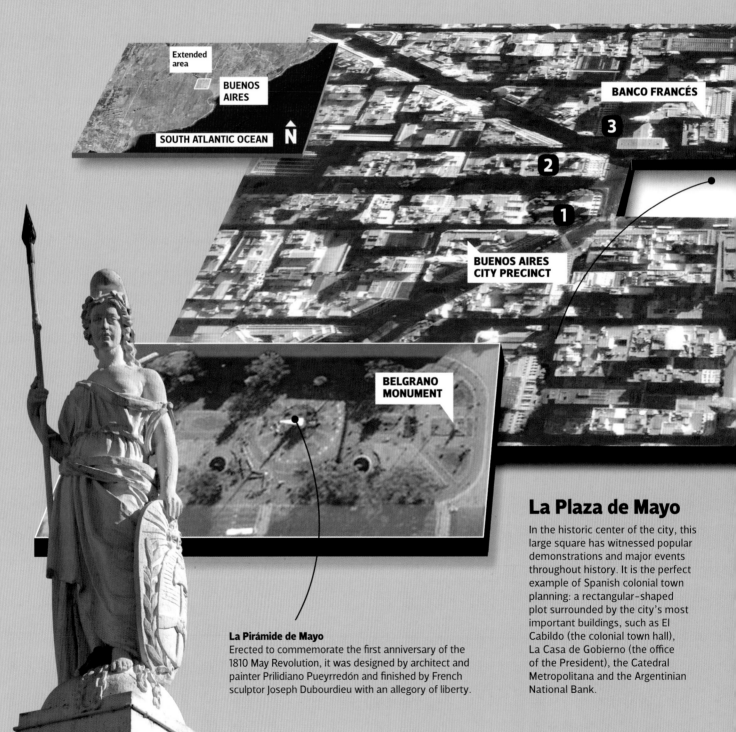

Extended
area

**BUENOS
AIRES**

SOUTH ATLANTIC OCEAN N

BANCO FRANCÉS

3

2

1

**BUENOS AIRES
CITY PRECINCT**

**BELGRANO
MONUMENT**

La Pirámide de Mayo
Erected to commemorate the first anniversary of the
1810 May Revolution, it was designed by architect and
painter Prilidiano Pueyrredón and finished by French
sculptor Joseph Dubourdieu with an allegory of liberty.

La Plaza de Mayo

In the historic center of the city, this
large square has witnessed popular
demonstrations and major events
throughout history. It is the perfect
example of Spanish colonial town
planning: a rectangular-shaped
plot surrounded by the city's most
important buildings, such as El
Cabildo (the colonial town hall),
La Casa de Gobierno (the office
of the President), the Catedral
Metropolitana and the Argentinian
National Bank.

⊕ KEY FACTS ABOUT BUENOS AIRES

FEDERAL CAPITAL ARGENTINA
Home to the federal government and state administrations, Buenos Aires is an autonomous city with a special status among Argentinian provinces.

LOCATION
Latitude 34° 36 '30" S
Longitude 58° 22' 19" W
Average altitude 82 ft (25 m) above sea level

IN FIGURES
Surface area 192 mi² (498 km²)
Population 2,900,000 (12.9 million—metropolitan area)
Population density 15,104/mi² (5,823/km²)

FOUNDATION
Foundation date February 3, 1536
Founder
The Spaniard, Pedro de Mendoza, founded the first settlement in the region in 1536.

It consisted of 250 square blocks, on the shores of Río de la Plata and was centered around the place where La Plaza de Mayo currently stands. Five years later, Mendoza abandoned the site having been besieged by indigenous peoples. Juan de Garay definitively re-established the city in 1580.

La Casa Rosada
It was built on land occupied by the Spanish Colonial military fort from 1594. The original Casa Rosada was built in the 19th century to house government offices from 1862.

GARAY MONUMENT

4

FORMER CONGRESS

1

El Cabildo
Restored several times since the 17th century, El Cabildo has occupied this location, as designated by Juan de Garay, since 1580. Spanish Colonial authorities lived on its top floor, whereas the ground floor was a dedicated prison and police station.

2

La Casa de Gobierno
Located on the opposite side of the square to La Casa Rosada, next to El Cabildo, this building was the creation of Italian architect Juan Cagnoni. It was built at the end of the 19th century in a French academic art style.

3

Catedral Metropolitana
Consecrated to the Holy Trinity, construction on the current temple, which lasted 150 years, began in the mid-18th century; various styles, from the original Baroque styling to neo-Romanesque styling, are visible throughout.

4

Argentinian National Bank
Founded in 1891 to overcome the financial crisis of the period, the Argentinian National Bank constructed this neoclassical-style building in the mid-20th century, designed by a follower of Nazi architect Albert Speer.

Latin spirit

Deeply Latin, Buenos Aires is a city full of contrasts, with a rich heritage and range of cultural activities to offer.

Vocal, arrogant, cultured, seductive, passionate, with a tendency for melancholy, psychoanalysis and, most of all, soccer... Few collective groups are more stereotyped than those from Buenos Aires. With every "porteño" (Buenos Aires local) you know—and everyone knows at least one given the migratory spirit imprinted in their genes—these characteristics become more apparent, even becoming a caricature that has little to do with the common idiosyncrasy of the actual founders of Buenos Aires.

Be that as it may, it cannot be denied that those born in the Argentinian capital have a very strong personality, meaning that they nearly always have an opinion to offer. Given their alleged vanity, Buenos Aires natives are not well-liked by the rest of Latin America and even by other Argentinians. Such is the disdain felt by Uruguayans, who share the same accent as their southern neighbors, that they often clarify their place of birth before speaking to foreigners.

And so why do so many Buenos Aires natives fulfill these stereotypes, when citizens of the Argentinian capital are the result of one of the most cosmopolitan integration processes on earth? Primarily comprised of descendants of Spanish and Italian immigrants, with important German, Central European, Russian, Ukrainian, Syrian and Lebanese (often dubbed Turkish) influxes, and with a large Jewish community, the population of Buenos Aires has melded homogenous and original character traits.

The gastronomy, packed with protein, is influenced by Italian flavors and the country's livestock heritage. The language, a dialect of Spanish that can be quickly identified by any Spanish speaker, always seems to be reinforced with exaggerated gesticulation that would appear to have been imported directly from Naples. A penchant for music, dance, animated conversations in doorways, simplistic hedonism, wiliness, family... Buenos Aires has ended up becoming the purest amalgamation of all things Latin on the shores of Río de la Plata.

European footprint

The Argentinian capital has always, justifiably, boasted being the most European of all great Latin American cities. As opposed to the majority of other cities on the continent, Buenos Aires always looked to Paris rather than New York for influence. Its architecture, brimming with impressive examples of art nouveau, art deco, neo-Gothic or neoclassic historicism, can clearly be seen in the perfect checkerboard style that the locals call *damero*, inherited from the original Spanish Colonial town planning in the Americas. This widely used method of town planning has not restricted the high level of diversity among the 47 neighborhoods that make up the federal capital, home to 40 percent of Argentinians. It is the fifth largest metropolitan area in the Americas and one of the widest spanning on earth, having grown north, east and south, throughout the Pampas (plains), without being hindered by any obstacle capable of slowing down its incredible development.

The period of splendor that the Argentinian capital experienced at the end of the 19th and start of the 20th centuries, during which a large part of the Italian and Spanish immigration took place that would influence the city's demographics forever, seemed to elevate Buenos Aires to the position of capital of the southern

hemisphere. However, the dynamism of its port, and thus its trade, supported by the immense agricultural and geological wealth of Argentina, collapsed after just a few decades.

The city with two faces

Today, Buenos Aires is a city full of contrasts that suffers from high levels of pollution (the Riachuelo River that bathes the popular neighborhood of Boca also serves as a garbage dump), high crime rates and traffic that can cause pedestrians nightmares. On the other hand this unique city enjoys a privileged climate, an enviable network of public parks, a lively urban atmosphere and a first-class cultural activity programme (headed by figures such as Jorge Luis Borges and Julio Cortázar, and institutions such as the Colón theater, one of the most renowned opera venues worldwide). Furthermore, it can proudly claim to have given the world two of its greatest ever soccer players: Alfredo Di Stéfano and Diego Maradona.

↖Casa Rosada
Views of the indoor courtyard, seat of the executive branch of the Argentinian government, across from La Plaza de Mayo.

↑La Boca
Colorful houses are the distinguishing feature of this popular neighborhood.

↖Puerto Madero
The skyscrapers on the shores of the river really make the city's most exclusive area stand out.

←Plaza Dorrego
Located at the heart of San Telmo, on Sundays it is filled with musicians, street vendors and tango dancers.

Colón Theater

Inaugurated in 1908, Buenos Aires' opera theater is considered one of the best in the world thanks to its excellent acoustics.

The curtain In 2011, the old curtain dating back to 1831 was replaced with a new one designed by plastic artist Guillermo Kuitca, which took 18 months to complete.

Facade The facade's 407,780 ft² (37,884 m²) combine three architectural styles. A slim gabled roof rises above the theater's terraces.

Interior The decor reflects the tastes of the bourgeoisie at the time, and in keeping with European style consists of: marble, golden capitals, crystal chandeliers, etc.

La Fuente de los Bailarines Opposite the Colón Theater, in Plaza Lavalle, this small monument is dedicated to the nine ballerinas of the Colón Ballet that died in an aircraft accident in 1971.

The stage Measures 157 ft (48 m) high and 115 ft (35 m) wide and deep. The scenery and background are changed using sophisticated technology.

The dome At 92 ft (28 m) high and with a surface area of 3,444 ft² (320 m²) the dome was decorated free-of-charge in 1966 by Argentinian painter Raúl Soldi.

Entrances There are four entrances. In the 19th century, there was an entrance for carriages, as was the case for many opera houses at the time.

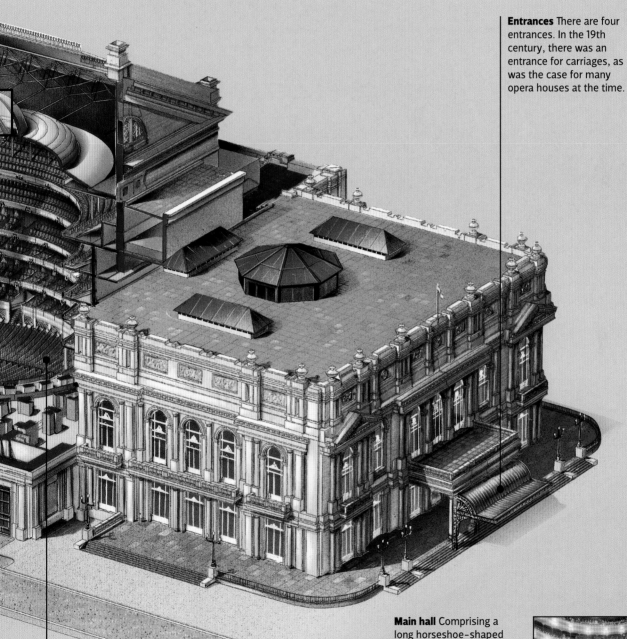

Main hall Comprising a long horseshoe-shaped curve, inside which the 22 rows of stalls seating are located. In total, the theater holds a capacity of 2,487 people seated, with a further 700 standing.

RIO DE JANEIRO

In the shelter of the bay

Located on the shores of Guanabara bay, the original heart of Rio de Janeiro has many buildings from the Portuguese Colonial period.

Brazil

Rio de Janeiro

Guanabara Bay

On 1 January, 1502, during an exploration voyage along the central coast of South America, Portuguese sailors entered a bay that made an ideal harbor, offering shelter from ocean storms. Believing it to be the mouth of a river, they named the area "Rio de Janeiro" (River of January). More than half a century later, the Portuguese soldier Estácio de Sá founded a settlement there, which is the origin of the city of today.

Enlarged area

RIO DE JANEIRO

ATLANTIC OCEAN

N

CATEDRAL DE SÃO SEBASTIÃO

La Candelária Church
The church was originally a hermitage, built in the 17th century. The Baroque facade dates from 1775. The rest of the building, including the white dome, was built in the 19th century.

Municipal theater
It was built in the early 20th century in an eclectic style, inspired by the Palais Garnier in París. It has a surface area of 45,424 ft² (4,220 m²) and a capacity of 2,400 people. Its golden age was in the 1920s.

National library
Located on the avenue of Rio Branco, this Neoclassical building, a work of Brazilian engineer and politician Francisco Marcelino de Souza Aguiar, was inaugurated in 1910. It houses nine million valuable volumes.

Arcos da Lapa
This 18th century aqueduct is one of the emblems of Colonial Rio. It was built to carry water from the river Carioca, the main source of fresh water for the Portuguese settlement. There remain 42 semicircular arches, 886 ft (270 m) long and 210 ft (64 m) high.

⊕ KEY FACTS ABOUT RIO DE JANEIRO

THE FORMER CAPITAL OF BRAZIL Rio de Janeiro was the capital of the country until 1960, when the Brazilian government moved to Brasilia, a new city built in the interior. Today it is the capital of the State of Rio de Janeiro, one of Brazil's 26 states.

LOCATION
Latitude 22° 54' 0" S
Longitude 43° 13' 59" W

Altitude 36 ft (11 m) above sea level
IN FIGURES
Surface area 456 mi² (1,182 km²)
Population 6,320,000 (11.8 million in the metropolitan area)

Population density 13,860/mi² (5,265/km²)
FOUNDATION
Foundation date March 1, 1565
Founder Estácio de Sá

Military origins The Portuguese soldier Estácio de Sá founded São Sebastião de Río de Janeiro as a naval base to attack a nearby French settlement and take control of the region. This objective was achieved in 1567.

Praça Quinze de Novembro

The heart of the old town of Rio, this square owes its name to the day in 1889 when Marshal Manuel Deodoro da Fonseca took office as the first provisional president of Brazil after the proclamation of the Republic. Many buildings from the Colonial period stand nearby. Further to the south, in the same area, Praça Floriano, named after the second president of the republic, Floriano Peixoto, although better known as Cinelandia, is the largest open public area in the center of Rio.

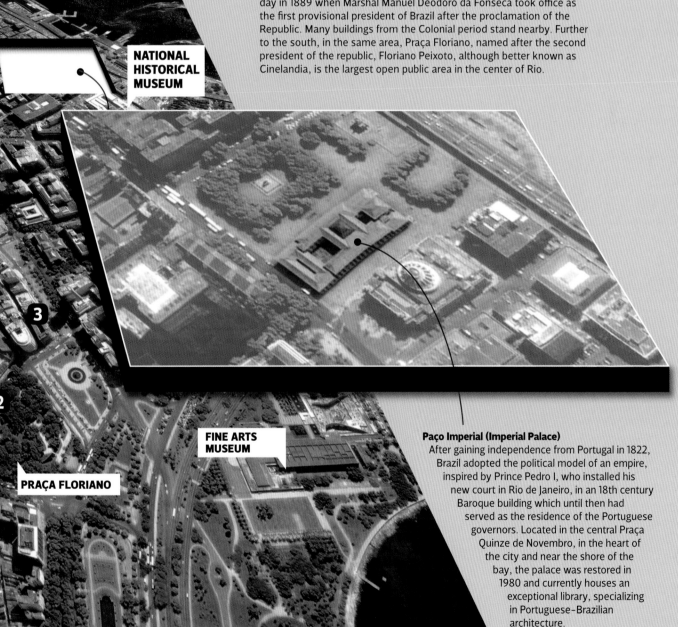

NATIONAL HISTORICAL MUSEUM

3

2

FINE ARTS MUSEUM

PRAÇA FLORIANO

Paço Imperial (Imperial Palace)
After gaining independence from Portugal in 1822, Brazil adopted the political model of an empire, inspired by Prince Pedro I, who installed his new court in Rio de Janeiro, in an 18th century Baroque building which until then had served as the residence of the Portuguese governors. Located in the central Praça Quinze de Novembro, in the heart of the city and near the shore of the bay, the palace was restored in 1980 and currently houses an exceptional library, specializing in Portuguese-Brazilian architecture.

To the rhythm of the samba

Rio de Janeiro occupies one of the grandest natural settings a city could dream of.

You can enjoy cities by wandering through their streets, getting to know their people, trying the cuisine, visiting the museums, palaces, churches and unique buildings... But a very select group of cities add something very special to these pleasures: they are cities, such as Naples or Cape Town, that are surrounded by hills, beaches, bays, islands, inlets... marvelous surroundings that must have captivated their original founders. From this exclusive list, one city stands out from the others: Rio de Janeiro.

Located between the Atlantic Ocean and Guanabara Bay, Rio uses the smallest nooks of the remarkable terrain of its setting to flourish on the slopes of its famous hills of rock, which are sometimes naked and sometimes covered in greenery. The slopes of some of these hills offer one of the most majestic spectacles of fusion between nature and civilization that can be admired on planet Earth. The landscape from Corcovado Mountain, from which rises the famous 98-ft (30-m) statue of Christ the Redeemer, is particularly suggestive. The views to the lagoon – surrounded by one of the most exclusive quarters of the city – the beaches of Ipanema, Copacabana, Botafogo and Flamengo, and the perfect natural dome of Sugarloaf Mountain, combine to make an image of Rio that has become as universal as those place names that have been imprinted in the collective memory of half the world as a paradigm of the good life in the tropics.

However, this is only the positive side of the story. In spite of the efforts and achievements of Luiz Inácio Lula da Silva and his successor, Dilma Rousseff, in their fight against poverty, the differences between social classes continue to mark the daily life of Rio and the whole of Brazil, almost as if the Indian caste system was in force. The comfortable middle classes live in the so-called

Zona Sur, or Southern Zone, in the districts closest to the ocean beaches. The working classes tend to populate the Zona Norte (Northern Zone), on the shores of Guanabara Bay and in the interior, where most of the region's industries are also concentrated. These generate high levels of pollution throughout the entire city, but especially in the Zona Norte. Finally, the "favelas" – the marginal shanty town districts – occupy the lower slopes of the hills, all along the city's upper limit. Half of Rio's population is of European origin. Portuguese roots predominate, as this was the former global power that gave Brazil its official language and its Catholic religion, although there are also German, Italian and Russian elements. The other half is Afro-American.

The beaches, the center of the social life
The 37 urban beaches are one of the few points of contact – along with soccer stadiums – where residents from all social strata come together, sharing the experience with tourists eager for the hot tropical climate sweetened by the breeze from the ocean. All the great passions of the "Cariocas" (as people from Rio are called) are catered for: sun, fresh air, the cult of the body, sports – especially soccer and volleyball – music and dance.

← **Sugarloaf Mountain**
The Sugarloaf Mountain is a granite hump 1,300 ft (396 m) high standing at the shore of the ocean. A visit offers one of the best views of the city.

↓ **Sambódromo**
The carnival parade in the Sambódromo da Marquês de Sapucái is the great fiesta of the year for Rio de Janeiro.

↓↓ **Lapa**
This central district with its bohemian atmosphere concentrates a good part of the cultural life of the city, as well as the nightlife.

Rio gave birth to two of the best-known musical styles of the 20th century: samba and bossa nova. With African roots, Samba was born in the favelas at the beginning of the 20th century. In 1917, the style transcended the slum districts following the success of the recording of the tune "Pelo telefone" by local composer Donga. With the passage of time, it was transformed into a phenomenon that cut across social classes and became a national symbol of Brazil. In 1984, the great Brazilian architect Oscar Niemeyer designed the Sambódromo in the Centro district, where the massive parades of the carnival take place.

Bossa Nova also originated in Rio, although in a more recent period—the late 1950s—and with a more elitist public. It was principally the fruit of the imagination of musicians Antonio Carlos Jobim, Joao Gilberto and Vinícius de Moraes, as a more sophisticated version of the samba. It reached global fame with the tune "The Girl From Ipanema", inspired by the atmosphere of the popular beach, and whose words transmit a characteristic mix of peacefulness, desire and melancholy. "...Ah... Why am I so lonely? Ah... Why is everything so sad now? Ah... The beauty that exists here... A beauty that is not only for me, that also passes by me..."

Christ the Redeemer

Inaugurated in 1931, this 125-ft (38-m) high statue was built to commemorate the centennial of Brazil's independence. Today it is one of the country's main tourist attractions.

The arms These weigh 30 tons (27 tonnes) each. The statue, designed by the Brazilian engineer Heitor da Silva Costa and made by French sculptor Paul Landowski, has a total weight of 1,262 tons (1,145 tonnes).

Corcovado Hill Christ the Redeemer is at the summit of Corcovado Hill, which is 2,326 ft (709 m) high. It stands on a base just 49 ft (15 m) wide, which made its construction a real challenge.

The pedestal This is 26 ft (8 m) high and has a chapel dedicated to Our Lady of Aparecida inside, with a capacity for 23 people, where weddings and baptisms are held.

LEDs The access path has 300 lights, operated by remote control, that highlight the statue.

The lookout Christ the Redeemer gets 1.8 million visitors a year, who enjoy one of the most magnificent panoramic views of the city of Rio and the Sugarloaf Mountain.

Head Slightly inclined downward, it is made up of 50 pieces. The figure of Christ is looking east, toward Jerusalem and Guanabara Bay.

The heart Situated on the 11th floor, on the outside of the statue, the heart measures 4.27 ft (1.3 m), which is proportionally rather small compared with the human body.

The outside The outside is covered by mosaics made from soapstone from Minas Gerais state.

The structure It is made of reinforced concrete and has 12 floors inside.

Access Escalators and three panoramic elevators were installed in 2002. Access on foot is by a stairway of 220 steps.

LONDON

The city on the Thames

The planet's biggest city from the mid–19th century up until 1925, London today is one of the most important financial centers in the world.

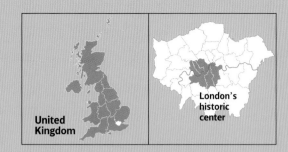

United Kingdom

London's historic center

Following the river

The course of the Thames marks the geography of London, several of whose principal places of interest are located on its banks, such as Parliament, the London Eye, the Tate Modern, and the Tower of London and its celebrated bridge.

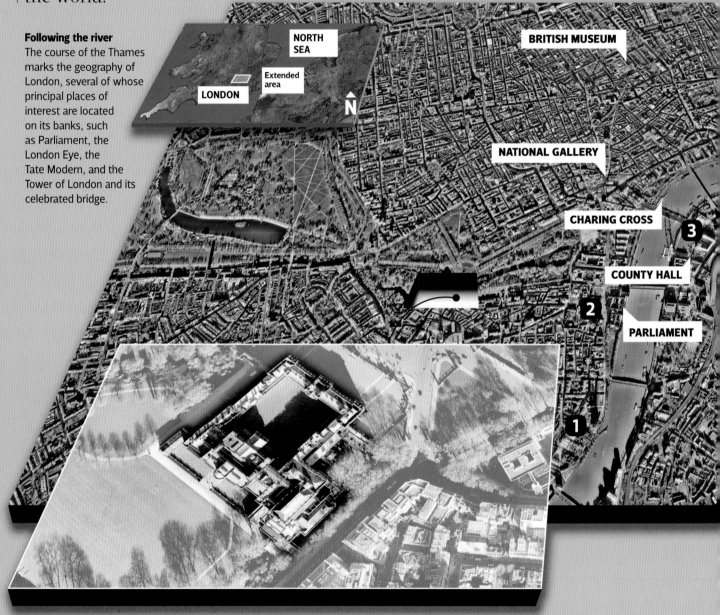

NORTH SEA

Extended area

LONDON

N

BRITISH MUSEUM

NATIONAL GALLERY

CHARING CROSS

3

COUNTY HALL

2

PARLIAMENT

1

Buckingham Palace

Official residence of the English monarch, it is located between Green Park and St. James' Park and was built in 1703 as a mansion for the first Duke of Buckingham. Sixty years later, having been acquired by King George III, it became royal property, and was renovated several times in the 19th and early 20th centuries, when the principal facade was made more extravagant. Every day at 11 o'clock the famous changing of the guard takes place.

⊕ KEY FACTS ABOUT LONDON

33 CITIES IN ONE
London is the sum of the 33 municipalities that make up Greater London, capital of England and of the United Kingdom.

LOCATION
Latitude
51° 30' 25" N
Longitude
00° 07' 39" W
Altitude
79 ft (24 m) above sea level

IN FIGURES
Surface area
659 mi² (1,707 km²)
Population
7,600,000
Population density
11,532/mi²
(4,452/km²)

FOUNDATION
Date
43 BC
Roman origins
Founded as Londinium and fortified by the Romans together with the Thames in what is today the City of London. During the Middle Ages, London saw the flourishing of various populations that in time would grow and begin to fuse together. The development of the Industrial Revolution in the 18th century converted London into the biggest city of the modern age.

St. Paul's Cathedral

In 1666, London suffered a fire that destroyed many of the city's buildings. Ten years later, the great English Renaissance architect Sir Christopher Wren designed the new cathedral, based on Saint Peter's in Rome.

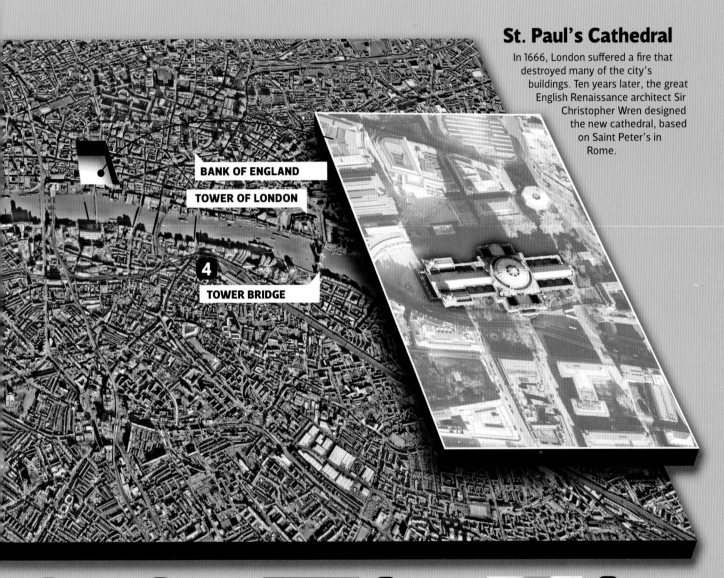

BANK OF ENGLAND
TOWER OF LONDON
4
TOWER BRIDGE

1 Tate Britain
Founded in 1897, this museum houses the collection of British art from the 16th to the 19th centuries, while the modern and contemporary art was transferred to the Tate Modern in 2000.

2 Westminster Abbey
A Gothic style building from the 18th century, the Abbey contains the remains of most of the Monarchs of England, as well as many important personalities from the country's past.

3 London Eye
With a diameter of 443 ft (135 m) and 32 cabins, this enormous Ferris wheel, inaugurated in 1999, turns at 0.6 mi/hr beside the River Thames. It takes half an hour to make one complete rotation.

4 Shard Building
This skyscraper, designed by Renzo Piano, was opened in June 2012. Shaped like a pyramid and coated in glass, it stands 1,017 ft (310 m) high and has 72 floors, housing an observation area at the top.

A world of great contrasts

The imperial past breathes in every corner of the great British capital that joins modernity and tradition in perfect equilibrium.

A short stroll around the corners of Westminster Abbey or the crypt of St. Paul's Cathedral is enough to give you an idea of the enormous importance that London had for humanity as the capital of the British Empire that dominated the world from the end of the 18th century until the first decades of the 20th century. In the city's two main churches lie the tombs or commemorative plaques of writers including Byron, Dickens and Kipling; scientists and inventors such as Newton, Darwin, Fleming, Watt and Stephenson; military and political leaders such as Nelson, Wellington and Churchill; and explorers such as Livingstone and Lawrence of Arabia. It provides a summary of what secondary school students in any corner of the planet might find in their textbooks.

The remains of an imperial past

Founded by the Romans on the banks of the Thames in 43 AD, the recent history of this city, has been etched in stone by the long centuries for which the planet's economy and diplomacy were decided from its palaces. London still breathes its imperial air thanks to an architecture that is perhaps less monumental than that of continental capitals like Paris, Vienna, or St. Petersburg. But it is replete with potent universal symbols like Tower Bridge, built in 1894, the great neo-Gothic complex of the Houses of Parliament, with its celebrated bell-tower, popularly known as Big Ben; the British Museum, housing many works that originated in the former colonies; and the Royal Observatory of Greenwich, a municipality of London from which the calculation of the earth's meridians began in 1884.

← **The Millennium Bridge**
In the background, St. Paul's Cathedral with its famous dome, one of the icons of the city.

↙ **Big Ben**
A classic image: the renowned clocktower veiled in the famous London fog.

↓ **British Museum**
The Queen Elizabeth II Great Court is one of the additions made in 2000.

However, far from resting on its laurels and basking in the eminent position it held at the beginning of the 20th century, London has maintained its classic entrepreneurial spirit. Without renouncing its tradition, the city has reinvented itself several times since then, most recently with the celebration of the Olympic Games in 2012, which served to improve some depressed districts in the eastern part of the capital.

In fact, London is a great city made up of many small towns, each with its own personality: a more or less crowded center with a large residential area around it. The distinguished area of Richmond, for instance, is very different from the alternative climate that we find around Camden Market. But only three subway stations away, in the same district of Camden, we find Hampstead, an area that maintains the peaceful, rural atmosphere of the isolated town it used to be. The most central areas–the City of London and Westminster–contain the best part of the capital's tourist attractions, but their streets and squares don't impress visitors for their grand scale as much as for

their human scale. To experience this sensation all you have to do is stand in the middle of Piccadilly Circus and turn your view to the west to admire the very elegant curve of the beginning of Regent Street, known as The Quadrant and designed at the beginning of the 19th century by the great English architect John Nash. With this curve, he executed a difficult and contradictory mixture of audacity and contentiousness that now stands as a pardigm of Victorian town planning.

The impulse of industrialization

The most indelible mark that the imperial period left in London, however, was without any doubt the Industrial Revolution, one of the principal causes of Britain's enormous power from the 18th century on. Today, fortunately, we can appreciate the extraordinary silhouettes of the electric power stations of Battersea– which starred on the cover of Pink Floyd's album *Animals*–and Bankside–the current home of the Tate Modern, the British contemporary art museum–without their veil of smog, the thick cloud of pollution that

➔Regent Street
An everyday image of Regent Street, one of London's most important commercial areas.

for many decades accompanied the classic images of industrial London. The Great Smog of December 1952, which in a few weeks caused 12,000 deaths in the city, made it necessary to take energetic measures against the severe pollution that then prevailed. This early awareness of ecological issues means that both the local inhabitants and the 15 million tourists a year who visit London can now enjoy the spectacle of its parks, which are the vestigial remains of the woods and country landscapes absorbed by the enormous demographic growth of its boroughs. Hyde Park, Regent's Park and Kensington Gardens keep a healthy place in the center of this enormous city, while other individual green spaces, such as the quiet Holland Park or the majestic Hampstead Heath, remain half-hidden from the general public.

The fact of being the imperial capital and the economic effects of the Industrial Revolution gave London a push forward as far as another phenomenon of the 20th century is concerned: immigration and cosmopolitanism. In the 1960s, the city was already an amalgam of dozens of ethnic and cultural groups, whose customs coexisted with the local traditions in an interaction that created totally original results in fields as different as music or cooking. In fact, this great power of attraction for people from distant lands remains the same. Just one example: almost 400,000 of the 7.5 million inhabitants of Greater London were born in one of the countries of the Indian subcontinent. For this new immigration, the city is still the capital of the Empire, a city that is at the same time old and young, and is still prepared to give an opportunity for the imaginative.

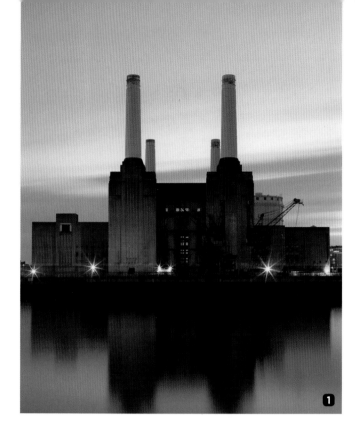

1.Battersea Power Station
A great symbol of London's Industrial Revolution, it has been closed since 1983.

2.Admiral Nelson's Tomb
You can visit this tomb in the magnificent crypt of St. Paul's Cathedral.

3.Liberty
One of the legendary establishments of Regent Street.

4.Camden
This area has a well-known market whose stalls have a very unique style.

5.Hyde Park
This is one of the most peaceful and attractive corners of the city.

6.Holland Park
In addition to the park, this high-class residential district is famous for its beautiful Victorian houses.

Tower Bridge

Built in 1894, this bridge allows vehicles and pedestrians to cross the Thames, while at the same time using an electro-hydraulic system to let shipping pass unhindered.

Original The bridge is an enormous steel structure with masonry cladding and a few details in iron or steel in the upper walkways.

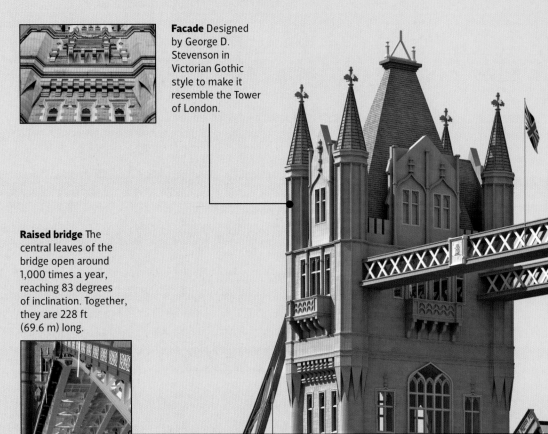

Facade Designed by George D. Stevenson in Victorian Gothic style to make it resemble the Tower of London.

Raised bridge The central leaves of the bridge open around 1,000 times a year, reaching 83 degrees of inclination. Together, they are 228 ft (69.6 m) long.

Upper parallel walkways
Originally these were designed to ensure pedestrian transit even when the central leaves were raised.

Tensors Extremely strong, they provide anchoring on shore and support the landward sections of the bridge.

Pillars The enormous foundations, standing on the bed of the Thames, weigh some 77,000 tons (70,000 tonnes).

BARCELONA

History and the avant-garde

Most of the places of interest in Barcelona can be found between the central districts of the Old Town and the Eixample.

Spain

Barcelona

Palau Reial
Located next to the cathedral, this was the residence of the Kings of the Crown of Aragon and the administrative headquarters of the realm during the Late Middle Ages.

The Cathedral
Work commenced on this cathedral in 1298. It was constructed in Catalan Gothic style characterized by its decorative restraint and solid buttresses.

Barri Gòtic

The original heart of Barcelona, the Gothic Quarter forms part of the Old Town district and contains the main administrative and religious buildings of the city and region. Its center is Plaça de Sant Jaume.

❶ Arc de Triomf
Built by Josep Vilaseca Casanovas in the historic neo-Mudéjar style, it served as the gateway into the showground of the International Exposition of 1888.

❷ La Rambla
This street has served as the center of the city since the 15th century and is the location of the Gran Teatre del Liceu and several bourgeois palaces.

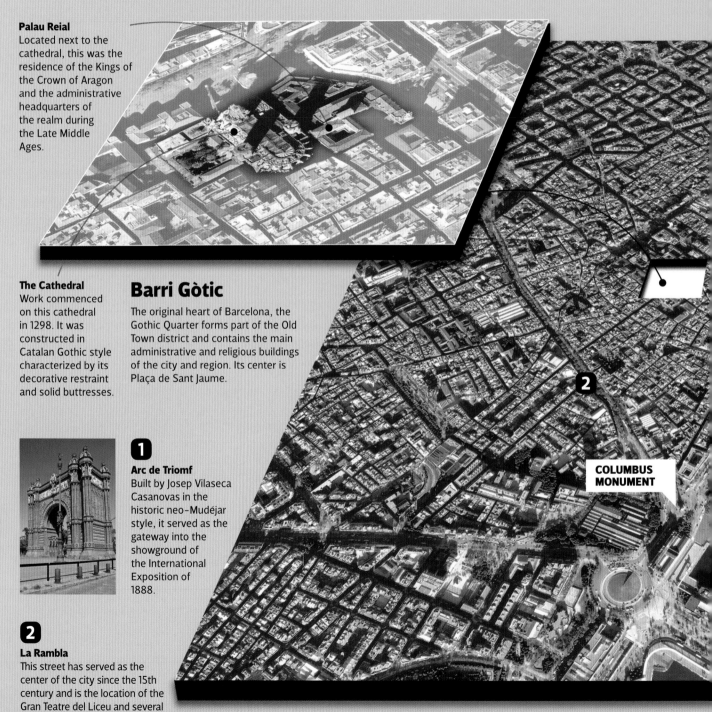

❷

COLUMBUS MONUMENT

⊕ KEY FACTS ABOUT BARCELONA

CAPITAL OF CATALONIA
Barcelona is the capital of the Catalonia Regional Community, which is on the northeast of the Iberian Peninsula and is the second largest city in Spain.

LOCATION
Latitude 41° 22' 57" N
Longitude 02° 10' 37" E
Altitude 30 ft (9 m) above sea level

IN FIGURES
Surface area
39.15 mi² (101.4 km²)
Population 1,616,000 (4.7 million in the metropolitan area)
Population density
41,277/mi² (15,937/km²)

FOUNDATION
Foundation date
Approx. 15 BC
Founders
The Roman Army
Iberian, Carthaginian and Roman
Despite Barcelona being officially founded—with the name Barcino—in the last few years before Christ and under the command of Roman emperor Augustus, it had previously had Iberian, Carthaginian—one legend attributes the founding to Hannibal—and possibly Greek settlements.

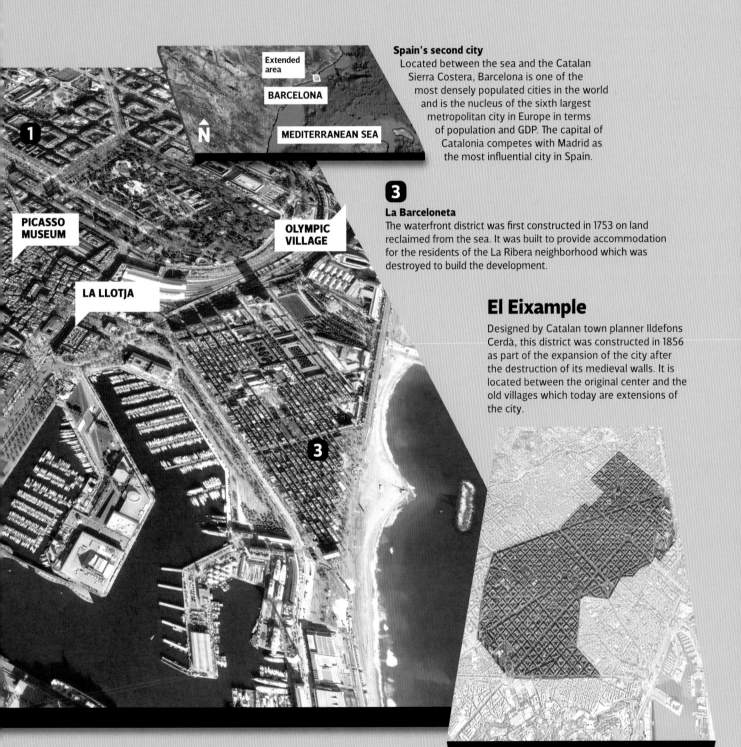

Extended area

BARCELONA

N

MEDITERRANEAN SEA

1

PICASSO MUSEUM

LA LLOTJA

OLYMPIC VILLAGE

3

Spain's second city
Located between the sea and the Catalan Sierra Costera, Barcelona is one of the most densely populated cities in the world and is the nucleus of the sixth largest metropolitan city in Europe in terms of population and GDP. The capital of Catalonia competes with Madrid as the most influential city in Spain.

3

La Barceloneta
The waterfront district was first constructed in 1753 on land reclaimed from the sea. It was built to provide accommodation for the residents of the La Ribera neighborhood which was destroyed to build the development.

El Eixample

Designed by Catalan town planner Ildefons Cerdà, this district was constructed in 1856 as part of the expansion of the city after the destruction of its medieval walls. It is located between the original center and the old villages which today are extensions of the city.

A Gothic and modernist jewel

Gothic and modernist architecture and the 1992 Olympic Games mark the personality of this welcoming and bright city.

All cities are the result of successive periods of magnificence and crises. The longer the period of prosperity, the more historically and socio-economically important the city. Despite not being the national capital, today Barcelona is one of the most dynamic cities in Europe, which is largely thanks to the wealth accumulated over three defining periods: the Late Middle Ages, the second half of the 19th century and the last decades of the 20th century.

Founded by the Romans toward the end of the 1st century BC, the city began a slow albeit sustained development in the 9th century, which transformed it within four centuries from the capital of a small earldom to the capital of the kingdom of Aragon. This is largely thanks to the commercial activity of its port which is one of the most active on the Mediterranean. This development, which can be seen on a map in the successive extensions of its walls, saw the construction in the Gothic Quarter of the much celebrated Cathedral and Basilica of Santa María del Mar—paradigms of the so-called Catalan Gothic, which was more austere than the French Gothic—the palaces of the king and the bourgeois families who became rich in that period of prosperity, and the "drassanes," the shipyards in which ships for the Catalan commercial fleet were manufactured.

The industrial age and the modern age

At the end of the 15th century, the dynastic union between Aragon and Castilla coincided with the beginning of a long period of hardship for Barcelona, blighted by the discovery of America, which directed a lot of its commercial interests across the Atlantic. This lethargy lasted several centuries until the arrival of a belated Industrial Revolution which, in the 19th century, enabled the city to become the strongest asset of the Spanish economy thanks to its textile and metalwork factories, notable examples of which can still be seen in the districts of Sants Marti and El Poblenou.

This second period of splendor bought with it huge changes for the city. In 1854, the notable demographic increase forced the municipal authorities to demolish the walls which squeezed the population into narrow streets and unsafe buildings. With the aim of urbanizing the uninhabited plains surrounding the city, the town planner Cerdà designed the so-called Eixample, a network of some 500 beveled blocks which today form part of the character of the district. It is home to the majority of the modernist buildings which thousands of tourists visit each year. Led by the genius Antoni Gaudí, the great architects of the period began to design works of extraordinary sumptuousness, individuality and color for entrepreneurs who had, thanks to the emergence of industry, become rich and were keen to flaunt their wealth. Visit the La Pedrera or the Casa Batlló, both on the stately Passeig de Gràcia, and you will discover a style overflowing with originality and lifestyles based on luxury and ostentation.

Modern Barcelona

During the second half of the 19th century, one of the key factors in Barcelona's development came about when the city held the International Exposition of 1888, which stimulated the renovation of the area today occupied by the Ciutadella Park. A century later, another great international event, the 1992 Olympic Games, gave rise to

📷

←La Rambla
This popular boulevard with flower and souvenir stalls and kiosks in the heart of the city is a compulsory must-see for any visitor.

←Casa Batlló
Detail of a stained-glass window from one of the jewels of Catalan modernism by Antoni Gaudí.

↓The Gothic Quarter
One of the streets in the former heart of the city, which is one of the largest and best preserved Gothic districts.

↓↓The waterfront
Renovated thanks to the 1992 Olympic Games, the waterfront stands out for its avant-garde architecture and eateries.

a new period of growth in the city, this time following a 40-year period of dictatorship that was especially difficult for the people of Barcelona. Holding the Games permitted the modernization of the city infrastructure, the renovation of Montjuïc as a large urban park and the transformation of La Poblenou from an industrial to a residential area, in addition to promoting a profound restoration of the monumental heritage and a large proportion of residential properties blackened by decades of neglect.

This general reorganization, in addition to the redevelopment of the waterfront, is the main reason for the exponential increase in tourism in Barcelona in the last few years. The 2.5 miles (4 km) of beach, the prevailing climate—mild winters and hot summers—the Gothic and modernist heritage and the excellent hotels and restaurants have transformed the city—whose human dimensions make it a paradigm of the Mediterranean lifestyle—into one of the preferred destinations in the world, despite the existence of entrenched problems such as noise and air pollution.

La Sagrada Familia

Designed by Antoni Gaudí in 1882, this monumental, modernist-style basilica is still under construction today.

The completed works When it is finished, the Sagrada Familia will have 18 towers: four on each of the three entranceways with the remaining six forming a spire with a great tower dedicated to Jesus as the central feature.

Nativity facade (east) This facade was built by Gaudí as a guide and example for his successors. It has a large portico with three doorways and four bell towers in honor of the Apostles Saint Barnabas, Saint Simon, Saint Jude Thaddeus and Saint Matthew.

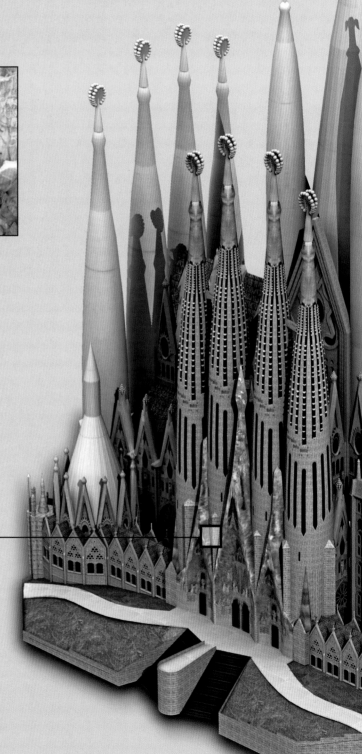

Passion facade (west) Located on the opposite side from the Nativity facade, there is also a large portico and four bell towers. The iconography, created by sculptor Josep Maria Subirachs, is dedicated to the passion and the death of Jesus Christ.

Forest of columns
The central space of the basilica is spectacular with beautiful stained glass windows, numerous columns with geometric trunks and original capitals. Branches at the top support the structure of the temple vaults.

Bell towers These spikes or pinnacles of the towers, decorated with mosaics, represent those who continue the work of the apostles. They will house 60 bells in total.

Windows The walls of the Sagrada Familia have many openings —windows, rose windows and arches— which help to reduce their weight.

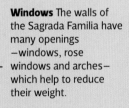

Organic figures There are an infinite number of human forms – biblical figures–and natural forms on all the walls of the temple.

Glory facade (south) Construction began in the year 2000 with the laying of the foundations and, like the others, it has symbolic decorative elements and four tapering towers, dedicated to the apostles Andrew, Peter, Paul and James.

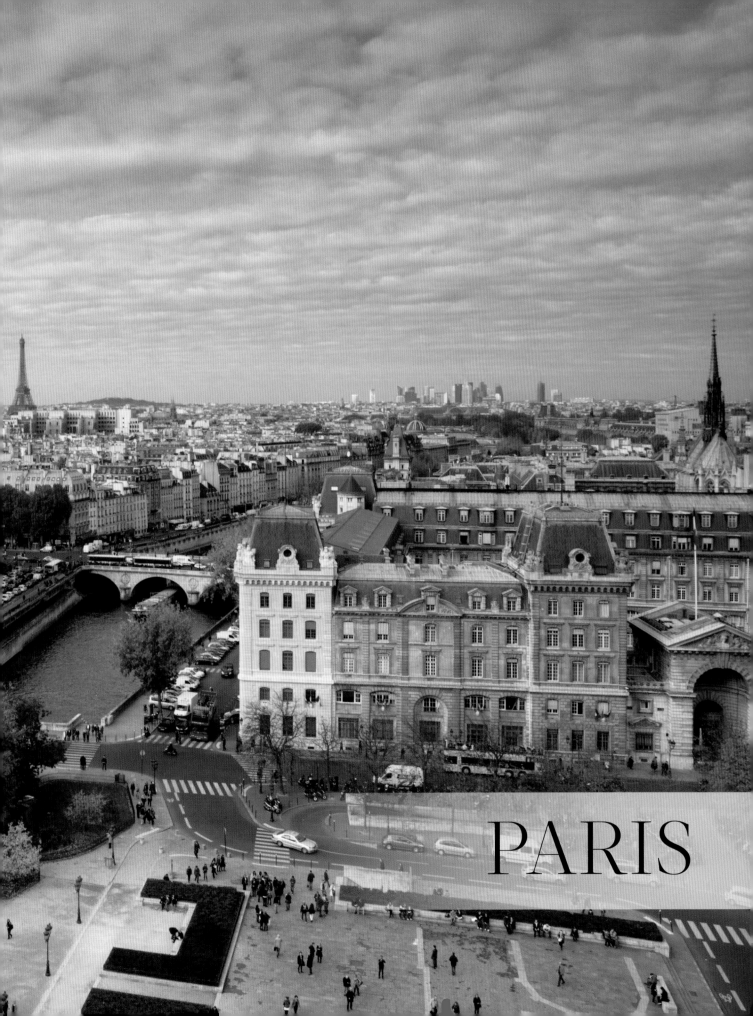

PARIS

Grandeur on the banks of the Seine

The Seine, which flows into the Atlantic Ocean, frames the geography and history of the French capital.

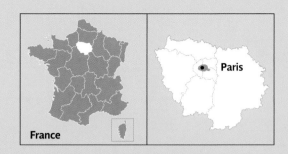

France

Paris

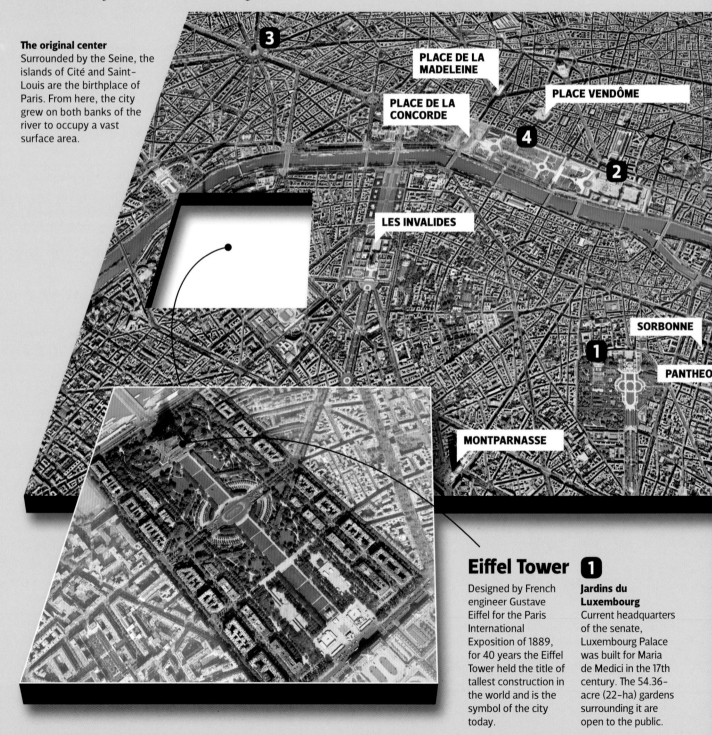

The original center
Surrounded by the Seine, the islands of Cité and Saint–Louis are the birthplace of Paris. From here, the city grew on both banks of the river to occupy a vast surface area.

3

PLACE DE LA MADELEINE

PLACE VENDÔME

PLACE DE LA CONCORDE

4

2

LES INVALIDES

SORBONNE

1

PANTHEO

MONTPARNASSE

Eiffel Tower **1**

Designed by French engineer Gustave Eiffel for the Paris International Exposition of 1889, for 40 years the Eiffel Tower held the title of tallest construction in the world and is the symbol of the city today.

Jardins du Luxembourg
Current headquarters of the senate, Luxembourg Palace was built for Maria de Medici in the 17th century. The 54.36–acre (22–ha) gardens surrounding it are open to the public.

⊕ KEY FACTS ABOUT PARIS

CAPITAL OF FRANCE
The metropolitan area of Paris is located in the province and region of Île-de-France, and is the headquarters of the French government.

LOCATION
Latitude
48° 51' 44" N
Longitude
02° 21' 04" E
Altitude
108 ft (33 m) above sea level

IN FIGURES
Surface area
41 mi² (105.4 km²)
Population
2,260,000
(11.9 million in the metropolitan area)

Population density
55,122/mi² (21,442/km²)
FOUNDATION
Foundation date
3rd century BC
Founders
Parisii Gauls

From Lutetia to Paris
Julius Caesar defeated the Gauls in 52 BC and took the city which was then in the hands of the Parisii tribe. Caesar named it

Lutetia. Later, in the 4th century, and with Imperial Rome in crisis, the town became part of the Frankish kingdom, regaining its former and current name.

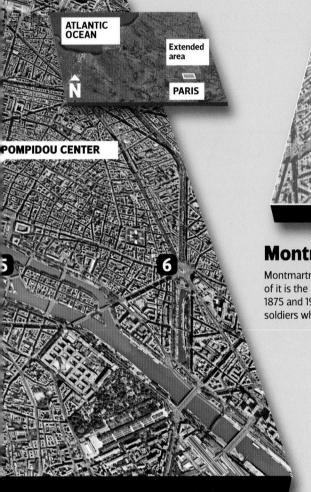

ATLANTIC OCEAN

Extended area

N̂ PARIS

POMPIDOU CENTER

Montmartre district

Montmartre Hill is 426 ft (130 m) high and atop of it is the Sacré-Cœur constructed between 1875 and 1919 as a dedication to the French soldiers who fell in the Franco-Prussian War.

The district that has established itself on the slopes of the hill is traditionally home to professional and amateur artists who give it a bohemian atmosphere.

3
Arc de Triomphe
Napoleon promised his army that they would return home "under triumphal arches" if they were victorious in the battle of Austerlitz. The Emperor fulfilled his promise and ordered the construction of this neoclassical archway.

4
Jardins des Tuileries
Situated parallel to the Seine, this garden was the first public park in Paris. Prior to this, it was part of the palace constructed in the 16th century at the request of Catherine de' Medici, wife of Henri II.

2
The Louvre
Opened during the middle of the French Revolution, the Louvre houses the most important art collection in the world, including works such as *La Gioconda* (the Mona Lisa), by Leonardo da Vinci. It is located in the old Louvre palace.

5
Notre Dame
Located in the heart of the Cité island and begun in 1163, this cathedral, with its high naves, towers, supports and flying buttresses, is the most famous Gothic temple in the world.

6
Place de la Bastille
On July 14, 1789, the Parisian people attacked the prison that was built there, instigating the French Revolution. Today, without the prison, the square is dominated by the Colonne de Juillet, which commemorates the Revolution of 1830.

The city of lights

The Paris of today is the result of a profound urban restructuring carried out in the second half of the 19th century.

The most visited city in the world, according to the World Tourism Organization, Paris is the paradigm of a city in terms of aesthetic norms and a destination which no self-respecting traveler can afford to miss. There are cities of such beauty and with such high standards of living that it is difficult to bring to mind one significant building or monument. The French capital, however, has probably the most international urban symbol in the world, the Eiffel Tower. It is this unique construction, as well as others such as the Arc de Triomphe, Notre Dame and the Louvre pyramid which more than fulfill emblematic roles to a great metropolis. Although it is not the extraordinary intuition demonstrated when building symbolic buildings that most distinguishes Paris from other large cities which, like Rome, for example, have great historic heritage, but it is the open, light and ordered urbanism that is respectful of its citizens.

The capital of France is the result of a long history which began 23 centuries ago with the meanderings of the Seine River. But no French hero, whether Carlos Martel, Joan of Arc, Louis XIV, Napoleon Bonaparte or Charles de Gaulle, has had such an influence on the appearance of Paris as the Baron Georges-Eugène Haussmann. In the middle of the 19th century, Emperor Napoleon III charged Haussmann, a civil servant and local politician, with the design of a profound urban restructuring. It would allow the city to do away with a past marked by the Old Regime and prepare it for a promising future with more prominence given to the burgeoning bourgeoisie, whose early progress came to fruition in the successive International Expositions held in Paris during the second half of the 19th century.

↖Pont des Invalides
Built in 1854,
it is one of the
37 bridges and
walkways which
cross the Seine. The
oldest is Pont Neuf
which dates back
to 1578.

↖Montmartre
The famous
bohemian district
of Paris still retains
some of its former
charm. In the Place
du Tertre, artists
and portrait painters
work in the open air.

↑Sainte Chapelle
This is one of the
largest Gothic jewels
in the world. It has
some 6,458 ft^2
(600 m^2) of beautiful
stained glass.

←Louvre Pyramid
With 8.8 million
visitors each year,
the Louvre museum
is one of the city's
greatest tourist
attractions.

→**Sacré-Cœur**
Located in Montmartre, it is one of the most celebrated and visited buildings in the city.

→→**Saint-Germain-des-Prés**
This district was home to the intellectual and the artistic during the 1950s and 1960s. Its cafes and other establishments today retain a certain atmosphere from that era.

→**Eiffel Tower**
(Opposite page) This gigantic iron structure 1,082 ft (330 m) high, which opened in 1889, is the symbol of the city.

In the years between 1852 and 1870, Haussmann erased a good part of the narrow and labyrinthine urban areas of the city—of which only a few traces on the Île de la Cité and in the district of Marais remain—and created a new framework in which order, geometry, health and ventilation became the leitmotiv. Very soon the evident modernization of the city—with its wide avenues and boulevards, the construction of a complete sewer system network, the installation of gas lighting, the arrival of the raidroad and the transformation of the Boulogne Forest into an urban park—more than compensated for the initial criticisms made over the destruction of the rich Medieval Parisian heritage.

The wide tree-lined boulevards, which today are admired by millions and millions of tourists, were designed in that period. Twelve of these avenues meet, forming a star in the Place Charles de Gaulle known as L'Étoile. It is famous for the skill and speed with which Parisian drivers usually tackle it. The Arc de Triomphe, on which construction began in 1806 under the orders of Bonaparte to celebrate his victory in the battle of Austerlitz, occupies the center of the square. It is visible from multiple perspectives offering an almost cinematographic effect which Haussmann sought to repeat several times in his urban designs in order to highlight the historic beauty of several of the most important buildings in the city. La Rue Royale meets at the neoclassical Madeleine church, while the narrow Baroque dome of Les Invalides, one of the largest constructions of the golden age of Louis XIV, can be admired from afar at the end of the L'avenue de Breteuil.

A city philosophy still in existence today

However, the best thing about the Haussmann reform is that much of his urban designs have been followed to the letter, without interruption, to the present day. Today, in the interests of harmony, proportion, public health and modernization in general, municipal authorities still require new constructions to respect the alignment and heights decided more than 150 years ago.

In fact, this great urban reform is nothing short of confirmation of a triumph, after many decades, of the ideas of the Ilustración and the Révolution born in the French capital during the 18th century. The rationalism which Haussmann injected into his project and the power of Napoleon III to carry it out—to adapt the city to the needs of the emerging bourgeoisie and the marked demographic increase—are legacies of the ideas of Voltaire, Montesquieu, Rousseau and Diderot. Indeed it is the legacy of all those thinkers whose reflections culminated in the slogans of Liberty, Equality and

Fraternity shouted by the revolutionaries on 14 July, 1789 during their storming of the Bastille, the now ruined prison, their occupation of which triggered one of the key developments by which the modern world is understood. The light which Haussmann successfully sought in his wide boulevards and which gave the city its deserved nickname is the same as that which inspired the great enlightened philosophers, the great impressionist painters—whose first innovative exhibition was held in Paris in 1874—and the avant-garde artists such as Matisse, Braque, Picasso, Duchamp and Kandinsky, who lived or exhibited in Paris during the first decades of the 20th century and transformed the course of international art.

Today, these avenues and boulevards that the Baron designed gather together an enormous amount of commercial and financial activity which makes Paris one of the most important centers for economic decision making on the planet. Its metropolitan area, the third most populous in Europe, generates almost a third of the wealth of France and if it were an independent state, would place it among the top 20 most prosperous. Educated, elegant and with a certain famous standoffishness, Parisians are conscious of this power and unique aspect of the capital and are proud to belong to the latest generation of this unique city.

Notre Dame

Situated on the Île de la Cité, this enormous cathedral dating from 1345 and dedicated to the Virgin Mary, is one of the prime examples of Gothic art.

North side rose window The cathedral has three rose windows: one on the main facade and the other two, 42 ft (13 m) in diameter, on the north and south faces.

Lower level The lower level is simple. It has a Latin cross with a long central nave and choir crossed by a large transept and two aisles.

Chimeras These statues can be found around the great towers. The name comes from Khimaira, a mythical Greek monster.

Flying buttresses These are external structural elements in the form of a half arc which absorb the pressure of the vault and transmit it to a buttress or support attached to the walls of the aisles.

The point It was decided to build this 314 ft (96 m) structure during restoration work undertaken by Viollet-le-Duc.

The towers Reaching a height of 206 ft (63 m), the north tower was completed around 1240 and the south tower some decades later.

The bells The largest and oldest, known as Emmanuel, can be found in the south tower. Its sound is associated with great events, such as coronations or the end of world wars.

The west facade The west facade has two high towers and three large portals—the Virgin, the Last Judgment (image) and Santa Ana. Above these is the Gallery of the kings, a horizontal strip with 28 statues depicting the Kings of Israel and Judea.

The Virgin In the mullion of the Virgin doorway, Mary is depicted with the Child in her arms. Over them, the figures of two angels are represented in a posture of consultation.

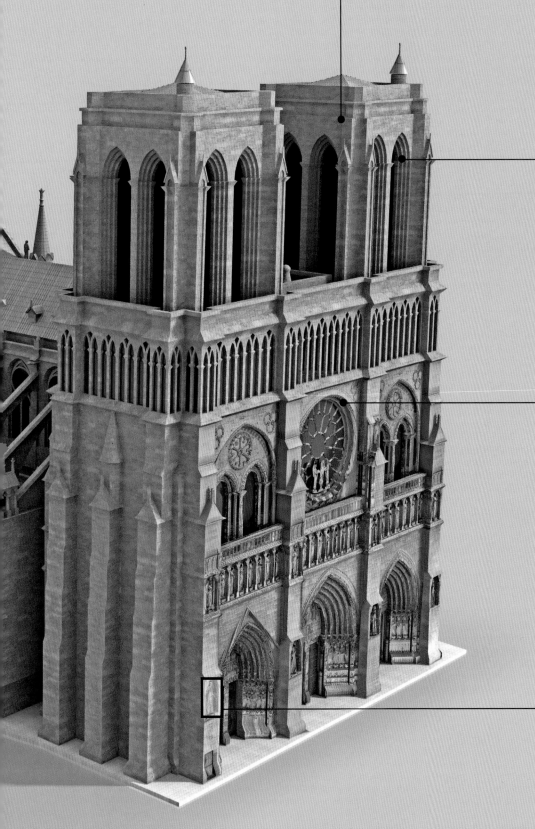

ROME

Where the stones speak

Ancient Rome extended to the banks of the Tiber River between the famous seven hills, an area which subsequently became flooded.

Italy

Rome

The Vatican City
The Pope has controlled the central territory of the Italian peninsula since the 16th century. After the unification of Italy, the Vatican State was limited to St. Peter's Basilica and the surrounding areas, within the city of Rome.

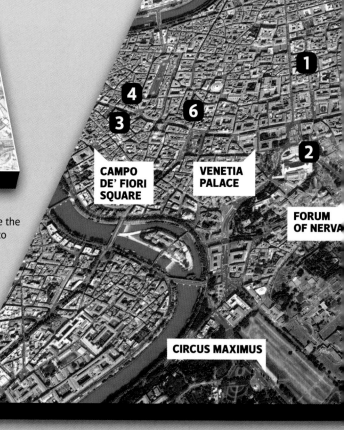

CAMPO DE' FIORI SQUARE

VENETIA PALACE

FORUM OF NERVA

CIRCUS MAXIMUS

1

The Trevi Fountain
The largest baroque fountain in Rome, the Trevi Fountain is located at the end of the old aqueduct, the sources for which, according to legend, were found with the help of the Virgin Mary. The monument is the work of 17th century Neapolitan sculptor Gian Lorenzo Bernini.

2

Forum Traiani
Built between 107 and 112 AD during the reign of the emperor Trajan, it is the largest of the Imperial Rome Fora and houses the porticoed square, Basilica Ulpia, Temple Traiano and Colonna Traiano.

3

Museum of Rome
Situated between the Piazza Navona, the Campo de' Fiori square and the Corso Vittorio Emanuele, the Palazzo Braschi is a neoclassical building dating back to the end of the 18th century.

4

Piazza Navona
This square was, until the Middle Ages, a Roman circus, the Stadio di Domiziano. It is the site of various churches and the famed Fountains of Bernini, the most well known of which is the Fontana dei Quattro Fiumi or Fountain of the Four Rivers.

5

Piazza di Spagna
This staircase with 135 steps, dating back to the beginning of the 18th century, which rise up to the church of Trinità dei Monti, has turned this square into one of the most visited in Rome. Fontana della Barcaccia, in the center of the square, is by Pietro Bernini.

⊕ KEY FACTS ABOUT ROME

CAPITAL OF ITALY
Rome is the headquarters of the Italian executive, legislative and judicial powers, and the capital of the autonomous region of Lazio and Catholic Christianity.

LOCATION
Latitude 41° 54' 0" N
Longitude 12° 30' 0" E
Altitude
121 ft (37 m) above sea level

IN FIGURES
Surface area
496 mi² (1,285 km²)
Population 2,785,000
Population density
5,613/mi² (2,167/km²)
FOUNDATION
Foundation date

April 21, 753 BC
Founders
Romulus and Remus
Myth or reality?
According to legend, Romulus and Remus— nursed by a she wolf—competed to

found the city. The first killed the second and became the first king. Historical and archaeological studies do not differ much in the date proposed by the Roman myth.

However, the exact foundation date is difficult to specify because for years the region was inhabited by Latin, Sabine and Lazio tribes.

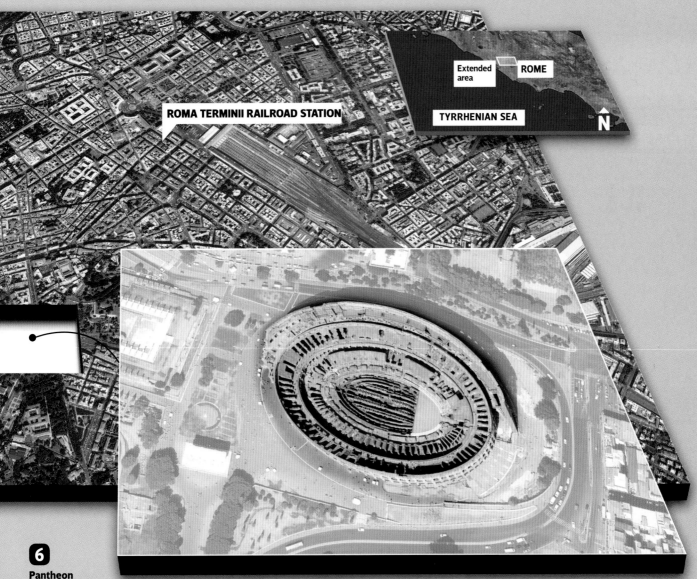

ROMA TERMINII RAILROAD STATION

Extended area — **ROME**

TYRRHENIAN SEA

N

6
Pantheon
Built in the 2nd century AD, this circular temple dedicated to the Roman gods is one of the landmarks in the history of architecture. It inspired the construction of Florence cathedral and St. Peter's Basilica.

The Colosseum

With a capacity of 50,000 spectators, the largest amphitheater of Imperial Rome was built in the 1st century AD to house wild beasts, gladiatorial fights, mock sea battles and other public spectacles usually held to celebrate

great military victories. Called the Colosseum after the colossal statue of Nero erected at the same time as the facade, in subsequent centuries it was the scene of the martyrdom of Christians, which is why it was later converted into

a shrine. This action also served to halt the plundering which the population had subjected it to since it fell into disuse in the 6th century. It is still spectacular today and is one of the city's main tourist attractions.

The great imperial legacy

The Eternal City naturally and confidently supports the weight of a glorious past which can be seen around every corner.

No city plays a leading role in the history books of the Western world quite like Rome. With a biography spanning some 3,000 years, the current capital of Italy was the first great metropolis in the history of humanity. At the height of its splendor, in the golden age of the Roman Empire, it had over a million inhabitants in a period in which the world's population was only 200 million. Rome controlled territories extending 2.5 million mi² (6.5 million km²), a surface area which is smaller than only six of the current countries of the world, and 27 times the size of the United Kingdom.

With such a scope, it is understandable that a good part of the legacy formed over two millennia on the banks of the Tiber River is bequeathed with such enormous vitality. The Romance languages–inherited from Latin–dominate southern Europe, Latin America and a good part of Africa; Roman law decisively pervades the laws of our communities; Christianity–adopted as the official religion by the Empire in the 4th century– is the religion with the most followers in the world; the alphabet, which is employed in the West is Latin, and many states incorporate a Senate into their legislative system. Art, engineering, thought... almost all disciplines of human activity feed on ingredients originating in Rome.

A city with two states

Rome is the only city which governs two states at the same time – Italy and The Vatican – and has served as the capital throughout three very distinct territorial entities: the Roman empire, the Papal states and Italy itself. It is known as the Eternal City, a classical nickname which conceals surprising information. If it were not for the establishment of the Pope, the marvelous imperial city of Augustus and Trajan could easily have become a ghost city, a collection of venerable ruins without life, like Babylonia, Petra, Egypt's Memphis, or Aztec Teotihuacán.

Rome was, in effect, destroyed by Barbarians in the 5th century, and for around 1,000 years it was nothing more than a small town of some 15,000 to 20,000 inhabitants. They crowded around the original Basilica of St. Peter, while the imposing buildings of the former Empire languished on the unpopulated outskirts, victims of the pillaging and the passage of time. It is not surprising, then, that the city of the Tiber is home to some rare medieval ruins among its rich heritage.

Thanks to the expansion of Christianity in the Old World during the Middle Ages, and the determined efforts of Pope Nicholas V (1397–1455), Rome was resurrected from a prolonged lethargy in the 15th century which coincided with the emergence of the Renaissance. Nicholas V built new walls, paved streets, restored old aqueducts and ordered the construction of beautiful buildings worthy of the site where the apostle Peter, first father of the Christian church, died

1. Historic Rome
The Colosseum and the Arch of Constantine, located next to the Roman Forum, are two buildings which best represent the Imperial era.

2. The Pantheon
Built by the Emperor Hadrian in 126 BC, this majestic temple is defined by its enormous dome measuring (142 ft) 43.3 m) in diameter.

3. Castel Sant'Angelo (Mausoleum of Hadrian)
Located close to The Vatican, legend has it that Pope Gregory I saw the archangel St. Michael at the top of this popular fortress.

4. Fontana dei Quattro Fiumi
This is a detail from Bernini's famous fountain, in the Piazza Navona.

5. Vatican museums
The Vatican's museums have countless artistic jewels collected by the papacy over hundreds of years, including the magnificent Sistine Chapel.

6. Trastevere
This popular district on the western banks of the Tiber is the main area for enjoying the city's nightlife.

as a martyr. The success of the enterprise, continued by subsequent Popes with colossal initiatives such as the new St. Peter's Basilica and the Sistine Chapel, was such that history has forgiven them for taking and using the marble which dressed the fabulous Colosseum for these beautiful restoration projects.

Famed tourist attraction
This Rome, reborn in a little over five centuries, is a real lesson in art history, with a new surprising example around every corner. It is this that attracts hundreds of thousands of tourists every day who saturate the streets and rouse the anger of local residents. They, in turn, insist on moving through them on private transportation – especially mopeds – causing monumental traffic jams and high levels of pollution in a metropolitan area of over three million people. No suitable underground system can be built beyond the existing two lines because any excavation encounters valuable relics of the past. However, despite all these inconveniences, the heritage of the city is so immensely rich, its streets and squares so captivating and the pulse of the citizens so alive and open that today it can be said, without fear of contradiction, that Rome really is an Eternal City.

St. Peter's Basilica

Built between 1506 and 1626, some of the best artists of the Renaissance and Italian baroque periods helped with the construction.

Dome Designed by Michelangelo, it is the tallest in the world (448 ft/136.57 m above ground level) and stands out for the sensation of lightness which emanates from it despite its huge size. (It has an inner diameter of 136 ft/41.47 m.)

Papal altar This work by Lorenzo Bernini, designed in Baroque style and standing 30 m (98 ft) high can be found underneath the dome protected by the historic baldaquin (canopy) of St. Peter. It is located just above the tomb of St. Peter.

The Pietà St. Peter's Basilica houses countless sculptural and religious treasures. One of these, Michelangelo's "Pietà," in marble, is one of the most famous and a must-see for all those who visit the temple.

The nave There is a central nave (613 x 147 ft/187 x 45 m), separated from the North Aisle and the South Aisle by enormous pillars.

The apse Built under the direction of Michelangelo, it is a monumental semicircular space with a seat which uses the curved wall as a backrest. During the service, this space is used by religious authorities.

Central loggia (balcony) This is where the new Pope is announced, and from where the Pontiff gives his blessing *Urbi et orbi*.

Bells The Basilica has six bells, the oldest of which dates back to the 13th century. On important occasions they ring out in unison (plenum).

Facade Built at the beginning of the 17th century, it is the work of Carlo Maderno and measures 377 ft (115 m) wide by 151 ft (46 m) high.

VENICE

The city of canals

The unique city of Venice is built on a group of islands crossed by canals on an extensive lagoon in the Adriatic Sea.

Italy

Venice

A protected lagoon

Located between the Piave estuary and the Po Delta, the Venetian Lagoon is a coastal lake region with 118 islands and islets and is virtually cut off by sandbanks. This strategic position allowed Venice to grow enormously during the Middle Ages. The inhabited islands are crossed with canals, which in many cases are used as streets.

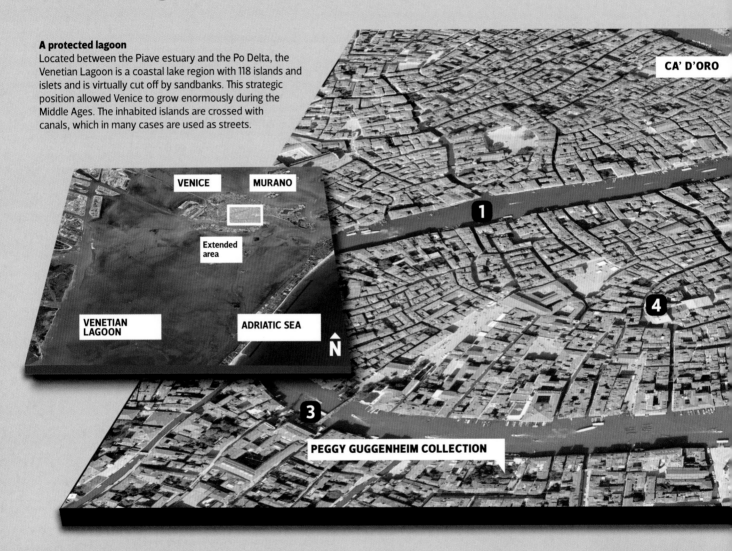

CA' D'ORO

VENICE   MURANO

Extended area

VENETIAN LAGOON

ADRIATIC SEA

N

PEGGY GUGGENHEIM COLLECTION

1

Grand Canal
At almost 2.8 miles (4 km) long, this is the longest canal in Venice. It traverses the main island of the city and is crossed by only four bridges: Rialto, Costituzione, Accademia and Scalzi (Bridge of the Barefoot [monks]).

2

Rialto Bridge
The oldest of the Grand Canal bridges, it was designed by Antonio da Ponte and completed in 1591. It has two inclined ramps which support a large central portico.

3

Gallerie dell'Accademia
This art gallery houses Italian Gothic through to neoclassic era works of art by artists such as Leonardo da Vinci, Tintoretto, Tiziano, Tiepolo, and Canaletto.

4

Teatro La Fenice
This Venetian opera house opened its doors in 1792 after a serious fire, hence its name (the Phoenix). Fire consumed it again in 1836 and 1996. It reopened in 2003, redesigned by Aldo Rossi.

KEY FACTS ABOUT VENICE

CAPITAL OF VENETO
Today Venice is
the capital of the
autonomous region
of Veneto, which
spans a large part of
the extreme
northeast of Italy.

LOCATION
Latitude
12˚ 20' 20" E
Longitude
45˚ 26' 03" N
Altitude
3.33 ft (1 m)
above sea level

IN FIGURES
Surface area 160 mi^2
(415 km^2)
Population
58,000 on the
island; 280,000
in the entire
municipality

Population density
1,709/mi^2 (660/km^2)
FOUNDATION
Foundation date
Beginning of the 5th
century AD
Founders
Latin settlers

**The lagoon as a place
of refuge**
A few Latin settlers
from the northeast
of Italy sheltered in
the marshy lagoons
located between
the Piave estuary

and the Po delta to
protect themselves
from invasion by
the Huns and other
tribes from the
north and east of
the continent. The
city began on stilts.

Murano

Located 0.6 mile (1 km) to the north of
Venice, the island of Murano—in reality
a group of seven small islands linked
by bridges—is home to a population
of some 6,000 inhabitants, many
of whom are glasswork artisans,
the craft for which the city
is famous.

St. Mark's Basilica
Built in the 11th century,
this Byzantine style
Venetian cathedral
underwent important
changes in the 13th,
15th and 17th centuries.

CAMPANILE

Doge's Palace
This Gothic building, built
between the 10th and
15th centuries, subverts
the laws of architecture
by placing the heavy,
almost solid walls, over
the light arches.

Lido

The Lido is one of the sandbanks which separates the
Venetian Lagoon from the Adriatic Sea, and which has
for centuries protected the city from foreign attack. It is
7 miles (12 km) long and barely 328 ft (100 m) wide at its
narrowest point. On its eastern coast, pleasant beaches
look out onto open sea. It has a population of 20,000
and each year hosts the prestigious Venice International
Film Festival.

A city of waterways

During the Middle Ages, a large part of trade on the Mediterranean was directed toward Venice, a small island in the Adriatic Sea.

The history of Venice is the story of how a small island, which can be traversed in little over an hour, came to control trade on the Mediterranean throughout the entire Late Middle Ages. The first Venetians settled on the islands of the Venetian lagoon at the beginning of the 5th century, fleeing attacks from peoples of the north and east of Europe. Sheltered in simple properties constructed on wooden posts, the Venetians were able to survive attacks from the Barbarians thanks to the protection of the lagoon and the surrounding sandbanks. This same strategic location was decisive in the city's development.

In the first centuries of its existence, it formed part of the Byzantine Empire, but Venice gradually achieved independence without the need to break with the empire. Its territorial limits, from the very beginning, obliged Venice to establish constant commercial contact with other Mediterranean communities who could supply it with the general basics that could not be produced on the lagoon. This commercial enterprise and the good relations with Byzantium allowed the Venetians to develop a wide network of allied ports and create an extensive fleet of ships captained by skilled sailors. More interested in trade than in wars and religion, the Venetians became the ideal business partners for the authorities of the eastern Mediterranean, who were Christian, Arabic and Jewish.

However, with the passing of the centuries, the economic and naval power accumulated by Venice enabled it to make great progress toward becoming a military power. The safety of the lagoon, together with the protection offered by the friendly ports in the Adriatic and the progressive decadence of Byzantium, gave the Venetians the opportunity to annex large islands of the

Mediterranean and dominate various strategic ports on the Black Sea. From here they could control the coveted Silk Road of China, in which the Venetian merchant and adventurer Marco Polo, of Dalmatian origins, played a leading role. These 500 years of development materialized in the form of the Doge's Palace, a building which initially began as a castle in the 10th century and was converted into an elegant palace in the Gothic period and adorned with bold elements which heralded the Renaissance.

Birthplace of great artists

After living through the peak of its magnificence during the first half of the 15th century—a period in which Serenissima (the Republic of Venice) had 3,300 ships and the city was, after Paris, the second-most populous in Europe—Venice entered a period of crisis coinciding with the taking of Byzantium by the Ottomans and the flourishing Atlantic trade. Paradoxically, this decline coincided with a period of cultural excellence for the city which, between the 16th and 18th centuries, encouraged the sponsorship of important artists such as the architect Andrea Palladio—creator of the churches Il Redentore and San Giorgio Maggiore—musicians Antonio Vivaldi and Tomaso Albinoni, painters Tiziano, Tintoretto, Tiepolo and Canaletto, and the writer and adventurer Giacomo Casanova, the embodiment of the decadent,

1. **The Rialto Bridge**
The oldest and most famous bridge which crosses the Grand Canal in Venice. Inside are two rows of craft shops.
2. **Burano**
This town next to Venice, also crossed by canals, is known for its colorful houses and beautiful lace.
3. **Carnival of Venice**
Venice holds one of the most popular carnivals in the world. For ten days, the city is filled with masqueraders and sophisticated costumes inspired by the 18th century.
4. **Palazzo Contarini**
This 15th century building is famous for its beautiful external spiral staircase replete with arches.

18th-century city. This period also saw the Duchy look to gambling to bring in money which no longer came in through trade. The costumes and masquerades, which can be appreciated each year during the famous Carnival, are inspired by this period of debauchery and self-indulgence. After forming part of the Austro-Hungarian Empire and later part of a unified Italy, as well as becoming a symbol of romanticism for 19th-century Europeans, Venice knew how to capitalize on its fame and heritage in order to experience a revival as a popular tourist destination. Today, it's great enemies are not the Turkish navy, nor commercial competition from Genoa, but climate change and the drastic demographic decline.

Already well accustomed to the phenomenon of high water, which regularly floods St. Mark's Square – preventing visitors from enjoying the Caffé Florian's terrace, one of the most distinguished cafes in the world – global warming now threatens the very existence of this city. After overcoming a critical period during the first half of the 20th century, when industrial activity dried the aquifers which keep the foundations of the city stable, Venice today fights against the sea level – the costly MOSE system of mobile dams is still unfinished – and against the exodus of young people fed up with high property prices and the scarcity of work on the fringes of tourism.

St. Mark's Basilica

The temple seen today is from the 11th century, although its history dates back to the year 828 when construction first began to house the St. Mark reliquaries.

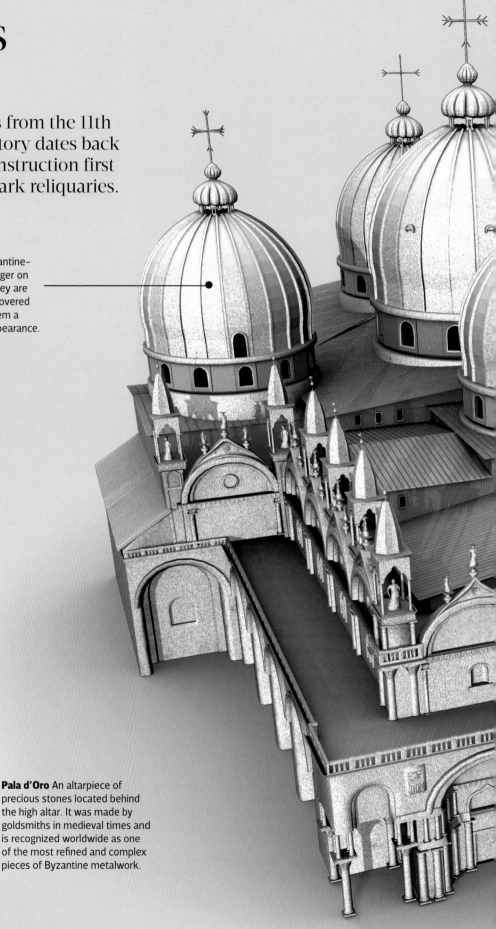

Dome The five Byzantine-style domes are larger on the outside than they are on the inside and covered with lead giving them a very distinctive appearance.

Narthex The atrium or vestibule situated at the entrance of the Basilica is finished with polychrome marble and mosaics and consists of six small domes. The 13th-century mosaics illustrate scenes from the Old Testament, eg the Creation on the dome of Genesis.

Pala d'Oro An altarpiece of precious stones located behind the high altar. It was made by goldsmiths in medieval times and is recognized worldwide as one of the most refined and complex pieces of Byzantine metalwork.

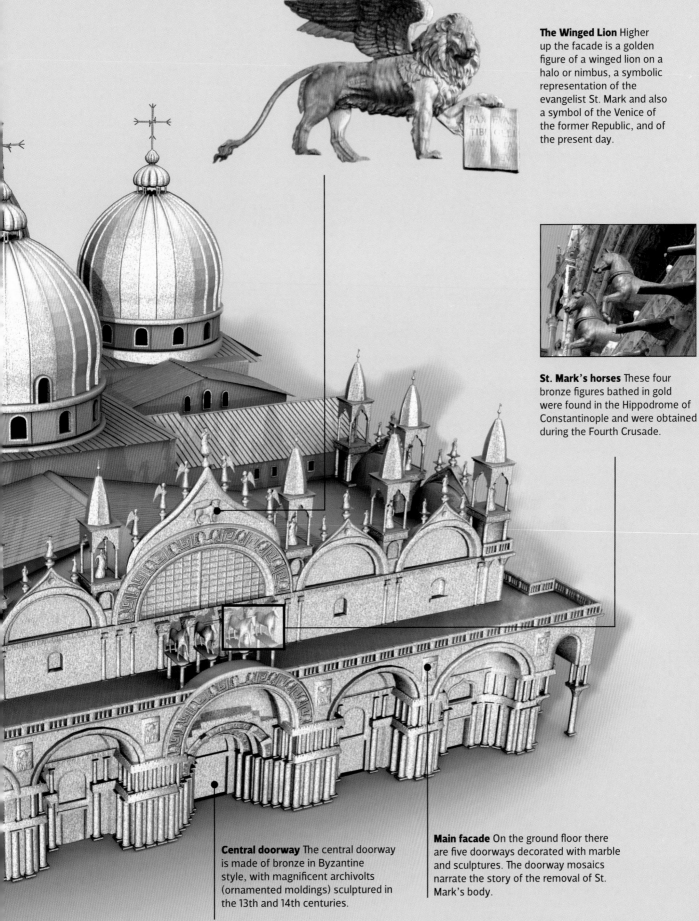

The Winged Lion Higher up the facade is a golden figure of a winged lion on a halo or nimbus, a symbolic representation of the evangelist St. Mark and also a symbol of the Venice of the former Republic, and of the present day.

St. Mark's horses These four bronze figures bathed in gold were found in the Hippodrome of Constantinople and were obtained during the Fourth Crusade.

Central doorway The central doorway is made of bronze in Byzantine style, with magnificent archivolts (ornamented moldings) sculptured in the 13th and 14th centuries.

Main facade On the ground floor there are five doorways decorated with marble and sculptures. The doorway mosaics narrate the story of the removal of St. Mark's body.

VIENNA

A rich heritage

Being the historical imperial capital, this city on the Danube has a vast artistic, architectural and monumental heritage.

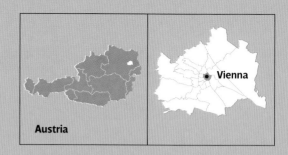

Austria

Vienna

In the heart of Europe
Vienna is less than 250 miles (400 km) by road from five national capitals: Bratislava, Budapest, Prague, Zagreb and Ljubljana, all of which were on the other side of the Iron Curtain before the fall of the Berlin Wall in 1989.

Old Vienna

With medieval roots, and dominated by the stylized needle of St. Stephen's Cathedral, the old heart of Vienna, restricted by the popular Vienna Ring Boulevard and its magnificent buildings, is made up of a dense network of little streets and small squares, filled at night with tourists and residents looking for entertainment.

Extended area

VIENNA

N

PARLIAMENT

THE MUSEUM DISTRICT

Hofburg Palace
The Hofburg imperial Palace was the Habsburgs' winter residence for six centuries. It is made up of ten buildings in which all European artistic styles are found, from Mediaeval Gothic to the historicism of the 19th century.

The Vienna State Opera
Inaugurated on May 25, 1969, the Staatsoper is one of the most prestigious stages for bel canto opera in the world. In 1945, a World War II shell scored a direct hit on this neo-Renaissance building, and it had to be restored at the end of the conflict.

⊕ KEY FACTS ABOUT VIENNA

CAPITAL OF AUSTRIA
Throughout its history, Vienna has been the capital of the Germanic Holy Roman Empire, the Austro-Hungarian Empire and the Republic of Austria.

LOCATION
Latitude
48° 12' 0" N
Longitude
16° 22' 0" E
Altitude
495–1,780 ft (151–543 m) above sea level

IN FIGURES
Surface area
160.19 mi² (414.90 km²)
Population
1,712,903
Population density
10,692/mi² (4,128/km²)

FOUNDATION
Foundation date
13 BC
Founders
Roman Army
The third largest city
Vienna experienced a period of great political, economic and cultural magnificence in the second half of the 19th century, to the extent that its population grew tenfold, reaching 2.3 million in 1916. At that time, it came to be Europe's third greatest city, after London and Paris, and the fourth in the world if New York is taken into consideration.

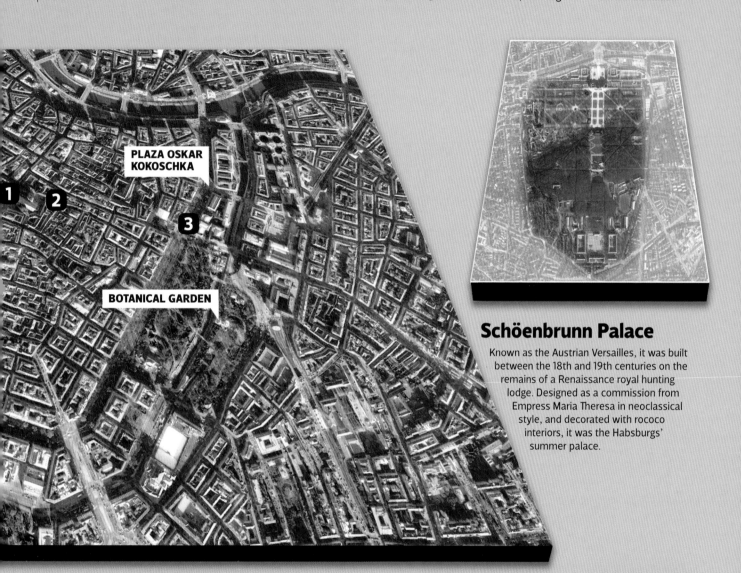

PLAZA OSKAR KOKOSCHKA

BOTANICAL GARDEN

Schöenbrunn Palace
Known as the Austrian Versailles, it was built between the 18th and 19th centuries on the remains of a Renaissance royal hunting lodge. Designed as a commission from Empress Maria Theresa in neoclassical style, and decorated with rococo interiors, it was the Habsburgs' summer palace.

1 **St. Stephen's Cathedral**
Located in the historical center, the Stephansdom is a Romanesque church dating from the 13th century, enlarged over the following two centuries in Gothic style, and also re-worked in later styles.

2 **Figarohaus**
Between 1784 and 1787, the first floor of this building from the baroque era was the residence of the great Austrian composer Wolfgang Amadeus Mozart. Today it is a museum dedicated to him.

3 **Museum of Applied Arts**
Founded in 1864 as a gallery of applied arts from all over the world, and renovated in 1993, it houses a large collection of objects, Islamic and oriental art, and avant-garde works.

The crown of the Empire

Debate and controversy have impelled the evolution of this cultured and educated city to the number one ranking in terms of quality of life.

Beautiful, orderly and elegant, Vienna gives a first impression of a peaceful, conservative city, whose inhabitants await the first measures of the next waltz by enjoying a delicious sachertort in a welcoming café in Kärntnerstrasse. Holding first place in the rankings of cities with the best quality of life, Vienna is, thanks to its enviable current situation and its local image of calm, a city full of contrasts. It has a long history of conflicts, largely a consequence of its strategic position in the geographical center of Europe and on the banks of the Danube, from which the city's canal carries water to the Medieval heart of the city.

Indeed, few cities can challenge Vienna for the title of the heart of the continent. Located in the extreme eastern part of Austria, for 40 years it was a bulwark of Western Europe, penetrating the Iron Curtain like an arrow. With this position, the country maintained strict neutrality, which enabled it to become one of the host countries for the United Nations and to house offices of international importance such as the Organization of Petroleum–Exporting Countries (OPEC).

The city of the Habsburgs

Vienna has been a site of constant tensions throughout history. It was founded by the Romans as a center for the defense of the Empire at a key point on the border with the Barbarian lands, and from the 16th century was home to the court of the Habsburgs, the reigning dynasty in central Europe and as far away as Mexico.

Vienna thus governed the destinies of the Holy Roman Empire and the Austro–Hungarian Empire. The power that accumulated in the hands of the Emperors of the house of Habsburg is manifested today in the Hofburg, an enormous complex which joins more than seven centuries of architecture, and in the Schöenbrunn Palace, built between the 18th and 19th centuries. This period, dominated by baroque and neoclassical styles, represents one of Vienna's most brilliant ages, and is visible in a good part of the heritage that can be admired today in Austria's capital. It was also at this time that Vienna created its reputation as the world capital of music, with the appearance of geniuses such as Joseph Haydn, Franz Schubert, Johann Strauss and above all, Wolfgang Amadeus Mozart, whose rivalry with Antonio Salieri is almost as memorable as his talent.

There have been many such antagonisms throughout Vienna's history. In the second half of the 19th century, a group of young artists led by the painter Gustav Klimt made their break with the official institution's public as they sought to create a new, free art movement based on modernism. It was called Secession and found a home in the building of the same name, today the primary example of the type of architecture the movement championed. At the same time, architect Adolf Loos became one of the precursors of constructive rationalism, rejecting not just the historicism of the old school, which was the dominant style in the magnificent Vienna of the time, but also the Secession movement's tendency for ornamentation.

←The Café Central
Meeting places for intellectuals and politicians in the 19th century, Vienna's cafes still maintain their welcoming, elegant atmosphere.

↓Hundertwasserhaus
This municipal residential complex, built between 1983 and 1986, shows off the city's architectural creativity.

↓↓Parliament
This building, built in the 19th century and modeled on a classical Greek style, is one of Vienna's main monuments.

In the 20th century, the old controversies spilled over into politics. In 1918, the city experienced a revolution that saw the downfall of the monarchy and the beginning of 15 years of rule by the Socialist Party, a time when the capital came to be known as Red Vienna. Annexation by the Nazis was a parenthesis in the idyll the city maintained throughout most of the 20th century thanks to its social democracy: an atmosphere of tolerance that nurtured important works such as Sigmund Freud's psychoanalysis and Karl Popper's philosophy.

The list of great Viennese of the 20th century must not bypass the ultimate evidence of the city's contrasts, as personified in economist Friedrich Hayek, the father of modern neo-liberal theory and the enemy of socialism. This is another example of the atmosphere of respect and plurality that characterizes the Austrian capital. It is seen today in such contemporary interests as caring for the environment, the taste for international cuisine, and experimental art, aspects of life that the Viennese of today cultivate with a great capacity for self-criticism, a marked tendency for black humor, and by applying their educational levels, which are among the highest on the planet.

←Secession Building
This unique building was built in 1897 by Joseph Maria Olbrich to house the exhibitions of the movement's artists.

St. Stephen's Cathedral

This temple is one of the most recognizable symbols of Vienna. Thanks to numerous modifications, it boasts Roman, gothic and baroque styles.

The interior The central nave is 118 ft (36 m) wide and 351 ft (107 m) long. The choir and side chapels are Gothic. Inside, there are several altars and valuable works of art donated by individuals over the centuries.

Roof Rebuilt after being destroyed in a fire in 1945, it is made up of 250,000 tiles of various colors. The roof covers the entire central nave and inclines at 64 degrees, although in some places it reaches 80 degrees.

Pagan Towers The towers are part of the original 13th–century building. Rising 210 ft (64 m) high, they flank the main entrance.

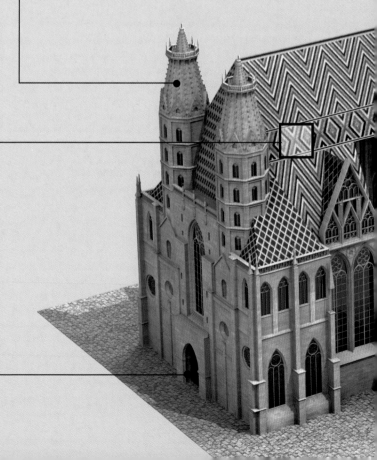

Giant's Door The west facade of the temple is one of the few remaining sections of the original Romanesque building built between 1240 and 1263.

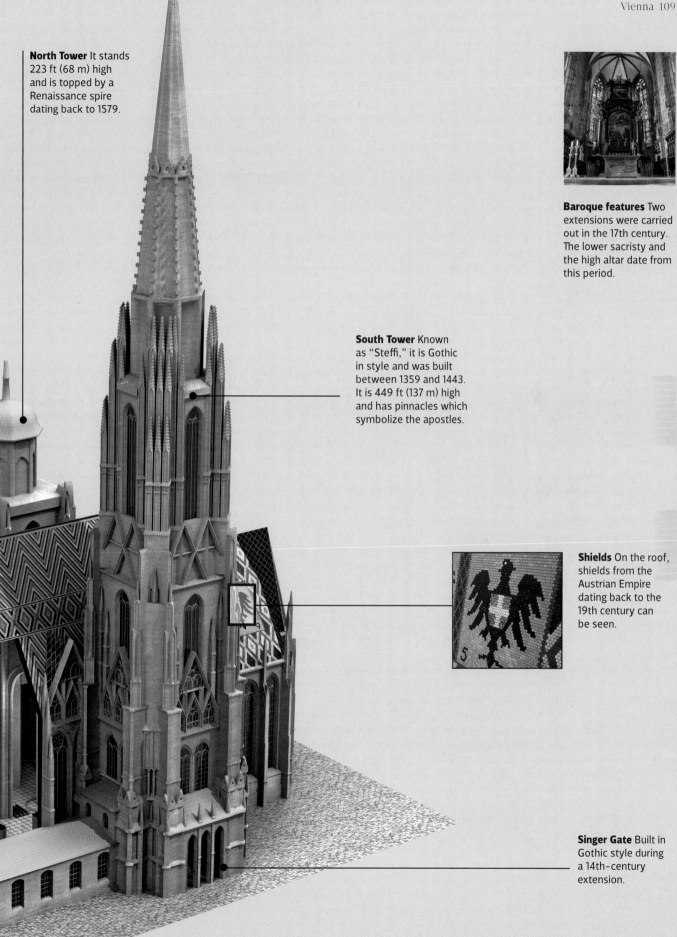

North Tower It stands 223 ft (68 m) high and is topped by a Renaissance spire dating back to 1579.

Baroque features Two extensions were carried out in the 17th century. The lower sacristy and the high altar date from this period.

South Tower Known as "Steffi," it is Gothic in style and was built between 1359 and 1443. It is 449 ft (137 m) high and has pinnacles which symbolize the apostles.

Shields On the roof, shields from the Austrian Empire dating back to the 19th century can be seen.

Singer Gate Built in Gothic style during a 14th-century extension.

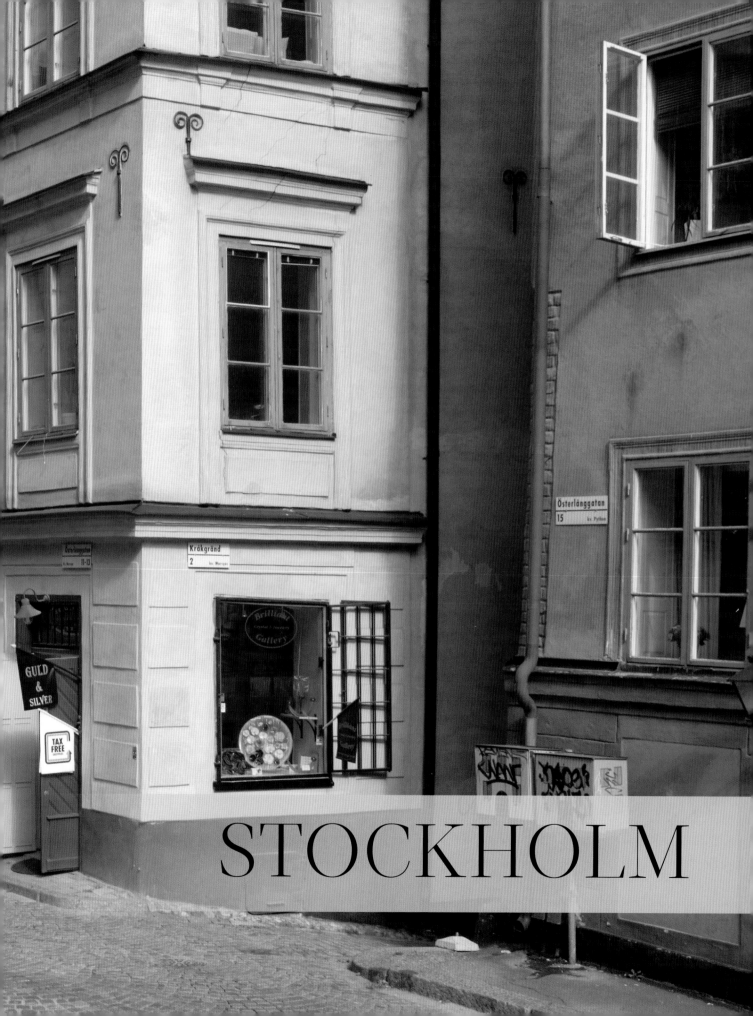

STOCKHOLM

The essence of Scandinavia

Stockholm has been the capital of Sweden since the beginning of the 15th century, and, from the Middle Ages, has housed the sites which most represent the Scandinavian kingdom.

Sweden

Stockholm

14 islands and 57 bridges

The municipality of Stockholm covers 14 inhabited islands, linked by 57 bridges which allow the city to be traversed entirely on foot, crossing over the canals that connect the Baltic Sea to the east, with the salty waters of Lake Mälar to the west. The metropolitan area, which is much more extensive, occupies up to 24,000 islands of different sizes, although only 150 are inhabited.

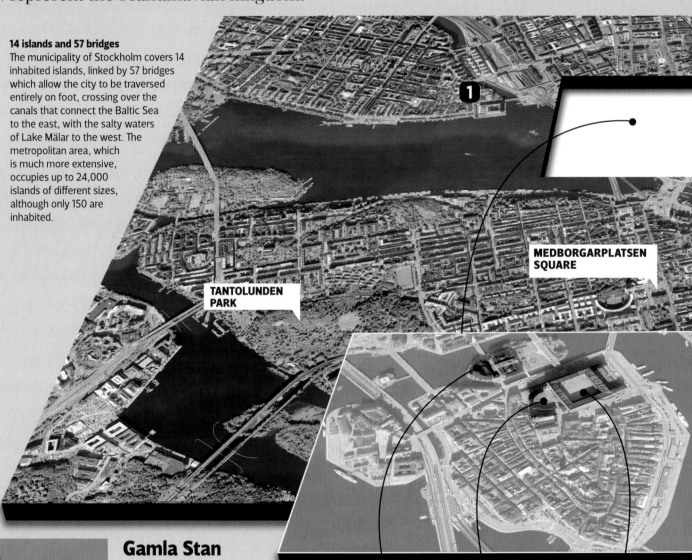

MEDBORGARPLATSEN SQUARE

TANTOLUNDEN PARK

Gamla Stan

Situated on the small island of Stadsholmen, the Old Town (*Gamla Stan* in Swedish) is the original center of the capital. Its medieval layout, restored in the 20th century, houses the church of St. Nicholas (Storkyrkan)—where the monarchs of Sweden are crowned— the Royal Palace (Kungliga Slottet), the Riddarhuset (or House of Nobility) and the Swedish Academy, which awards the Nobel prizes.

The Swedish Parliament
The Riksdag or Parliament has its roots in the 15th century and is located on the small island of Helgeandsholmen, situated between Stadsholmen and the district of Norrmalm.

Church of St. Nicholas
Known as Storkyrkan and built in plastered brick, it has a 13th-century gothic interior and an 18th century baroque facade.

The Royal Palace
This is one of the largest royal residences in the world and was built in the middle of the 18th century on the site where Jarl Birger built the fort which gave rise to the city.

KEY FACTS ABOUT STOCKHOLM

CAPITAL OF SWEDEN

Stockholm is the capital of Sweden and the largest city in the country, as well as being the center of Sweden's most extensive and inhabited metropolitan area.

LOCATION

Latitude 59° 19' 0" N
Longitude 18° 04' 0" E
Altitude 144 ft (44 m) above sea level

IN FIGURES

Surface area 73 mi² (188 km²)
Population 1,288,000 (2 million in the metropolitan area)
Population density 17,744/mi² (6,851 /km²)

FOUNDATION

Foundation date 1252
Founder Jarl Birger
Military fort Tired of attacks from foreign fleets, the *Jarl* (the title held by the Swedish nobility) Birger decided to build a military fort on an island, called Gamla Stan, located in the center of the largest canal which connects the Baltic Sea to Lake Mälar. The city of Stockholm emerged around this fort. In 1419 it was proclaimed the capital of Sweden.

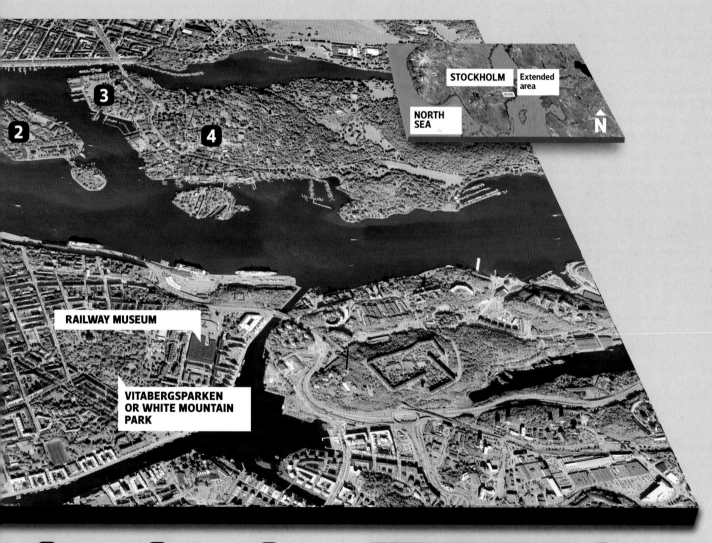

STOCKHOLM   Extended area

NORTH SEA

N

RAILWAY MUSEUM

VITABERGSPARKEN OR WHITE MOUNTAIN PARK

1

The Town Hall
Situated on the island of Kungsholmen, the Town Hall was built between 1911 and 1923 in red brick in the romantic style. It houses the Blue Hall, where each year the Nobel Prize banquet is held.

2

The Museum of Modern Art
Located on the island of Skeppsholmen, the Modern Museum exhibits great works of geniuses of the 20th century such as Picasso and Dalí. The current building (1998), is the work of Spaniard Rafael Moneo.

3

The Vasa Museum
The most visited museum in Scandinavia is situated on the island of Djurgården. It displays the well-preserved 17th-century warship *Vasa*, and has several exhibitions on the ship's history and the period.

4

Skansen
This museum contains about 150 buildings from different parts of Sweden, and displays Swedish life in the 19th century when it experienced a period of transformation from a rural agrarian to an industrial society.

The city of wellbeing

Stockholm began as a little island in a strategic location between the Baltic Sea and Lake Mälar.

A study of the city on Google Maps explains a lot about Stockholm. A simple look at its large metropolitan area shows a complex tangle of channels between the Baltic Sea and Lake Mälar, created through the action of the glaciers that covered the region until a few tens of thousands of years ago. Obviously, the image explains a lot about its geography: some 24,000 islands and islets have been created in this land tortured by ice. But this also explains a lot about its history: In 1252, Jarl (Count) Birger ordered the construction of a fort on a small island which was strategically situated in this region, in order to defend against the incursions of enemy forces. This island, then called Stadsholmen, was the beginning of what is today known as Gamla Stan or the Old City, the medieval heart of Stockholm. It is surrounded by the districts of Norrmalm, the modern city center; Södermalm, with the best views of the city and a lively area for evening entertainment; Östermalm, the upmarket district; and Djurgården, a woody island that houses the distinguished open-air museum Skansen.

This strategic position was one of the main reasons for the city's growth and development between the end of the Middle Ages and the beginning of the Modern Age. However, after a magnificent 17th century, in which the population grew by a factor of seven to reach 100,000 inhabitants, there came the long centuries of decay resulting from the Great Northern War, which left the capital half destroyed. It was a difficult period not just for Stockholm but for the whole of Sweden, many of whose inhabitants had to emigrate to North America to escape the widespread poverty.

When we look at the city's enviable current situation, it is surprising to think of the long crisis that the country experienced up until only a century ago. Today,

Stockholm, the cradle of Alfred Nobel, Greta Garbo and Ingrid Bergman, of ABBA and Henning Mankell, is a rich city, with a high standard of living, only moderated by the traditional Nordic sense of austerity. In addition to the headquarters of locally based multinationals such as Ericsson and Electrolux – found in the technological district of Kista – and the clothing retailer H&M, the capital has an active port. It has connections to all the Baltic cities, and has recovered from the severe economic crisis that shook the foundations of Swedish society in the 1990s threatening the traditional social democracy, which was the dominant ideology in the country throughout most of the 20th century and largely responsible for the successful state model of well-being enjoyed by its inhabitants.

Frozen winters and summers in the open air
Like all the cities located in the higher latitudes, Stockholm has two personalities, almost opposed to each other: its dark, frozen winters encourage a domestic, indoor life, which is why one of the Swedes' greatest desires is to have a comfortable living space, always furnished with a good library and fast Internet access. In contrast, summers are an explosion of life that the inhabitants of Stockholm live to the full outdoors, participating in the many parties,

1.Stortorget
This is the main square of the old city and the oldest square in Stockholm.

2.Skansen Museum
Located on the island of Djurgården, this open-air museum, founded in 1891, shows the architecture and traditional way of life of Sweden.

3.Gamla Stan
The historical center is characterized by its medieval and Renaissance houses and streets.

4.The House of Nobility
Also called Riddarhuset, this palace was built between 1641 and 1674 as a meeting place for the Swedish nobility.

5.Skogskyrkgarden
A World Heritage Site since 1994, the Cemetery Woodland was built in 1915, to integrate graves with nature.

6.Royal Palace
It has more than 600 richly decorated rooms, some of which may be visited.

concerts and festivals that are organized in the city, or moving out to the little vacation homes that many of them own in the countryside. Personal safety is among the best in the world, although the murder of two political leaders – that of the historic social-democratic leader Olof Palme in 1986 and that of the Minister of Foreign Affairs Anna Lindh in 2003 – continue to haunt the peaceful inhabitants even years later.

Perhaps it is the experience of seeing nature fall silent for more than seven months each fall that makes the Swedes so careful about the environment. Or perhaps it is just the opposite: the privilege of being there every spring for the miracle of seeing nature reborn, the disappearance of the white mantle that has covered the city and its surroundings and its transformation into a carpet of deep green which comes to dominate the parks and the woods of the metropolitan area between May and October. The reality is that the residents of Stockholm – with the highest rate of immigration in the country, especially with the neighboring Finns – put ecological issues at the top of the political agenda. For example with the urban toll that cars have had to pay since 2006 when they enter the city, a measure designed to reduce traffic and therefore pollution.

Royal Palace

Today the official residence of the Swedish monarchy, it was built in baroque style on the site of the old Fortress of the Three Crowns and completed in 1754.

Roof Covered in copper and completely surrounded by a balustrade, it inclines slightly inward.

External courtyard Located on the west facade, it is surrounded by two semicircular wings.

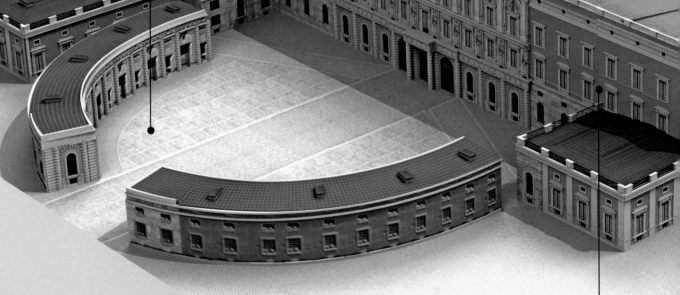

Museums The palace is home to several museums: Gustav III's Museum of Antiquities (photo), the Three Crowns, the Treasury, the Royal Armory and the Royal Apartments.

Facades The facades are red brick with some sections covered in sandstone.

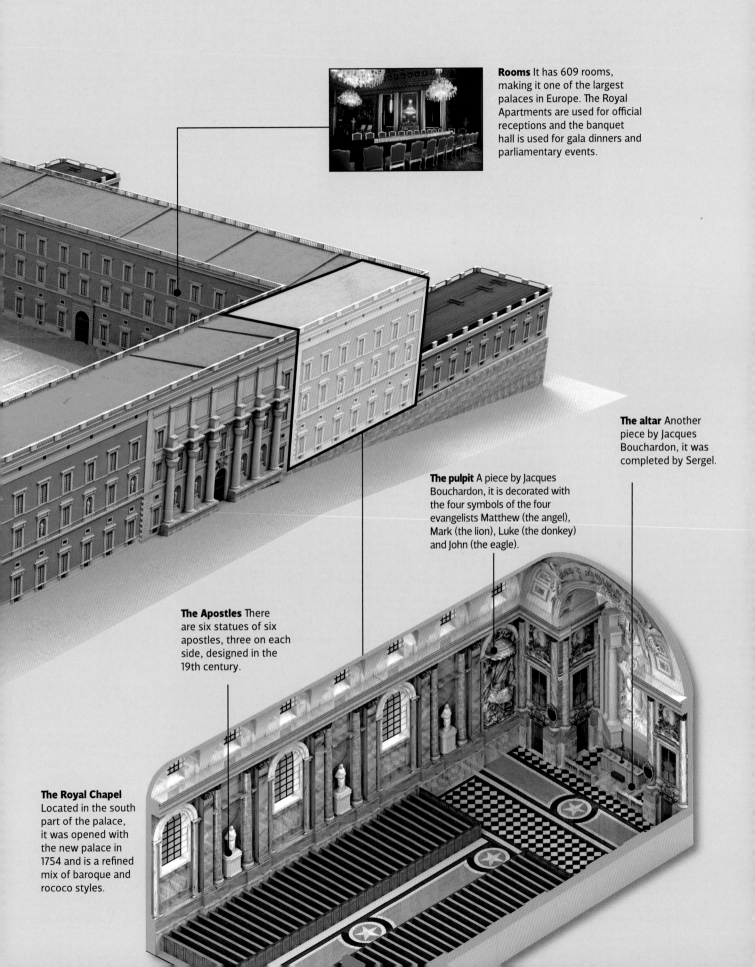

Rooms It has 609 rooms, making it one of the largest palaces in Europe. The Royal Apartments are used for official receptions and the banquet hall is used for gala dinners and parliamentary events.

The altar Another piece by Jacques Bouchardon, it was completed by Sergel.

The pulpit A piece by Jacques Bouchardon, it is decorated with the four symbols of the four evangelists Matthew (the angel), Mark (the lion), Luke (the donkey) and John (the eagle).

The Apostles There are six statues of six apostles, three on each side, designed in the 19th century.

The Royal Chapel Located in the south part of the palace, it was opened with the new palace in 1754 and is a refined mix of baroque and rococo styles.

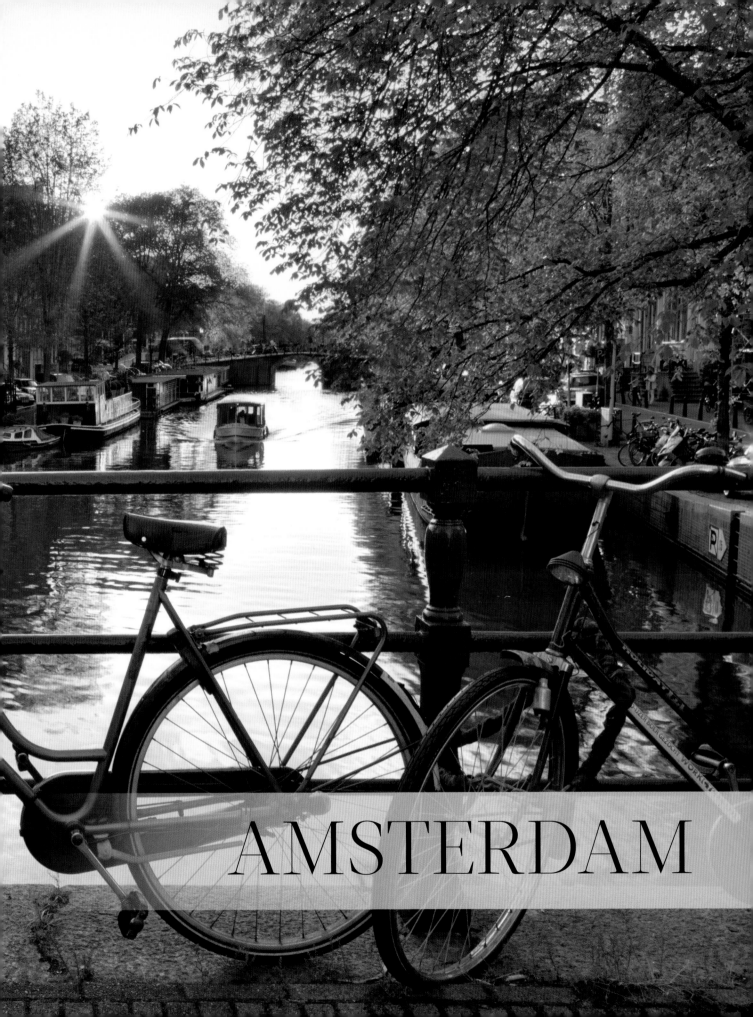

AMSTERDAM

The Venice of the North

Built on land reclaimed from the sea, Amsterdam is crisscrossed by 160 canals which give it a very distinguished personality.

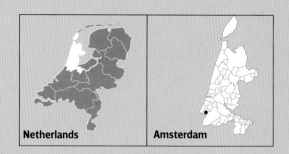

Netherlands | Amsterdam

NORTH SEA

AMSTERDAM
Extended area
MUSEUMPLEIN
Ñ

Connected to the North Sea

Amsterdam is located next to the waters of the IJ bay dykes, which connect it, through the dykes that protect the city, with the North Sea. To facilitate the barge traffic, a canal was opened to make a direct link between the port and the North Sea, across the peninsula of North Holland.

1

House of Anne Frank
The house in which the Jewish girl Anne Frank hid from the Nazis is now a museum recounting her isolation and subsequent death in a concentration camp.

NATIONAL MONUMENT

OPER

Dam Square

The origin and heart of Amsterdam, Dam Square is the place where the first containing dyke was built, making it possible to build the city's first buildings. It has an irregular shape and contains important buildings such as the Royal Palace, the New Church and the National Monument.

2

Royal Palace
Built in the mid-17th century, the Royal Palace housed parliament until 1808, when it was converted into the Royal Residence for Louis Bonaparte.

3

New Church
The Nieuwe Kerk was built at the beginning of the 15th century to provide for the growing number of believers in the city. In the 17th century it was rebuilt in Gothic style.

KEY FACTS ABOUT AMSTERDAM

COCAPITAL OF THE NETHERLANDS
Amsterdam is the largest city in the country and shares the status of capital with The Hague, where the legislative, executive and judicial branches of government sit.

LOCATION
Latitude 52° 22' 0" N
Longitude 4° 53' 0" E
Altitude –13 to 46 ft (–4 to 14 m) below sea level

IN FIGURES
Surface area
84.56 mi² (219 km²)
Population 760,000 (1.5 million in the metropolitan area)
Population density
8,987/mi² (3,470/km²)

FOUNDATION
Foundation date
12th century
Medieval origins
It is recorded that a group of Friesian fishermen settled in the area in the 12th century. However, the first written documents mentioning Amsterdam date from 1275. Today, with Rotterdam, Utrecht and the Hague, it is part of the populous conurbation of Randstad, with 6.5 million inhabitants.

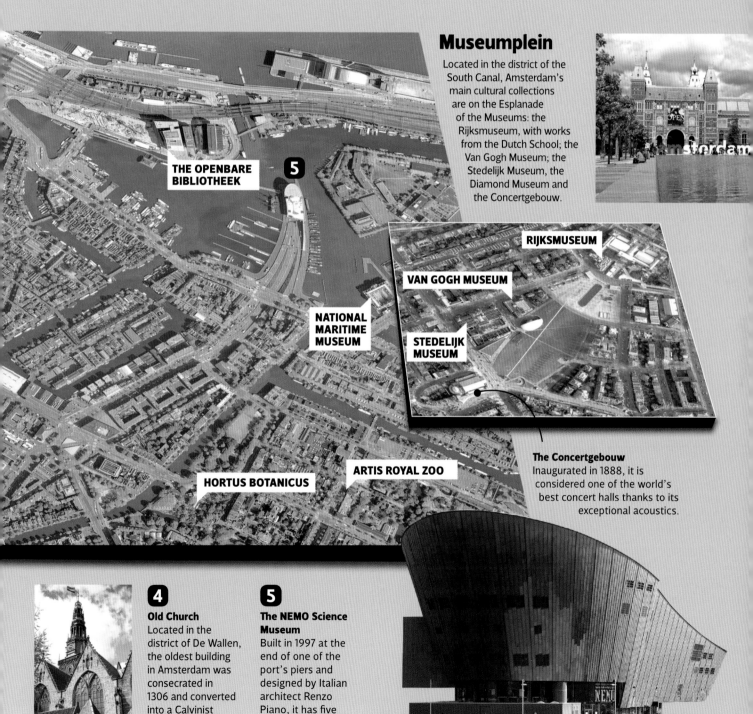

Museumplein

Located in the district of the South Canal, Amsterdam's main cultural collections are on the Esplanade of the Museums: the Rijksmuseum, with works from the Dutch School; the Van Gogh Museum; the Stedelijk Museum, the Diamond Museum and the Concertgebouw.

THE OPENBARE BIBLIOTHEEK

5

NATIONAL MARITIME MUSEUM

RIJKSMUSEUM

VAN GOGH MUSEUM

STEDELIJK MUSEUM

The Concertgebouw
Inaugurated in 1888, it is considered one of the world's best concert halls thanks to its exceptional acoustics.

HORTUS BOTANICUS

ARTIS ROYAL ZOO

4
Old Church
Located in the district of De Wallen, the oldest building in Amsterdam was consecrated in 1306 and converted into a Calvinist temple during the Reformation, in 1578.

5
The NEMO Science Museum
Built in 1997 at the end of one of the port's piers and designed by Italian architect Renzo Piano, it has five floors of scientific exhibits.

Living on the water

Open, tolerant and liberal, Amsterdam is the dynamic capital of one of the most unusual countries on the planet.

The Netherlands is unique: half its surface area is below sea level and Amsterdam, its capital, is a good example of this peculiar system: the houses of its large original center were built on a bed of wooden wedges which were pushed into the sandy soil like concrete foundations: sound evidence of the tenacious and imaginative character of its inhabitants.

Amsterdam was founded in the 12th century by fishermen and peasants, who built dykes and then drained the land reclaimed from the sea – called "polders" – in order to grow crops. Dam Square, the city's crowning glory since its foundation, was the first dyke (dam in Dutch) to be constructed to contain the waters which are today channeled into the river Amstel, which explains the name of the city. Thanks to its strategic situation sheltered from the North Sea, Amsterdam grew rapidly. In 1300 it was granted the status of city and in the 16th century it received a considerable number of Jews who had been expelled from Spain and Portugal, plus Protestants fleeing from Flanders and Huguenots from France.

The arrival of these dynamic communities meant a great leap forward for the city, both in social and economic terms, and this founded a tradition of tolerance which has been maintained to the present day. It is no coincidence that the Netherlands was the first country to legalize euthanasia and gay marriage – indeed, it has the most active and powerful gay collective in Europe. Soft drugs are permitted – hashish and marijuana are consumed in the city's popular coffee shops – and prostitution is also tolerated, institutionalized in the famous Red Light District, to the east of Dam Square.

Amsterdam experienced its own Golden Age in the 17th century, when it became the leading port in Europe, thanks to the Spanish conquest of the city of Antwerp in Flanders, its main regional rival. Without this competition, the Dutch capital intensified its sea trade with the Baltic countries, North America, Brazil, Africa and Indonesia, until it had achieved a position of hegemony.

The demographic growth of the city during this brilliant period led the local authorities to make profound changes to the medieval city center, designing a semi-circular network of concentric canals around the center, to house the new arrivals. Today, thanks to a strict policy of protection, both the heart of the city and the new belt of construction from the 17th century are conserved almost intact, with more than 7,000 buildings catalogued as national monuments. Many are identifiable by their characteristic redbrick facades, which, like the well-known Casa Bartolotti, are reflected in the peaceful waters of the canals.

Open-minded
Traditionally open-minded and liberal, in recent years the Dutch have taken a more conservative turn in their habits. Nevertheless, Amsterdam continues to be a hospitable city, and continues to offer good opportunities for immigrants, who make up 12 percent of the population, with the largest numbers coming from Surinam, Indonesia, Morocco and Turkey.

Lovers of the excellent local beer and passionate followers of Ajax, the soccer team that has been the champion of Europe four times and home to the brilliant Johan Cruyff, one of the best soccer players

1. De Waag
This medieval building is located in the New Market Square, an area full of terraces and with a varied market.

2. Living on the canal
Amsterdam has more than 600 mi (1,000 km) of canals, on the shores of which barges are moored, including some houseboats.

3. Bicycles everywhere
Circulating in traffic or parked on the sidewalks or by the canals, bicycles are everywhere in the city.

4. Typical houses
Built in the 17th century, they are characterized by being extremely narrow, and by their bell-shaped eaves.

5. Permissiveness
The permissive attitude to the sale and consumption of marijuana and hashish is also a tourist attraction.

6. Queen's Day
Queen's Day is on April 30, a national holiday celebrated on the canals on board boats with music at full volume.

in history, the residents of Amsterdam also enjoy the exceptional collections of art that are exhibited in the city, mostly grouped in the Esplanade of Museums, close to Vondelpark, the largest green space in the city center.

Amsterdammers are also addicted to shopping in the area of the Nine Little Streets (Negen Straatjes, in Dutch), located in the district of Jordaan, in the marvelous antique shops of Nieuwe Spiegelstraat and in the lively market of Waterlooplein, always traveling– it's true!–by bicycle, the typical and characteristic means of transportation in Amsterdam. For the nearly 800,000 inhabitants of the city there are some 700,000 bicycles, many of which are in terrible condition. It is a good way of making sure they don't get stolen, this being a crime against which the local authorities struggle without much success: every year some 80,000 bicycles go missing. About half of these end up rusting in the waters of the canals.

The Begijnhof Court

This site, built in the 14th century, was the residence of a Catholic sisterhood (the Beguines) who were dedicated to charity.

Engelse Kerk The English church, built in 1419, passed into the hands of the Calvinists in 1578, and then to the Presbyterians, so the women of the congregation then built secret churches at numbers 28 and 29 of the square.

Houten Huis Located at number 40, Houten Huis was built in 1470 and is the oldest house in Amsterdam, and one of only two wooden buildings that still remain in the city.

Courtyard The buildings are arranged around a carefully landscaped central courtyard.

Entrances The area is semihidden in the middle of the city. It is accessed by the arch of Gedempte Begijnensloot. Although it is private property, it can be visited for free as long as the prevailing silence is respected.

Residents The last Beguine died in 1971, and today the houses are occupied by up to 140 single women and students.

Gable end Frequently seen on Amsterdam houses, these facade finishes could be rectangular, staggered or bell-shaped.

Houses There are 47 houses. Originally they were made of wood, but in 1521 it was forbidden to use this material to build properties as it easily caught on fire. In fact the majority of the current houses date from the 17th and 18th centuries, as the older, wooden buildings were destroyed by a fire.

BRUSSELS

Medieval heart

The name Brussels probably comes from a medieval Dutch term meaning "hermit in the marsh," referring to the religious building that gave rise to the city.

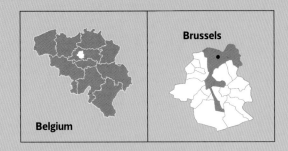

Belgium

Brussels

The city center

A ring of boulevards in the shape of a pentagon, built in the 19th century, marks the historic sector of Brussels, with the Grand Place as the center.

NORTH SEA

Extended area

BRUSSELS

N

Grand Place

The Grand Place has held the city's market since the Middle Ages. The buildings surrounding it, among others the Gothic Town Hall from the 15th century and the King's House, rebuilt in the 19th century in neo-Gothic style, make this square one of the most elegant in the world.

Town Hall Tower, 314 ft (96 m) high.

LAW COURTS

KING'S HOUSE

TOWN HALL

1
La Monnaie
The Royal Theater of the Mint was built in the 19th century. It hosts one of the most prestigious opera companies and was the headquarters of the famous 20th-century ballet company, directed by Maurice Béjart.

KEY FACTS ABOUT BRUSSELS

CAPITAL OF BELGIUM AND OF THE EU
Brussels is the capital of the federal state of Belgium, and hosts the main European Union and NATO institutions.

LOCATION
Latitude
50° 51' 0" N
Longitude
4° 21' 0" E
Altitude
164 ft (50 m) above sea level

IN FIGURES
Surface area:
62 mi² (161 km²)
Population
1,125,000
Population density
18,125/mi² (6,988/km²)

FOUNDATION
Foundation date
Bronze Age
Origin uncertain
Remains of settlements from the 3rd millennium before Christ and

the 7th century were found in the area of present-day Brussels. However, the Belgians commemorate the foundation of the city in 979, the year in which the

Duke of Brabant supposedly ordered the construction of a fortress there at the request of the Emperor Otto II, to defend the town square.

BOTANICAL GARDEN

2

EUROPEAN PARLIAMENT OF BRUSSELS

ROYAL THEATER OF THE PARK

ROYAL PALACE

The Royal Palace and Brussels Park

Located at the eastern edge of the Old City, the Royal Palace is the official residence of the royal family, even though they actually live at the Castle of Laeken, on the outskirts of the city. It was built at the beginning of the 19th century, although its facade, which looks out onto the great green expanse of Brussels Park, is from the beginning of the 20th century.

The Royal Palace by night

2
Brussels Cathedral
The Cathedral of St. Michael and St. Gudula is a Gothic building dating from between 1226 and 1500 that did not attain the category of a cathedral until 1962.

3
Manneken Pis
The "urinating boy" is a small bronze statue 24 in (61 cm) tall, located in a corner of the medieval city, and is one of the symbols of Brussels.

The capital of Europe

Brussels acts as a link between the Walloons and Flemish people in Belgium and as capital of the 27 member-state European Union.

As capital of a small state and a great continent, Brussels is, more than host to the majority of Europe's institutions, a magnificent symbol of what Europe represents. Bruxelles to some and Brussels to others, the city is the main mechanism of cohesion between the two communities that make up the state of Belgium—Flemish and Walloon—and struggles to keep them together because of their notable differences (cultural, linguistic, social and economic) the same sort of thing that happens, on a much larger scale, with the 27 states making up the EU.

The metropolitan area of Brussels is, together with Flanders and Wallonia, one of the three federal regions that make up Belgium. They reflect the political decentralization that was undertaken in 1993 with the aim of curbing the progressive drifting apart of the Dutch-speaking Flems from the north and the French-speaking Walloons of the south. Twenty years later the tensions continue, making it extremely difficult for the country's government, despite the unifying role of the capital, which is at the same time the seat of the North Atlantic Treaty Organization (NATO).

Even though it is officially bilingual, French-speakers now predominate in Brussels. But it wasn't always like that. Founded during the High Middle Ages on a small hill that dominated a swampy area, the Belgian capital was an almost exclusively Dutch city for the whole of the Middle Ages and a large part of the Modern Age. However, from the 18th century onward it underwent an intense period of French development, which turned its situation completely upside down. Today, 57 percent of its inhabitants have French as their mother tongue and only 7 percent come from Dutch-speaking families. The remainder of the residents come principally from the Maghreb, Turkey and

the Congo—formerly a Belgian colony—or are EU officials, whose habitual use of French as lingua franca increases the existing linguistic imbalance still further.

One thing the Walloons, Flems and foreign residents all agree on is enjoying the beer and the chocolates that have made Brussels world famous. Choosing from among the hundreds of local beer brands in one of the city's excellent pubs is one of the greatest pleasures in the Belgian capital, together with enjoying the typical and popular mussels with fries (moules et frites), a simple dish that in the taverns of central Brussels is transformed into a ritual worthy of a gourmet.

The historic center

Always lively and bubbling, the old city center spreads out around the Grand Place, the city's medieval heart, bound by a ring of boulevards called La Petite Ceinture (Little Belt). Flanked by beautiful examples of Gothic, Renaissance and Baroque architecture, the cobbled streets of the center hide surprises like the little statue of the Manneken Pis, a symbol of the city through which the inhabitants express their special sense of humor. It is something seen day after day in a thousand different ways, with the same imagination that made Brussels the comic capital of Europe: Hergé (Tintin), Morris (Lucky Luke), Franquin (Spirou), Peyo (The Smurfs) or Jacobs (Blake and Mortimer), all local artists, are one of the prides of the country, with their work collected and displayed in the Belgian Comic Center, to the northeast of the Grand Place.

In the mid-19th century, the building of the Quartier Léopold (Leopold Quarter) meant the first expansion of the city outside of its medieval core, projecting toward

←The city of comics
Brussels being the home of some of the greatest comic artists has many facades of the old town decorated with their drawings.

←The King's House
Located in the Grand Place, this former office of the duke's, and then the king's, tax-collector, today houses the Museum of the City of Brussels.

↓Atomium, symbol of Brussels
This structure, 338 ft (103 m) in height, was built for the 1958 World's Fair and reproduces the atomic structure of an iron crystal.

the southeast and absorbing the town of Ixelles. A few decades later, at the end of the 19th century, this area of metropolitan Brussels, birthplace of people as famous as the actress Audrey Hepburn or the writer Julio Cortázar, produced a new style, art nouveau, invented by the brilliant Belgian architect Víctor Horta, some of whose best works–the Tassel House and the Solvay House–stand in the district. And just half a mile further north, around the large Schuman Plaza, is the so-called European District, from whose main buildings–the seats of the European Commission, the Council of Europe and the European Parliament–the destiny of more than 500 million inhabitants of the Old Continent is decided. That challenge is so complicated that the local disagreements between Flemish and Walloon citizens seem something tiny in comparison.

Grand Place

This is a collection of buildings with huge architectural value. It includes structures of different styles, some of which such as the Town Hall, are real gems.

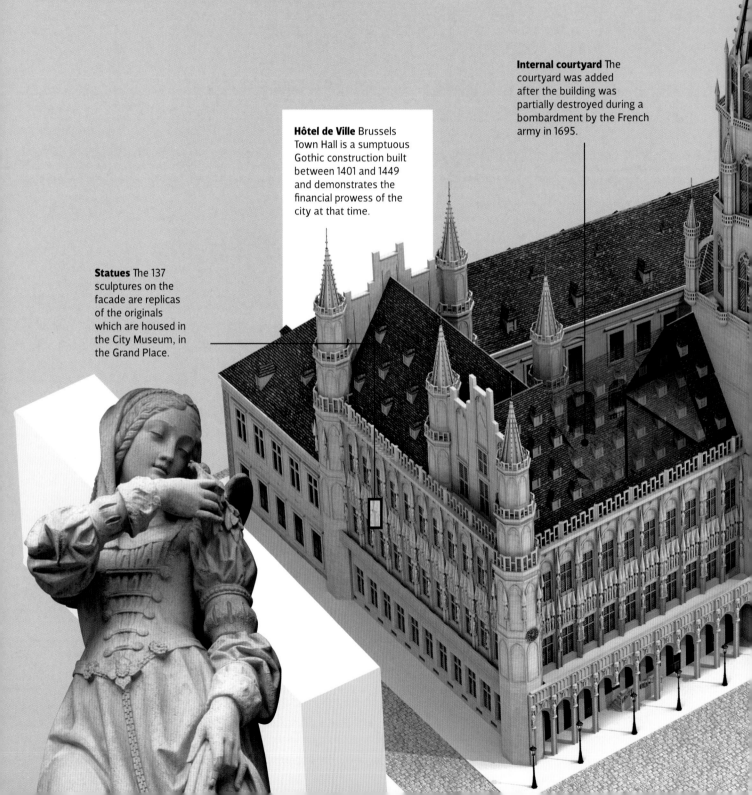

Tower Built in 1455 in Gothic style, it measures 315 ft (96 m) high. At its summit there is a 16-ft (5-m) high gilded statue of the archangel Michael, patron of the city, slaying a dragon.

Internal courtyard The courtyard was added after the building was partially destroyed during a bombardment by the French army in 1695.

Hôtel de Ville Brussels Town Hall is a sumptuous Gothic construction built between 1401 and 1449 and demonstrates the financial prowess of the city at that time.

Statues The 137 sculptures on the facade are replicas of the originals which are housed in the City Museum, in the Grand Place.

La Louvre (The She-Wolf) Former headquarters of the archer's guild, featuring a phoenix.

Renard (The Fox) The headquarters of the haberdashers' guild displays a fox on its facade.

Roof This gable roof is filled with dozens of attic rooms with skylights.

Le Sac (The Bag) Headquarters of the cabinet-makers' guild.

Le Cornet (The Horn) Headquarters of the boatmen's guild, its facade emulates the stern of a galleon.

The Guild Houses Grand Place was the location of the former industrial unions. The majority of the buildings date from the end of the 17th century and the beginning of the 18th century, when they were rebuilt in record time after being bombed.

Portico Following the model of the period there is a facade with a portico, the function of which was to house the city market.

Modernization Some buildings have hardly changed in 200 years. Others have been updated and house businesses, cafes and restaurants on the lower levels.

La Brouette (The Wheelbarrow) House of the grease-maker's guild, who transferred their merchandise with wheelbarrows.

Le Roi d'Espagne (King of Spain) So-called because of the bust of Carlos II, the King of Spain, which adorns the facade. It used to be the baker's headquarters.

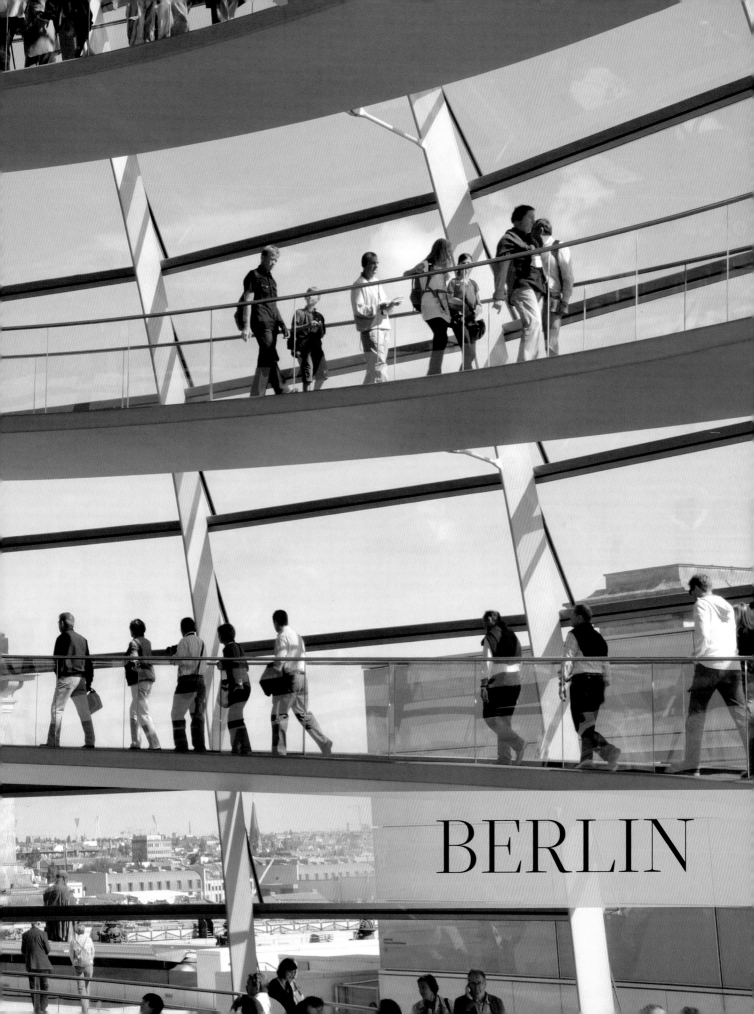

BERLIN

Two cities in one

Expansive and flat, Berlin is a city whose most central district–Mitte–stands on both banks of the Spree River.

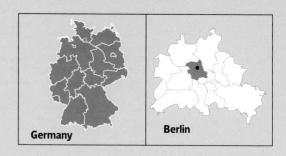

Germany | Berlin

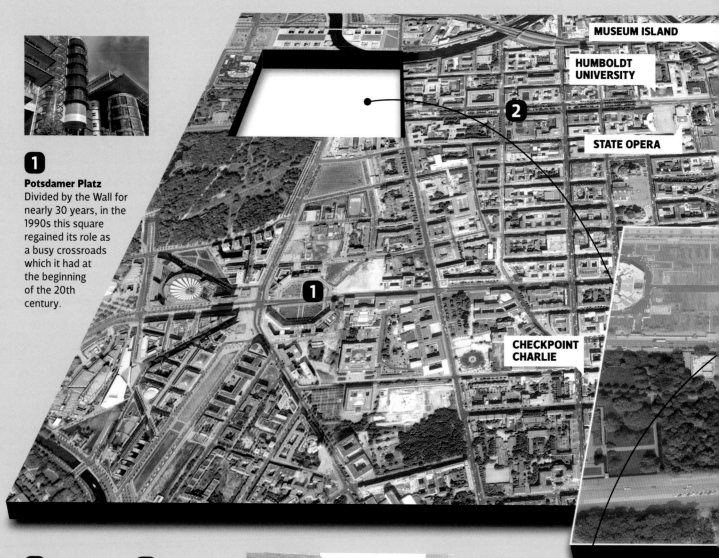

MUSEUM ISLAND

HUMBOLDT UNIVERSITY

STATE OPERA

CHECKPOINT CHARLIE

1

Potsdamer Platz
Divided by the Wall for nearly 30 years, in the 1990s this square regained its role as a busy crossroads which it had at the beginning of the 20th century.

2

Komische Oper
The Komische Oper is a small theater built in 1892 with room for 1,300 spectators. Its modern facade in the shape of a cube hides a neo-baroque interior.

3

Alexanderplatz
Located in old Berlin, it has retained its typical socialist urban planning. The city's largest Nazi bunker was recently discovered underneath it.

The Bundestag
At the end of the 20th century the building housing the Reichstag was fundamentally rebuilt to hold the Bundestag–the Federal German parliament. The original building, built at the end of the 19th century at the time of German unification, was left practically in ruins by World War II and was redesigned by British architect Norman Foster.

KEY FACTS ABOUT BERLIN

CAPITAL OF GERMANY
Berlin recovered the status of capital of Germany in 1990, after reunification. It is one of the 16 federal states of Germany.

LOCATION
Latitude
52° 31′ 0″ N
Longitude
13° 24′ 0″ E
Altitude
141 ft (34 m) above sea level

IN FIGURES
Surface area
344 mi² (892 km²)
Population
3,445,000
Population density
10,003/mi²
(3,862/km²)

FOUNDATION
Foundation date
1307
Founder
Otto III
Origins
Two towns founded at the beginning of the 13th century— Berlin and Cölln (a settlement that used to stand on the current Museum Island)— united in 1307 to form one city, with the name of the former.

CASTLE SQUARE

BALTIC SEA

BERLIN

Extended area

The Central district
The geographical and historical heart of the capital, the new district of Mitte, where many of its tourist attractions are located, includes areas formerly located in East Berlin, such as the district of Mitte itself, with parts of West Berlin, such as Tiergarten or Wedding.

Victory Column
Located at the intersection of five avenues in Tiergarten park, this monument 226 ft (69 m) high, was inaugurated in 1874 to commemorate the successive Prussian victories against Denmark, the Austrian Empire and the reign of Napoleon III.

The Brandenburg Gate
The work of Carl Gotthard Langhans, the Brandenburg Gate is built in neoclassical style inspired by the atria of the Acropolis in Athens. It was the monumental entry to Berlin from when it was finished in 1791 until the enlargement of the city in the 20th century.

Monument Center

On the south bank of the Spree River is the area of Berlin with the highest density of monuments: The Bundestag, the former Reichstag, and the Brandenburg Gate, which marks the beginning of the Unter den Linden (Under the Linden Trees), the city's main avenue.

The memory of the Wall

After almost 30 years of division and isolation, in 1989 Berlin was reunified and became the capital of a united Germany.

"Definitive exits are now possible through all the frontier points of the German Democratic Republic to the Federal Republic of Germany. As far as I know effective immediately, without delay." These were the words of an official of the Unified Socialist Party of Germany, Günter Schabowski, in a press conference on November 9, 1989. It meant the end of 28 years of the Berlin Wall, the uncrossable frontier that split the old German capital, converted during the Cold War into a symbol of the painful division of Europe and, from that precise moment, also of the reunification of the city, the country and the continent.

The happiest day

A consequence of the general breakdown in the Soviet Union and its satellite states, the day the Wall fell was the happiest day in the lives of several generations of Berliners: those who had seen it being built and those who had been born when the barrier already prevented natural things like brothers and sisters getting together for a celebration, or that two old friends could meet at the café on the corner to have a cup of coffee, or that a family could go for trips around their own country as tourists.

A few months later, the reunification was consummated and the federal capital was once more Berlin, a city which had already been the seat of the court of the medieval state of Brandenburg, of the modern Kingdom of Prussia and of the different versions of Germany up until the Third Reich, and whose failure left Berlin in ruins. So, to recuperate its stature of old, work had to be done. On the one hand, the need arose to design new government buildings or restore those already there to house the federal institutions. On the other hand, the destruction of the Wall—work in which the Berliners had joined in enthusiastically, armed with pickaxes, sledgehammers and anything else they could find—left an unoccupied strip of land from tens to hundreds of yards wide, which crossed the city center from north to south. And additionally, one-third of the surface area of the city—the former Soviet Sector—was opened up to capitalism, with a consequent revolution of commerce and construction.

Reconstruction after the fall of the Wall

With these conditions, post-Wall Berlin turned into a real laboratory for all kinds of planning experiments. The reconstruction affected all the districts, but the areas that saw the most profound changes were those around the Reichstag, the neo-Renaissance building now converted into the Bundestag, or German Parliament, where the highest telecommunications tower in the European Union was erected; and, especially, the Potsdamer Platz, a large area that had known its most splendid period in the 1920s, had been destroyed in World War II, and then left as no-man's-land by the transit of the Wall. After the Wall was demolished, a very large area of 150 acres (60 ha) was

📷

1. East Side Gallery
The remains of the Berlin Wall have been converted into an open-air museum where various artists have been developing their vision of the world since it fell.

2. Sony Center
This complex of buildings in the Postdamer Platz was finished in 2000 and contains many shops and offices.

3. Tiergarten
A wintertime image of the most central and popular park in Berlin with the Victory Column in the background.

4. Checkpoint Charlie
The reconstruction of one of the main border crossings of the Wall is today one of Berlin's tourist attractions.

5. Holocaust Memorial
This monument to the Jews murdered in Europe, which stands close to the Brandenburg Gate, is made up of 2,711 blocks of cement.

opened up, and various star architects (Arata Isozaki, Renzi Piano, Rafael Moneo and Helmut Jahn, among others) designed iconic buildings.

However, after a few years of initial euphoria, Berlin –and in general all the states of the former German Democratic Republic– went into an alarming period of economic stagnation which even today, more than 20 years later, continues to hamper economic activity in the German capital, despite the considerable government grants provided by the rich federal states of the West.

Civilized, educated, liberal and very fond of nightlife, clubs and techno music–Tangerine Dream, the fathers of electronic music, were born here–the Berliners look at this new situation with the calm attitude that comes from the experience of having lived buried away, isolated from the rest of the world for nearly three decades. With a very high figure of 10 percent of residents being of foreign origin–with a high proportion of Turks–the inhabitants of this city which aims to be the capital of Europe look forward with some worries, above all, about the integrity of their immediate surroundings, the green belt that their predecessors guarded a century ago, and that they now care for as if it were their own private garden.

The Reichstag

Built at the end of the 19th century in neo–Renaissance style and remodeled at the end of the 1990s, the Reichstag is the current headquarters of the Bundestag, the German Parliament.

The main facade Designed by Paul Wallot in 1895 in neo–Renaissance style, the main facade's entrance is decorated with a staircase and Corinthian columns.

Interior The inside was completely redesigned between 1994 and 1996, using concrete, glass and steel. Brightness, energy efficiency and modernity prevail, with a range of colors in the different areas.

DEM DEUTSCHEN VOLKE

The Plenary Hall
Located in the center of the building, this hall is approximately 3,937 ft^2 (1,200 m^2). Completely remodeled, while respecting its historic heritage, it is presided over by the Federal Eagle. Sessions can be observed from the upper dome.

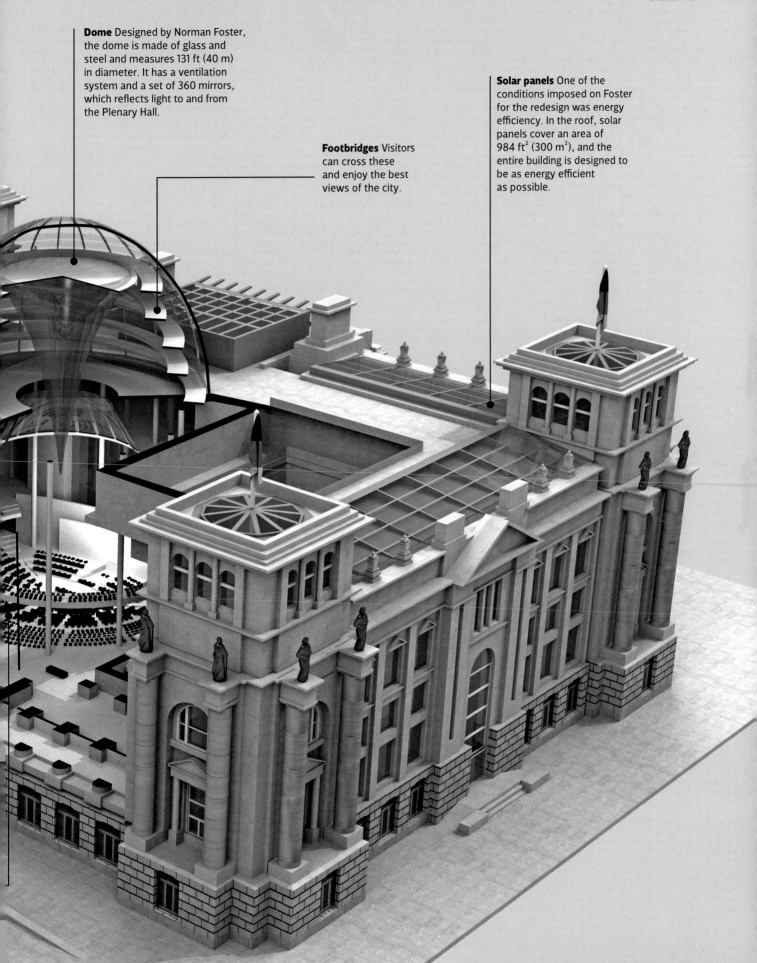

Dome Designed by Norman Foster, the dome is made of glass and steel and measures 131 ft (40 m) in diameter. It has a ventilation system and a set of 360 mirrors, which reflects light to and from the Plenary Hall.

Footbridges Visitors can cross these and enjoy the best views of the city.

Solar panels One of the conditions imposed on Foster for the redesign was energy efficiency. In the roof, solar panels cover an area of 984 ft^2 (300 m^2), and the entire building is designed to be as energy efficient as possible.

PRAGUE

At the foot of the castle

Located on the banks of the Vltava River, Prague has one of the greatest concentrations of historical monuments in Europe.

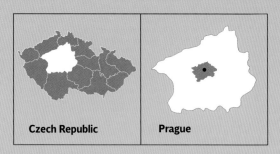

Czech Republic Prague

Prague Castle

The largest Medieval fortress in Europe, it was built in the 9th century, enlarged in Gothic style and restored between 1920 and 1934. It has a surface area of 840 ft^2 (78,000 m^2), an area equivalent to 100 standard football fields, with a length of 1,870 ft (570 m) and an average width of 426 ft (130 m). Inside the castle is the St. Vitus Cathedral, the largest example of Gothic art in the city, St. George's Basilica and the Royal Palace.

ST. VITUS CATHEDRAL

St. Nicolas Church
Built between 1673 and 1752 for the use of the Jesuits, St. Nicholas is the baroque jewel of Prague. From its tower, 213 ft (65 m) high, you can see the whole district of Malá Strana, one of the city's oldest areas.

1

Charles Bridge
This Gothic style bridge over the Vltava, the oldest in Prague, joins the Old Town to Malá Strana. Construction began in 1357 under the orders of King Charles IV.

Statue of St. John the Baptist
This is one of the 30 mainly Baroque sculptures that decorate Charles Bridge.

⊕ KEY FACTS ABOUT PRAGUE

THE CAPITAL OF THE CZECH REPUBLIC
Capital of Czechoslovakia from 1918. On January 1, 1993 it became the capital of the new Czech Republic.

LOCATION
Latitude
50° 05' 0" N
Longitude
14° 25' 0" E
Altitude
587–1,310 ft (179–399 m) above sea level

IN FIGURES
Surface area
192 mi^2 (498 km^2)
Population 1,162,000
Population density
6,042/mi^2 (2,333/km^2)
FOUNDATION
Traces have been found of the Celtic village of Závist to the south of the city, dating from the 6th century BC, but Prague, correctly speaking was founded at the end of the 9th century, based on the building of the castle on the banks of the Vltava River.
The legend
The legendary origin of the city is attributed to Princess Libuse, leader of a Slavic tribe established in Vysehrad, to the south of today's Prague, in the 8th century. The princess predicted the city's greatness and ordered the building of the castle.

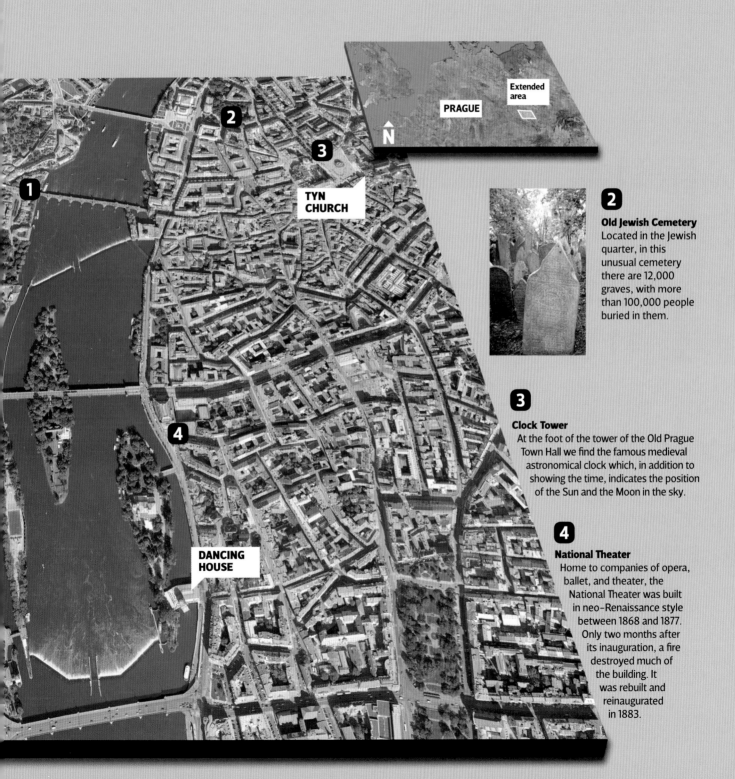

PRAGUE

Extended area

N

1

2

3

TYN CHURCH

4

DANCING HOUSE

2 Old Jewish Cemetery
Located in the Jewish quarter, in this unusual cemetery there are 12,000 graves, with more than 100,000 people buried in them.

3 Clock Tower
At the foot of the tower of the Old Prague Town Hall we find the famous medieval astronomical clock which, in addition to showing the time, indicates the position of the Sun and the Moon in the sky.

4 National Theater
Home to companies of opera, ballet, and theater, the National Theater was built in neo–Renaissance style between 1868 and 1877. Only two months after its inauguration, a fire destroyed much of the building. It was rebuilt and reinaugurated in 1883.

Majestic and evocative

Prague preserves almost intact the monuments and streets that attest to a past of great splendor and riches.

For those who didn't live through it, it is very difficult to imagine how Prague was in the 1970s. Today, the capital of the Czech Republic is a beautiful city of human proportions, full of color and crammed with great monuments from very different periods and with evocative corners. It has become one of the 20 most visited capitals of the world, in which it is now very expensive to buy or rent even a little apartment.

Just 40 years ago, Prague was a sad, gray, polluted city, punished by a combination of historical adversities, a consequence of its strategic situation in the geographical center of the continent. In just one century, since 1914, the city on the Vltava has suffered badly from two world wars followed by more than 40 years of communist dictatorship. The curious truth is that between 1939 and 1945, Prague was the victim of the three greatest military powers of World War II. It passed this six years under Nazi occupation, suffered bombardment from U.S. aircraft—whose pilots believed they were bombing the German city of Dresden—and was finally occupied by the Red Army.

Conflicts and revolutions

However, the character of Prague's people is not broken so easily. The joy and pleasure running through the streets of the Czech capital hide a history full of conflicts, starting with the Hussite wars of the 15th century, which pitted the supporters of theologian Jan Hus, a precursor of the protestant reform of Luther, against King Sigismund, who was faithful to the doctrine of Rome. With so much conflict in its past, it is not so strange that Prague should be known for three famous defenestrations, events in 1419, 1483, and 1618 that ended with the deaths of notable figures from the city after being thrown out of

the windows of different public buildings, and which set off important conflicts such as the Thirty Years' War (1618–1648), which involved most of the great European powers of the time.

Neither is it strange, with this past, that the citizens of the Czech capital should have learned to react to difficult situations with a civic pride worthy of the greatest praise. In 1968, after two decades of Soviet dominion, there was the so-called Prague Spring. The Czech communist leader Alexander Dubcek started to apply certain reforms designed to give "a human face" to Soviet socialism. Six months later, the experiment ended with the invasion of Czechoslovakia by the armies of the Warsaw Pact and the replacement of Dubcek by a leader who was faithful to Moscow. Two decades after that, Prague gave two new lessons in civic duty by leading the Velvet Revolution—a peaceful civic movement that led to the unseating of the Communist Party and the holding of free elections—and by agreeing with Slovakia on the division of Czechoslovakia into two sovereign states.

Prague, fortunately, has also experienced periods of wealth and stability. In the 13th century, King Ottokar II founded the district of Malá Strana (Lesser Town) at the

←Malá Strana
View of the castle and the characteristic Renaissance and baroque buildings of Malá Strana from the Charles Bridge.

↓The Dancing House
Modern Prague has its icon in this deconstructivist building developed in 1997.

↓↓Charles Bridge
The majesty and monumental character of Prague is manifested in the Gothic bridge that unites the areas of the city.

foot of the castle, on the opposite bank of the river from the Staré Mesto (the Old Town). A century later, Charles IV, one of the key monarchs in Prague's history, ordered the construction of the Nové Mesto (New Town) as an expansion of the Old Town. It connected the two centers, situated on opposite banks of the Vltava, by the bridge now known as the Charles Bridge, one of the most easily recognizable landmarks of the city of Franz Kafka.

Architecture, the sign of identity

Another period of great magnificence was the 18th century, which was when most of the baroque palaces and churches were built–buildings which have made such a contribution in earning Prague's fame as one of the most beautiful cities of Europe, with the Church of St. Nicolas in Malá Strana the most prestigious example from that period.

In the 1990s Prague, freed from the Iron Curtain, recovered a central role in the new Europe and the famous architect, the Canadian–American Frank Gehry, designed the renowned Dancing House. These and other "events" along with Prague's splendid heritage, allow, many decades later, the city to look optimistically at the future.

Cathedral of St. Vitus

Located inside Prague Castle, building began in the 14th century, although it was interrupted several times and not completed until the 20th century.

Interior The cathedral has a large central nave with narrow aisles that provide access to small chapels. The most famous of these is dedicated to St. Wenceslas.

The main facade Built in neo-Gothic style, it faces west and was the first to be completed. Its twin towers of 262 ft (80 m) stand out.

Rose Window The enormous Rose Window, which is 34 ft (10.4 m) in diameter, was designed in 1928 by Frantisek Kysela with scenes from the Creation.

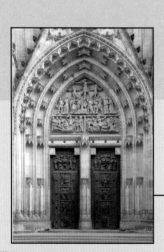

Main door This contains scenes relating to the process of building the cathedral.

Main tower The work of Peter Parler, dating from the 14th century. This is the highest point of the cathedral and is crowned by a neo-Renaissance balustrade and cupola from 1770.

The clock Added to the bell tower in 1552, it governs the life of the city.

Stained-glass windows Of great beauty, they belong to the period of the first Czechoslovak Republic, and are mostly the work of Frantisek Kysela and his pupils at the School of Decorative Arts of Prague.

Gilded door It owes its name to the color of its Venetian mosaics, which represent the Final Judgment. For centuries it was the main entrance to the cathedral.

ATHENS

Classical heritage

Located in the Greek region of Attica, Athens has a rich and ancient heritage, testament to its period of splendor 2,500 years ago.

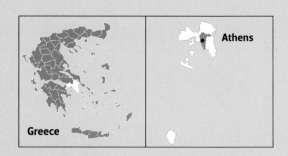

Greece

Athens

ATHENS

Extended area

N

AEGEAN SEA

CERAMICS

1

PARTHENON

A rugged landscape
Athens is surrounded by the Parnitha, Pendeli and Hymettus mountains and the port of Piraeus in the eastern Mediterranean. The urbanized plain on which Athens sits is dotted with eight hills, among which Mount Lycabettus and the Acropolis are worth special mention.

Erechtheion
Ionic columns in the Erechtheion temple at the Acropolis.

The Acropolis

The second highest hill, in the centre of the city, measures 511 ft (156 m) in height. The Acropolis houses buildings from ancient Athens such as the Parthenon, the Erechtheion, the Temple of Athena, Nike and the Propylaea, in addition to other buildings typical of the classical period. It is characterized by the use of lintel system architecture and the three orders (Doric, Ionic and Corinthian).

⊕ KEY FACTS ABOUT ATHENS

CAPITAL OF GREECE
Although the city of Athens is relatively small, the metropolitan area comprises 54 municipalities which multiply its population almost six-fold.

LOCATION
Latitude 37° 58' 40" N
Longitude 23° 43' 40" E
Altitude 230–1,109 ft (70–338 m) above sea level

IN FIGURES
Surface area
15 mi² (39 km²). 1,131 mi² (2,928 km²) in the metropolitan area
Population 6,655,000 (3.8 million in the metropolitan area)

Population density
49,503/mi² (19,133/km²)
FOUNDATION
Foundation date
Neolithic era
Ancient history
The area located

north of the Saronic Gulf has probably been inhabited for over 10,000 years, since the Neolithic period. The city has been important since

the Mycenaean period, around 1400 BC, although it enjoyed its period of greatest splendor during the classical period, in the 5th century BC.

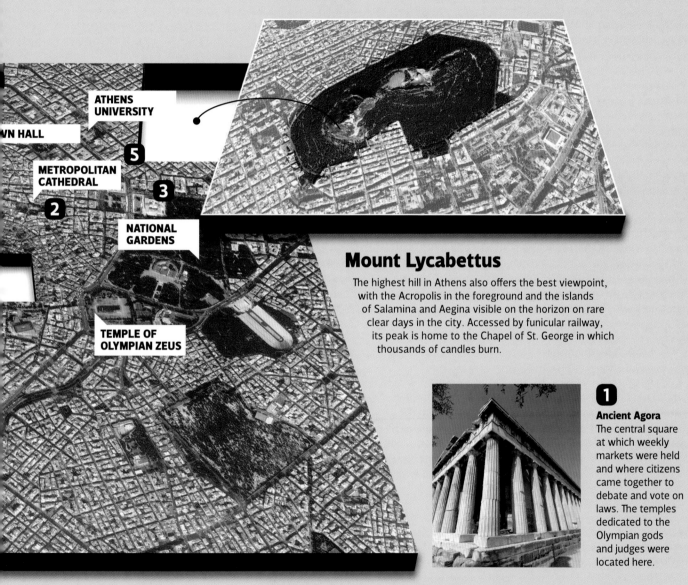

ATHENS UNIVERSITY

WN HALL

5

METROPOLITAN CATHEDRAL

3

2

NATIONAL GARDENS

TEMPLE OF OLYMPIAN ZEUS

Mount Lycabettus
The highest hill in Athens also offers the best viewpoint, with the Acropolis in the foreground and the islands of Salamina and Aegina visible on the horizon on rare clear days in the city. Accessed by funicular railway, its peak is home to the Chapel of St. George in which thousands of candles burn.

1
Ancient Agora
The central square at which weekly markets were held and where citizens came together to debate and vote on laws. The temples dedicated to the Olympian gods and judges were located here.

2
Plaka
When the city became the capital of modern Greece in 1834, Athens was approximately the size of this Ottoman-influenced central neighborhood.

3
Hellenic Parliament
Located in Syntagma Square, the Hellenic Parliament was constructed in neoclassical style following independence in 1830 and was the country's Royal Palace until the monarchy was abolished.

4
National historical museum
This neoclassical building housed the Parliament between 1875 and 1932. Currently, it displays works depicting the history of Greece from ancient times up until the 20th century.

5
Syntagma neighborhood
At the center of modern Athens and housing the city's financial district, Syntagma Square (or Constitution Square in English), houses the Tomb of the Unknown Soldier and the Hellenic Parliament.

The weight of history

The historical hardship suffered by the Acropolis symbolizes the historical evolution of the city in which democracy was born.

The majority of large cities that flourished before our time are today, at best, only visible in ruins. Only very few cities, the majority of which are in Asia, have ruins dating back over 3,000 years that are just a stone's throw from modern-day streets and squares. European and Mediterranean Athens is one of those cities. Not without its difficulties, the Attican city was successfully converted from an ancient Greek superpower city-state, whose legacy of democracy, philosophy, art, science and medicine is fundamental to understanding our current world, to the capital of modern-day Greece.

The monumental complex of the Acropolis is a unique symbol of the torturous path taken by Athens from the splendor of the Age of Pericles, 2,500 years ago, to the modern day city. Translating as "high city" in ancient Greek, it was constructed as a defense on one of the eight hills in the region; however, it quickly became a religious and ceremonial center. Following the destruction of temples previously erected on the hill by the armies of Persian king Xerxes, Pericles ordered the construction of the Parthenon. This was followed by other constructions at the Acropolis, during the 5th century BC, which marked the evolution of Classical architecture. They were reasonably preserved for almost 2,000 years, until the 16th century when the Turks converted the Parthenon into a mosque, the Erechtheion into a Gynaeceum and the Propylaea into an ammunitions store. The threat to these monuments grew during the attack on Athens by its neighbor in 1687, when the Parthenon was left roofless and partly destroyed.

As was the case with Rome, Athens experienced a critical period during which the Acropolis was ageing and Constantinople, modern-day Istanbul, was conquering the

eastern Mediterranean. During the late Middle Ages, with the city's population barely reaching 4,000, the bimillennial Greek city changed hands on a number of occasions; from the Byzantine empire to the Ottomans, falling under French, Italian, Aragonese and Sicilian rule in the interim.

Capital of independent Greece

Athens' luck changed with the War of Greek Independence between 1821 and 1829, following which the city became the capital of the new state, recovering its economic and demographic power, mainly due to large-scale internal migration during the 20th century. This resulted in disorganized urban growth on the outskirts, causing the chaotic traffic and pollution that has plagued Athenians for a number of decades.

Since the mid-20th century, migration has been a very reliable index of Athens' evolution. Traditionally a land of emigrants, with significant communities as far away as

📷

←Caryatids
The famous entrance to the Erechtheion, within the Acropolis.

↙National Guard
It is common to see the Evzones, the popular soldiers of the National Guard, wearing their traditional dress in Syntagma Square.

←Plaka
The narrow streets, open-air tavernas and a calmness that would be more commonly associated with a village rather than a European capital, are all features of this fully pedestrianized neighborhood.

↓Church of the Holy Apostles
One of the 11 Byzantine churches still standing in Athens today. Dating back to the 11th century, it is located in the ancient Agora.

Australia, Canada, Argentina and South Africa, the tide changed in the years following the 2004 Olympic Games which were held in the city. This period coincided with an unprecedented economic boom in the Greek capital as a result of the entrance to the Euro and the resulting cheap credit. Businesses in the Greek capital started to fill with Albanian, Romanian, Turkish and Bulgarian workers who, from 2008 onward, have been forced to return home or driven to poverty as a result of the economic crisis; young Athenians have also lived a similar experience in recent years.

Crisis or no crisis, 21st century Athenians can still be found drinking coffee on terraces located on the city's pedestrian streets and squares, taking refuge from the heat in the shadow of orange trees, just as their illustrious ancestors did 2,500 years ago in the Agora of Ancient Athens. The Agora's ruins can be admired today to the west of the Monastiraki neighborhood, an open and sociable meeting point in which democracy was born.

Acropolis

Conceived as military forts, acropoleis became religious centers in Greek cities. The spectacular architecture of the Acropolis in Athens really makes it stand out.

Erechtheion Unified by the use of the Ionic style, this temple was formerly more complex as it facilitated worshiping various gods and heroes, such as Athena and Erechtheus, at the same time.

Athena Promachos This is a bronze sculpture of Athena, the goddess of wisdom and warriors. According to the historian, Pausanias (2nd century AD), it served as a guide to Athenian sailors given its 29 ft (9 m) height.

Propylaea The monumental entrance door to the Acropolis. Doric in style, it was left unfinished due to the outbreak of the Peloponnesian War.

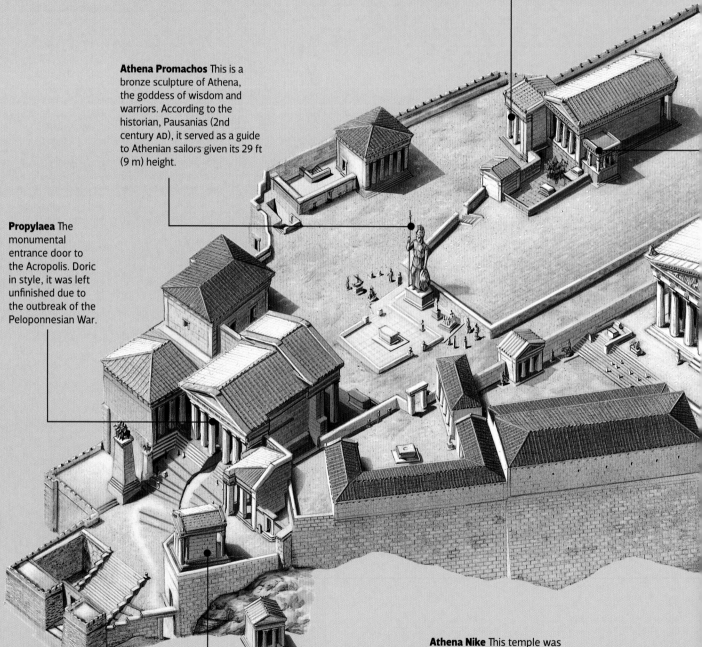

Athena Nike This temple was constructed in 420 BC on the foundations of a Mycenaean shrine. It contains a marble frieze with depictions of battles between the Greeks and the Persians.

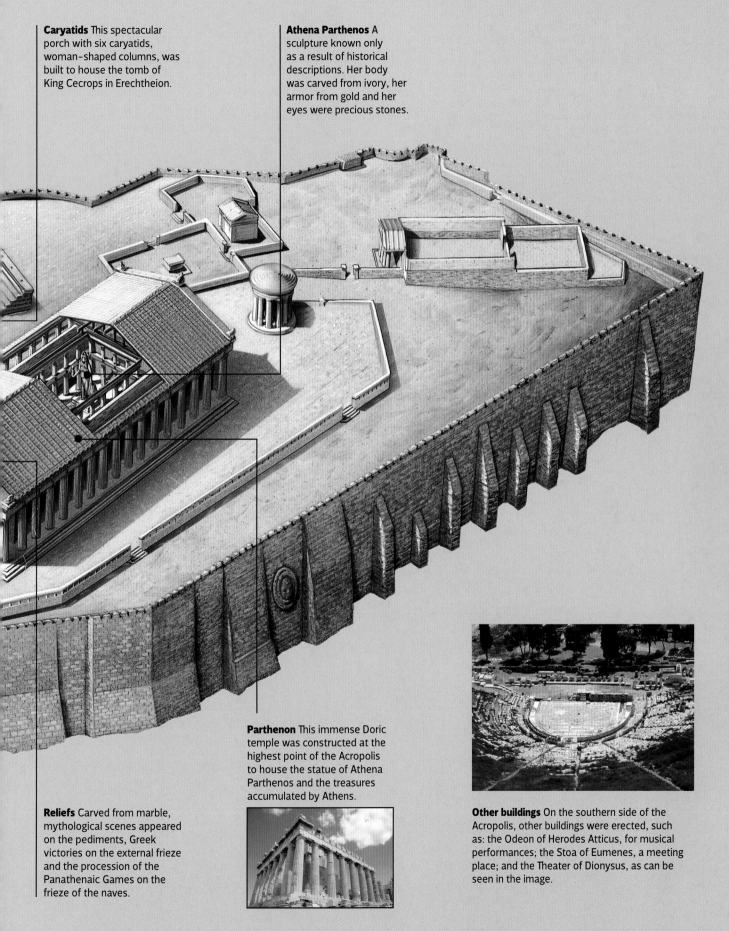

Caryatids This spectacular porch with six caryatids, woman-shaped columns, was built to house the tomb of King Cecrops in Erechtheion.

Athena Parthenos A sculpture known only as a result of historical descriptions. Her body was carved from ivory, her armor from gold and her eyes were precious stones.

Reliefs Carved from marble, mythological scenes appeared on the pediments, Greek victories on the external frieze and the procession of the Panathenaic Games on the frieze of the naves.

Parthenon This immense Doric temple was constructed at the highest point of the Acropolis to house the statue of Athena Parthenos and the treasures accumulated by Athens.

Other buildings On the southern side of the Acropolis, other buildings were erected, such as: the Odeon of Herodes Atticus, for musical performances; the Stoa of Eumenes, a meeting place; and the Theater of Dionysus, as can be seen in the image.

MOSCOW

European Russia

Red Square and the Kremlin, the main points of reference in Moscow, are located in the historic center, which sprung up on the banks of the Moskva River.

Moscow

Russia

Moscow

Great European city

The vast city of Moscow, the largest metropolitan area in Europe, is divided into concentric circles defined by wide circular avenues. At the heart of these major sections are Red Square, the Kremlin and one of the curves that the Moskva River cuts out as part of its route through the city.

N

Extended area

MOSCOW

Russian State Historical Museum

Built in neo-Russian style between 1875 and 1881, this redbrick building separates Red Square from Manege Square. The State Historical Museum's collection covers works of art and objects produced in Russia dating from prehistoric times to the present.

PUSHKIN MONUMENT

2

Red Square

In addition to the Kremlin, St. Basil's Cathedral, the Russian State Historical Museum and the GUM department store, the square is home to the tombs of Stalin and Yuri Gagarin, among others.

MOSCOW LIBRARY

ARBAT DISTRICT

PUSHKIN STATE MUSEUM OF FINE ARTS

St. Basil's Cathedral

Located at the far southeast end of Red Square, this Orthodox church is famous for its onion-shaped, colored domes. It was constructed between 1555 and 1561 under the orders of Ivan the Terrible to commemorate the conquest of the khanate of Kazan.

🌐 KEY FACTS ABOUT MOSCOW

CAPITAL OF THE RUSSIAN FEDERATION
Capital of the Russian Empire until 1712, when Peter the Great moved the capital to St. Petersburg. It was restored as the capital later in 1922.

LOCATION
Latitude 55° 48' 08" N
Longitude 37° 37' 56" E
Altitude
492 ft (150 m) above sea level

IN FIGURES
Surface area
965 mi² (2,500 km²)
Population 11,500,000 (16 million in the metropolitan area)
Population density
11,914/mi² (4,600/km²)

FOUNDATION
Foundation date
Unknown
Founder
Vyatichi Slavs
First reference
The Moscow area has been inhabited since Neolithic times and it is known that there was a well-established settlement during the late Middle Ages. However, the first Russian reference dates back to 1147, when Yuri Dolgorukiy mentioned Moscow. Stalin used this date to celebrate the 800th anniversary of the city in 1947.

Main Kremlin buildings

The Kremlin is an enormous fortified area of medieval origin located between Red Square and the Moskva River. Four palaces and four cathedrals dating back to different periods are housed inside its walls.

Grand Kremlin Palace
Located on a small pine-tree-covered hill and built during the mid-19th century on the orders of Nicholas I, it is currently the official residence of the president of the Russian Federation.

Cathedral of the Assumption
Finished in 1479, this white-colored temple adorned with golden domes houses the tomb of Ivan the Terrible. Coronation ceremonies to crown the tsars were held here.

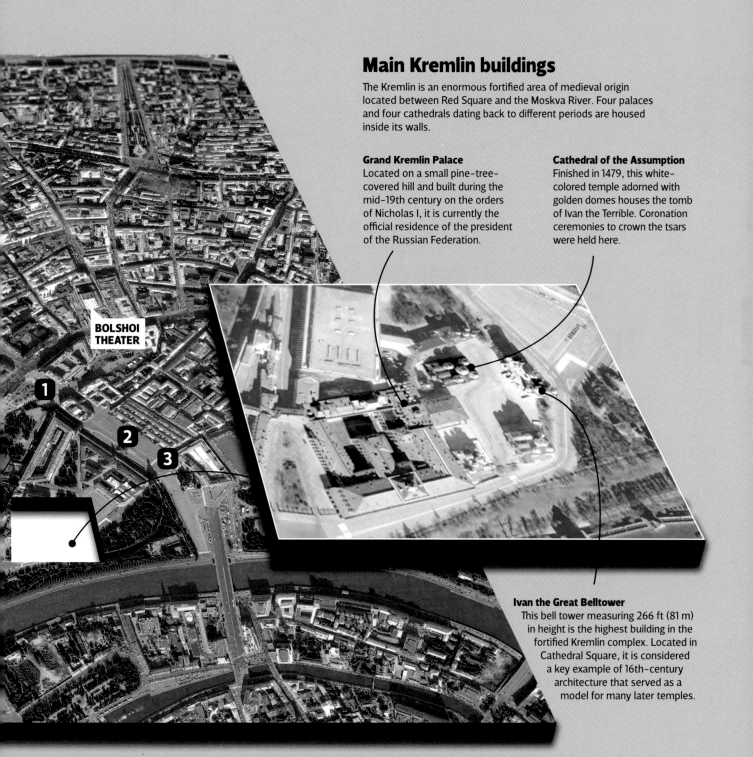

BOLSHOI THEATER

Ivan the Great Belltower
This bell tower measuring 266 ft (81 m) in height is the highest building in the fortified Kremlin complex. Located in Cathedral Square, it is considered a key example of 16th-century architecture that served as a model for many later temples.

Westward looking

The jump from strict communism to savage capitalism has transformed the face of Moscow in just a few short years.

However, the icy winters and the winding path of the Moskva River through its neighborhoods have remained unchanged. The colored domes of St. Basil's Cathedral are still a presence, as are the harsh walls of the Kremlin and Lenin's embalmed body. Everything else, however, has undergone one of the quickest and most radical changes that a city could possibly experience in such a short space of time. The dimly lit streets of Soviet Moscow were replaced by a veritable feast of electric power and LED lights; the depressing windows of communist shops were filled with Chanel dresses; and the relaxed procession of old Ladas was succeeded by Lexus and Mercedes filled traffic jams...

After months of tension, on Christmas Day 1991, reformist Mikhail Gorbachev, the last head of state of the Soviet Union, offered his resignation. As a result, the hammer and sickle disappeared from all official buildings. In just a few weeks, new laws were passed that repealed the collective dominance of production resources and the resulting assets. In its place, the new laws consecrated private property and free trade, starting a drastic program of privatization that in just a few short years transformed Moscow from the paradigm of a planned economy to the most extreme model of ultraliberalism with no room for an alternative middle ground.

Thus, anyone traveling to Moscow after a 20-year break will find a city that bears little resemblance to the former capital of the USSR. Today it is the most costly city in Europe, surpassing London, Zurich, Geneva and Oslo, and is one of the five most costly cities on earth. This is particularly true in terms of house prices and the luxury offices which have been occupied by multinational companies from all sectors of business.

This enormous increase in cost (it is worth remembering that accommodation was free in the USSR) and the quick accumulation of wealth among a minority of entrepreneurs has generated significant inequality between an elite that lives in permanent luxury (there is no other city on earth with as many limousines) and a working class that has seen its already humble living standards during the socialist period decrease.

Birthplace of millionaires

Having surpassed none other than New York, Moscow is now the city with the highest ratio of millionaires worldwide. This process has been stimulated by the ultraliberal policies of Boris Yeltsin and Vladimir Putin, the main protagonists of post-Soviet politics. Commonly called Moscow City, the International Business Center was created at the end of the 20th century in the Presnensky district. Its purpose was to create a city within the city, with offices, housing and entertainment centers for a brand-new generation of Russian executives; the embodiment of this new social group is Mikhail Khodorkovsky who, thanks to profits made by the Yukos Oil Company, quickly became one of the wealthiest people on the planet... before falling from grace at the hands of President Putin and being imprisoned.

←**Moscow City**
This is a large, 148 acre (60 ha) economic district conceived by the Moscow government in 1992. It is expected to be completed in 2020.
↓**Baroque subway**
Komsomolskaya Station, with its majestic yellow baroque ceiling is one of the most enchanting corners of Moscow.
↓↓**GUM department store**
Occupying a large 19th-century building, this is the biggest shopping center in the city and one of the main tourist attractions.

Politically vilified, the old yet highly interesting Stalinist architecture is gradually being ostracized by local authorities, who are keen to destroy entire blocks of building heritage from the 20th century in order to erect new skyscrapers, with a view to creating a similar landscape to those common among large North American metropoleis. Fortunately, the great works known as the Seven Sisters, monumental buildings constructed by Stalin between the 1930s and 1950s to house the most representative bodies of the Soviet regime, still remain in place. Furthermore, Red Square at the heart of the capital and the "zero mile marker" of Russia, has preserved the character that only a few select sites possess despite the significant changes experienced by the city. The square's 6 acres (2.3 ha) provide access to; the Kremlin, the former royal fortress; the Orthodox St. Basil's Cathedral, built in the 16th century; the Russian State Historical Museum; and the GUM department store, established during the Soviet period, which today is popular with Moscovites and tourists with a thirst for designer brands. The city's less fortunate residents can take solace in having the most extraordinary subway network on the planet, with exquisitely elegant stations designed in historical, modern and art-deco styles. The artistic value of the stations has seen them dubbed "the palaces of the people."

St. Basil's Cathedral

Ordered by Ivan the Terrible, this is one of the most beautiful and eye-catching Christian places of worship, given its stunning array of colors and decorations.

Central tower Measuring 156 ft (47.5 m) in height, it unites the whole assembly.

Onion shape The cathedral's domes represent the flame of a candle in reference to the words about Christ: "You are the light of the world."

Group of chapels St. Basil's Cathedral encompasses ten independent chapels or churches in total, each with its own treasures dedicated to different venerations.

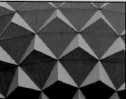

Colored domes The color of each dome represents a special significance: the golden dome, for example, alludes to heavenly glory, the blue to the Virgin Mary and the green to the Holy Trinity.

1. Church of the Holy Trinity
2. Church of Three Patriarchs of Alexandria
3. Church of Saint Martyrs Cyprian and Justina
4. Church of St. Gregory the Illuminator of Armenia
5. Church of St. Basil the Blessed
6. Church of the Intercession of Most Holy Theotokos
7. Church of St. Alexander Svirsky
8. Church of the Velikoretskaya Icon of St. Nicholas the Miracle-Worker
9. Church of the Entry of the Lord into Jerusalem
10. Church of St. Barlaam of Khutyn

Octagonal bell tower Dating back to the 17th century, this bell tower was constructed on the foundations of an older bell tower, about which information is scarce.

War scars The Church of the Entry of the Lord into Jerusalem shows scars of a missile that hit the building during the October Revolution in 1917.

Patriots Across from the cathedral is the popular bronze monument to Dmitry Pozharsky and Kuzma Minin, two patriots who expelled Polish invaders in 1612.

Interior All the chapels are united by a gallery that encircles the central church. The interior, which is more austere than the facade, is full of icons of the saints, mosaics and Orthodox paintings.

Facade The outside of the churches, in which redbrick predominates, was recently restored to celebrate the 450th anniversary of the cathedral, founded in 1561.

ISTANBUL

Between East and West

An imperial capital for more than 15 centuries and situated between two continents, Istanbul combines the heritage of Eastern and Western cultures.

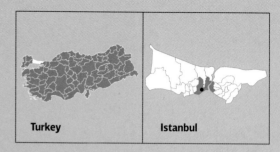

Turkey

Istanbul

Transcontinental conurbation
The Istanbul, or Bosphorus, Strait separates Istanbul on the west from Kadiköy (ancient Calzedonia) and Üsküdar (Crisópolis), on the east, which form part of this conurbation despite belonging to a different continent.

BOSPHORUS

ISTANBUL

Extended area

SEA OF MARMARA

N

1
Topkapi Palace
Built under the orders of Sultan Mehmed II in 1459, this palace has splendid views of the Bosphorus Strait. It combines landscaped areas with a structured complex of buildings which today houses exhibitions of objects and works of art from the imperial ages.

2
Blue Mosque
The mosque has a combination of Byzantine and Ottoman features and was built across from the Hagia Sofía at the beginning of the 17th century. The interior is lined with blue mosaics which create an unusual atmosphere.

3
Grand Bazaar
Built on the site of the old Byzantine market a few years after the Ottoman conquest, it is one of the largest markets on the planet. It has 58 streets with 4,000 shops.

NEW MOSQUE

3

⊕ KEY FACTS ABOUT ISTANBUL

IMPERIAL CAPITAL
Capital of the Eastern Roman Empire, the Byzantine Empire and the Ottoman Empire. When it became the Republic of Turkey in 1923, the capital moved to Ankara.

LOCATION
Latitude 41° 1' 0" N
Longitude 28° 58' 0" E
Altitude
131 ft (40 m) above sea level

IN FIGURES
Surface area
594 mi² (1,539 km²)
Population
13,700,000
Population density
23,054/mi²
(8,901/km²)

FOUNDATION
Foundation date 667 BC
Founders
Greeks from Megara
Name changes
Although the region has been inhabited since the Neolithic period, the first people to establish a population were settlers from the Greek city of Megara, near Athens, who named it Byzantium. It was renamed Constantinople in the 4th century, when it became the capital of Eastern Imperial Rome. In the 15th century it was under the rule of the Ottomans who renamed it Istanbul.

The Golden Horn

This estuary at the entrance of the Bosphorus is where the Greeks settled to found Byzantium in the 7th century BC. Today it separates the ancient city of Constantinople from the district of Beyoglu, formerly known as Galata. It forms a deep natural harbor and is crossed by four bridges.

GALATA TOWER

GALATA BRIDGE

THE GOLDEN HORN

Hagia Sofía

Dedicated to the Holy Wisdom, this large Christian temple is a fine example of Byzantine architecture. It was built between 532 and 537 under the orders of Emperor Justinian and converted into a mosque after the Ottoman conquest of 1453.

WALLS

1

2

Historic dome
The central dome, on spandrels which adorn the temple, is 104 ft (32 m) in diameter and 187 ft (57 m) above ground level.

The capital of the world

Whether under the name Byzantium, New Rome, Constantinople or Istanbul, the city of the Bosphorus has a magnificent history.

"If the world were just one country, Istanbul would be its capital." The French Emperor Napoleon Bonaparte, much given to quotes, was a huge admirer of past civilizations and recognized in the then Ottoman capital, the remains of centuries and centuries of powerful empires. Under any of the different names which it has adopted over its almost 3,000 years of existence, Istanbul is a unique city owing to its strategic location at the seam of two great continents; thus the world capital which Napoleon appreciated so greatly.

Some areas have played leading roles in history owing to their unique geographical location. On the eastern Mediterranean, two long and narrow straits connect the Black Sea with the Aegean Sea while separating Europe from Asia. Since the battle of the Granicus – the beginning of the incredible adventures of Alexander the Great through Asia – up to the Gallipoli campaign – during World War I – this region has been the object of desire for many peoples and empires because of its privileged position which allows it to control commercial traffic from east to west and from north to south.

Greek colony of Byzantium

Istanbul was founded in the 7th century BC at the entrance to the Bosphorus, one of the above-mentioned straits. It was named Byzantium because it was founded by Greek settlers from the island of Megara, whose king was called Byzas. Persians, Spartans, Athenians, Macedonians and even Celtic tribes from distant lands attacked and conquered the city until the arrival of the Romans in the 2nd century BC, which prompted a long period of stability. In the year 330 AD, Constantine the Great chose Byzantium to establish his imperial

court because of the profound crisis which Rome experienced as a result of constantly being besieged by peoples from the north and east of Europe. The emperor rebuilt the city according to Roman tastes, established a senate and called it New Rome, but his descendants decided to rename it Constantinople (Constantinopolis, the city of Constantine), a name which lasted in Europe until the beginning of the 20th century. Barely one century from its refounding, the new imperial capital went from 40,000 to half a million inhabitants.

The Eastern Roman Empire and its direct heir, the Byzantine Empire, dominated the eastern Mediterranean for more than 1,000 years following Constantine's decisive move. The city progressively abandoned Roman culture, welcomed Greek as its official language and exerted a great influence on the Christian world. This prestige allowed it to build the fabulous Hagia Sofía temple whose historic domes have, for almost 15 centuries, survived important historic events such as the Great Schism (which made Constantinople the capital of Orthodox Christianity from the 11th century), multiple lootings during the Crusades, conversion into a mosque when the city was conquered by the Ottomans in 1453 and finally

← The Golden Horn
This famous estuary, connected to the Bosphorus Strait, divides the European part of Istanbul between the old town and the Galata district.

↓ Basilica Cistern
This cistern dates back to 532 and is the largest of 60 constructed in the Byzantine era. It is 105,486 ft² (9,800 m²) and has 336 marble columns.

↓↓ Istiklal Cadessi
In the district of Beyoglu, an old tram line 1.8 mile (3 km) long runs along the most popular commercial street in the city.

its opening as a museum in 1935, after the founding of a modern, secular, republican Turkey, of which, strangely, Istanbul is not the capital.

Recreation

Far removed from the long history borne by the cobbled streets of the old quarters of the center, with its facades adorned with typical wrought-iron balconies, the inhabitants of 21st century Istanbul soak up the evening atmosphere in the tavernas of Nevizade Sokak, enjoy the shops of Istiklal Caddesi (Independence Avenue), or the constant comings and goings at the Grand Bazaar. Here, with the appearance of a teapot full of aromatic tea, the people go from hustle and bustle to complete relaxation and spend some time resting during conversation.

Mainly arriving from Asiatic Turkey in a migratory process which has quadrupled the population of the city in just 25 years and exacerbated urban and traffic chaos, residents—crazy for soccer and very attached to family life—sometimes cross the Golden Horn to enjoy the restaurants which surround the fishing market of Beyoglu. This district retains some of the cosmopolitan and Western ambience it had up until the beginning of the 20th century in order to accommodate the communities of foreign traders who worked in the city.

Hagia Sofía

A wonder of Byzantine architecture and engineering, for 1,000 years it was the largest cathedral in the world and served as inspiration for subsequent temples.

Spandrels The dome is situated over a rectangular base thanks to these structural components.

Semidomes These serve as buttresses to the central dome.

Mosaics The rich collection of Byzantine mosaics inside the building is the Hagia Sofía's greatest treasure.

Structure Hagia Sofía has a grand central nave measuring 229 x 242 ft (70 x 74 m) and two aisles.

Atrium It has five porticos with classical columns and a large receptacle for holy water.

Minarets These were added in the 15th and 16th centuries when the city was under Ottoman control.

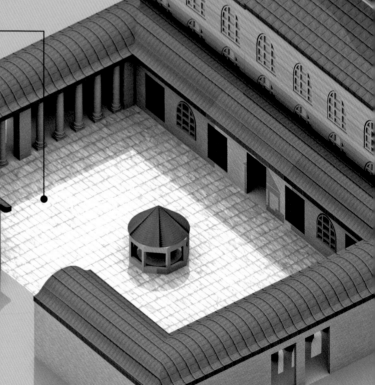

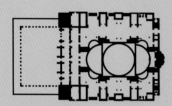

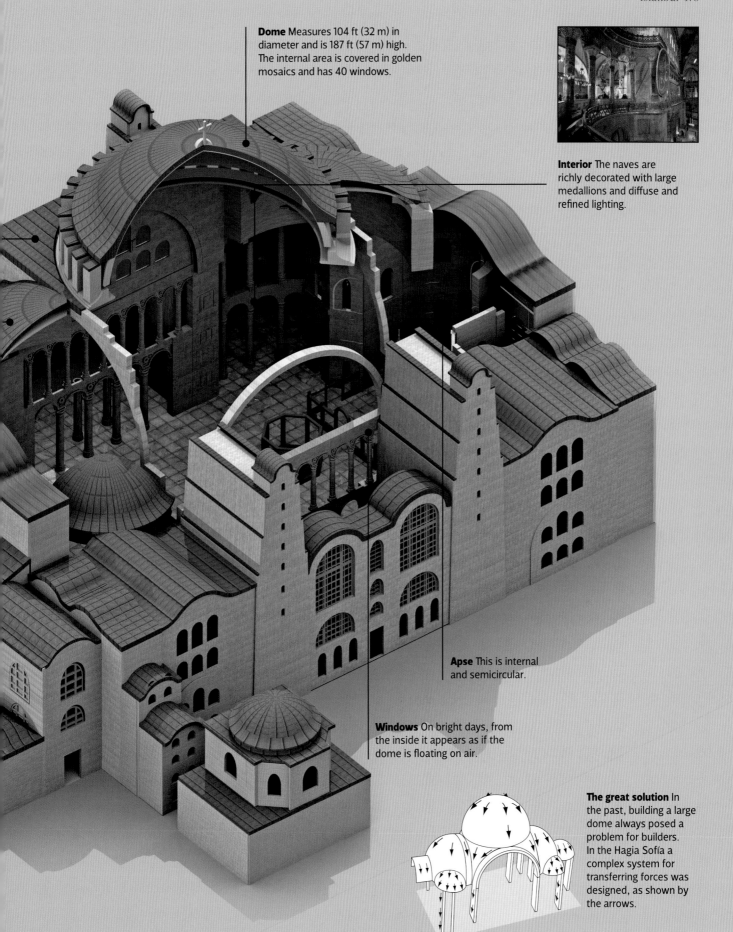

Dome Measures 104 ft (32 m) in diameter and is 187 ft (57 m) high. The internal area is covered in golden mosaics and has 40 windows.

Interior The naves are richly decorated with large medallions and diffuse and refined lighting.

Apse This is internal and semicircular.

Windows On bright days, from the inside it appears as if the dome is floating on air.

The great solution In the past, building a large dome always posed a problem for builders. In the Hagia Sofía a complex system for transferring forces was designed, as shown by the arrows.

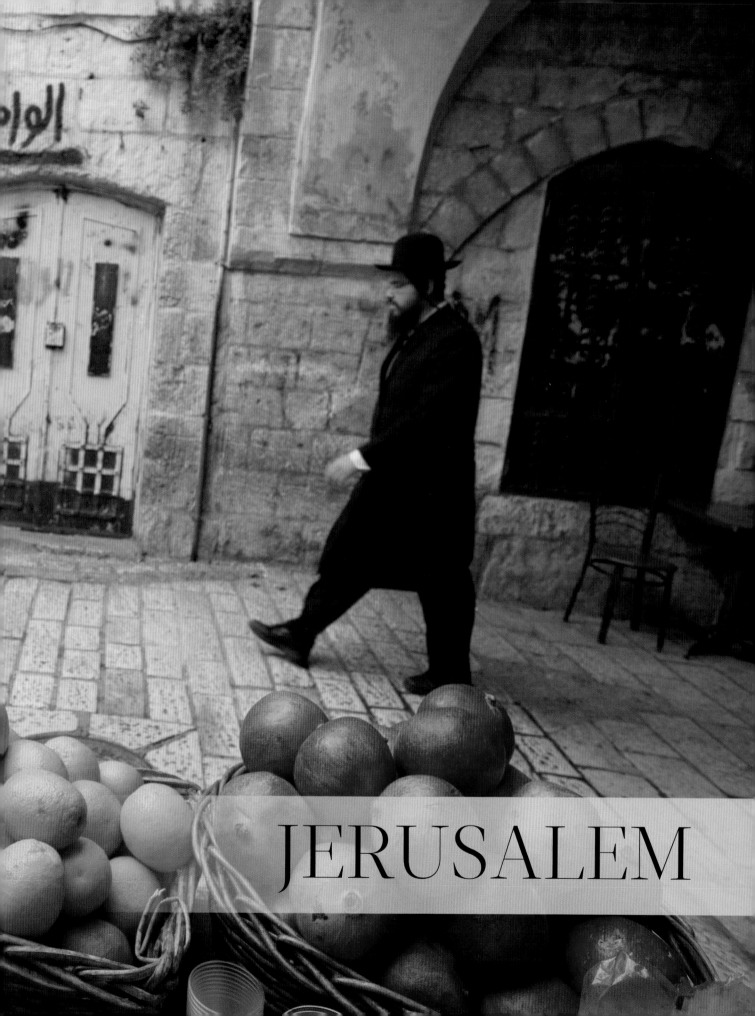

JERUSALEM

Holy Land

The sacred city of the three great monotheistic religions encompasses a large number of places, the names of which resonate in the collective memory of half of mankind.

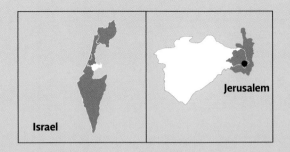

Israel

Jerusalem

Christian, Jewish and Muslim

In Jerusalem, Christians have the opportunity to follow the Via Dolorosa (Way of Grief)—the path which Jesus Christ followed toward Calvary (the crucifixion site)—and visit the church of the Holy Sepulchre, the Mount of Olives and the site of the Last Supper. Muslims can admire the Dome of the Rock and the Al-Aqsa Mosque and Jews can pray at the foot of the Wailing Wall.

MEDITERRANEAN SEA

JERUSALEM Extended area

N

SACHER PARK

1

The Knesset

Israel's Parliament is located in the modern city in the region of Sacher Park. Built after the founding of the state of Israel, the building was financed by the family of bankers, the Rothschilds.

2

Museum of Israel

The museum was founded in 1965 and houses collections of Israeli history and culture from prehistory to contemporary art. It displays some of the controversial Dead Sea Scrolls and has a model of the city of Jerusalem as it appeared during the period of Jesus Christ (photograph).

3

Monastery of the Cross

Located in the Valley of the Cross, this fortress-like building was built in the 11th century, under the orders of King Bagrat IV. According to Christian tradition, it was built on the site of the tree used to build the cross on which Jesus Christ died.

⊕ KEY FACTS ABOUT JERUSALEM

DOUBLE CAPITAL
The conflict between Jews and Palestinians is one of the harshest chapters in the history of Jerusalem, the city which both communities want as their capital.

LOCATION
Latitude 31° 47' 0"N
Longitude 35° 13' 0" E
Altitude
2,484 ft (757 m) above sea level

IN FIGURES
Surface area
48 mi² (125.2 km²)
Population
773,000 (3.8 million in the metropolitan area)
Population density
16,194/mi² (6,174/km²)

FOUNDATION
Foundation date
4th century BC
Founders
King David is the historic character who gave rise to the capital.

Thousand-year origins
Inhabited since the Neolithic or Copper age, by the middle of the 2nd century BC Jerusalem was already a considerably sized fortified town. Around the year 1000 BC, King David conquered it and made it the Jewish capital.

The Old City

Situated at the foot of Temple Mount and divided into four districts (Christian, Armenian, Muslim and Jewish), the Old City is the original center of Jerusalem. It is surrounded by a wall with eleven gates—seven open and four bricked up—built in the middle of the 16th century after the conquest of the city by the Ottomans.

Holy Sepulchre
The Church of the Holy Sepulchre or Resurrection was built in the 4th century in the Christian district, the supposed site of the Calvary or Golgotha where Jesus Christ was crucified and buried.

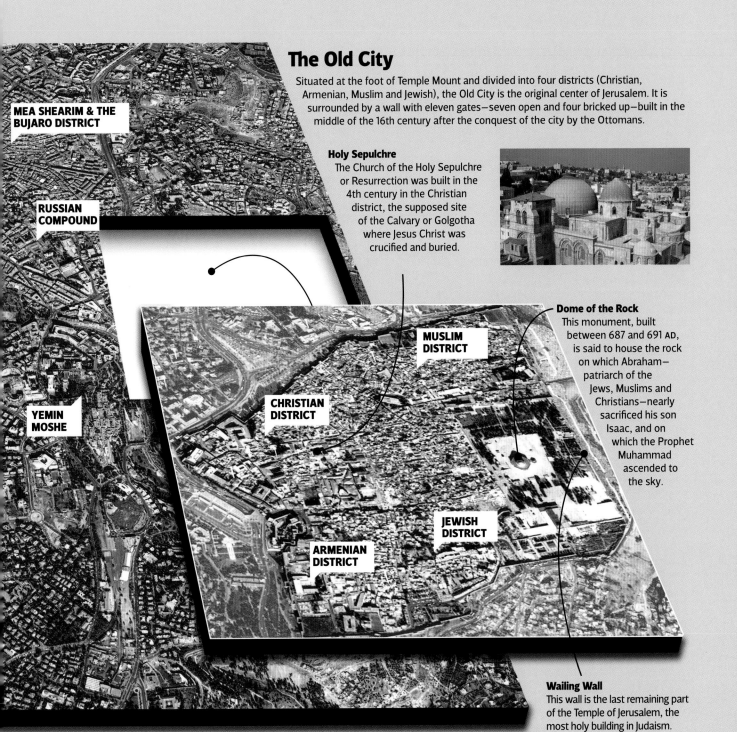

MEA SHEARIM & THE BUJARO DISTRICT

RUSSIAN COMPOUND

YEMIN MOSHE

MUSLIM DISTRICT

CHRISTIAN DISTRICT

ARMENIAN DISTRICT

JEWISH DISTRICT

Dome of the Rock
This monument, built between 687 and 691 AD, is said to house the rock on which Abraham—patriarch of the Jews, Muslims and Christians—nearly sacrificed his son Isaac, and on which the Prophet Muhammad ascended to the sky.

Wailing Wall
This wall is the last remaining part of the Temple of Jerusalem, the most holy building in Judaism.

The coveted city

Jews, Muslims and Christians have fought for three millennia for this small piece of land between the Mediterranean and Dead Seas.

Since ancient times, men have fought to the death for their own survival, for their family, their tribe, their king, or for the land which they believe is theirs. But there is an even more powerful reason to take up arms against your fellow man: religion. Despite sharing the same God, the people of the three monotheistic religions—Christians, Muslims and Jews—have for centuries fought for a small piece of fortified land located at the edge of the fertile plain between the Mediterranean and Dead Seas and, in particular, for a tiny piece of land within these walls: The Esplanade of the Mosques in the Old City of Jerusalem.

Barely 37 acres (15 ha) in size, this small plateau was the site chosen by King Solomon 3,000 years ago to build the temple which would house the Ark of the Covenant, the sacred chest containing the Ten Commandments. The Jews called this hill Temple Mount and identified it as the site where Abraham almost sacrificed his son Isaac. One thousand years later, at the beginning of our era, a Jewish prophet called Jesus proselytized a new message in the same Jerusalem and was, for this reason, martyred on the cross. Thought by his followers to be the Messiah, he gave rise to Christianity, the faith which the Romans adopted as their own in the 4th century and which today is the main religion in the world.

More than 600 years after Jesus, in the 8th century, the followers of another prophet—Muhammad—conquered the city and built sacred buildings on the site previously occupied by Solomon's Temple; the Dome of the Rock and the Al-Aqsa Mosque. The Muslims also had Abraham as a patriarch and they defended the sanctity of Temple Mount because it was the site on which Muhammad began his mystical journey through the

seven heavens. Fearful of the fate that could befall the sacred Christian sites under Muslim rule, the Popes of Rome promoted the crusades, a series of European Christian military coalition campaigns to liberate Jerusalem from Islam. The success of the crusades was short-lived and Jerusalem remained in the hands of Muslims until the beginning of the 20th century.

Capital of Israel

In 1948, the state of Israel was founded with Jerusalem as its capital and a population which mixed the resident Jews and Palestinian Arabs with Hebrews who had recently arrived from all corners of the world. Despite the experience of many centuries of reasonably harmonious co-existence in the Maghreb, Near East and Europe,

←←Christian district
A street in the Ad-Dabbagha Market, in the Christian district of the Old City.

←Dome of the Rock
The oldest of the Muslim buildings in the city, famed for its large golden dome.

↙The Wailing Wall
Orthodox Jews pray before the famous Wailing Wall.

↓The Via Dolorosa
One of the passages which forms part of the Via Crucis (Way of the Cross) of Jesus Christ.

good relations between Jews and Muslims living on the same land and between the State of Israel and its Arabic neighbors proved impossible and the following decades have passed with no solution to the conflict.

A glance at the map of the Old City reinforces the idea that there were long periods of peaceful cohabitation between the three religions. Over less than one-half square mile (one square kilometre) of fortified surface, upon which stands the Wailing Wall—the last remains of Solomon's Temple—Christians, Muslims, Armenians and Jewish districts coexisted. A simple walk through the streets of the city, however, reveals the tensions that exist between the Jewish and Arabic communities. There is also tension within the Hebrew collective with growing differences between the ultra-Orthodox—those in favor of closing nightclubs during the early hours of the Sabbath—and the secular Israelis, who follow Western fashions.

Although the state of Palestine does not actually exist, Jerusalem is in fact the only city in the world which simultaneously acts as the capital of two states. This translates into the existence of two centers separated by little more than a half mile (1 km): Western Jerusalem, the Jewish and modern city where the buildings representing the Hebrew state are located; and Eastern Jerusalem, the Muslim districts plus the Old City, poorer and more chaotic than the Hebrew districts and separated from the rest of Palestine by a security fence erected by the Israeli army in 2003.

Church of the Holy Sepulchre

Built as a sanctuary in the year 335 on the site of the martyrdom and death of Jesus Christ, it was completely redesigned by the crusaders in the 12th century.

Dome The dome reaches a height of 112 ft (34 m) and is 67 ft (20.5 m) in diameter. It was rebuilt in 1960 after being destroyed by an earthquake.

Walls The internal walls are built of stone, but the external walls are of baked brick to reduce the load.

The stone of Unction Located to the left of the main entrance, this stone dates back to 1808—the previous one was destroyed—and commemorates the stone on which the body of Jesus Christ was prepared before being buried, according to Jewish ritual.

Monastery The monastery was built in the 11th century by the Coptic Church, which had become independent in the Council of Calcedonia in 451. According to tradition, it has preserved the belief and the Orthodox Christian doctrine in their purest forms.

Monastic cells Incorporated into the structure of the basilica, throughout history they have been kept hidden.

The main entrance Built by crusaders in the 12th century.

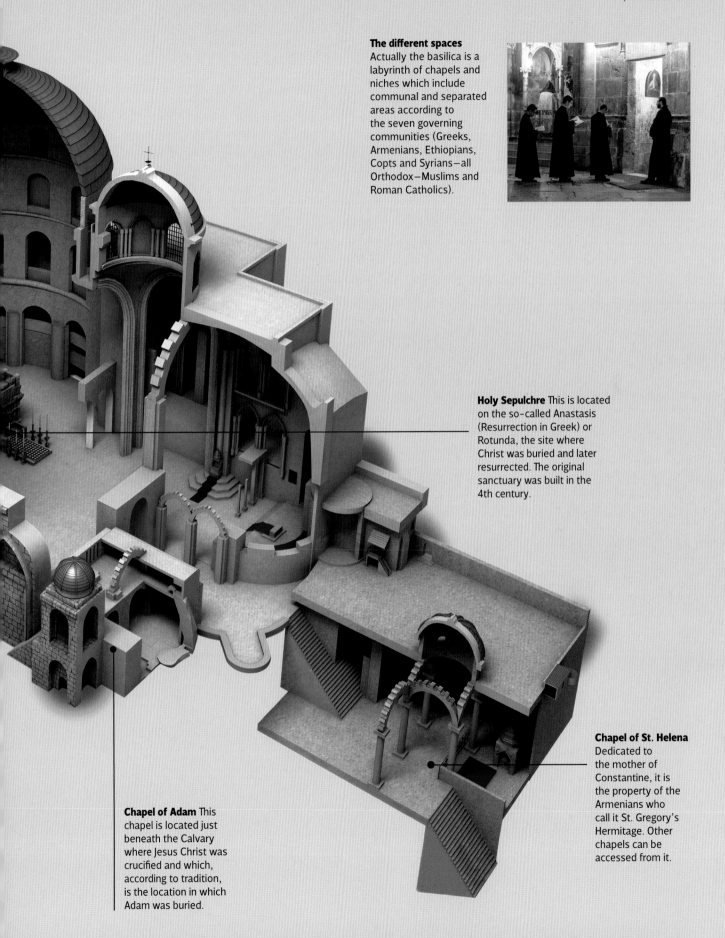

The different spaces
Actually the basilica is a labyrinth of chapels and niches which include communal and separated areas according to the seven governing communities (Greeks, Armenians, Ethiopians, Copts and Syrians—all Orthodox—Muslims and Roman Catholics).

Holy Sepulchre This is located on the so-called Anastasis (Resurrection in Greek) or Rotunda, the site where Christ was buried and later resurrected. The original sanctuary was built in the 4th century.

Chapel of St. Helena Dedicated to the mother of Constantine, it is the property of the Armenians who call it St. Gregory's Hermitage. Other chapels can be accessed from it.

Chapel of Adam This chapel is located just beneath the Calvary where Jesus Christ was crucified and which, according to tradition, is the location in which Adam was buried.

DUBAI

Artificial paradise

Rapid urbanization over the last few years has united the two historic centers of the city: Deira to the north and Dubai to the south.

United Arab Emirates

Dubai

The World

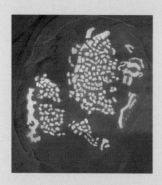

Among the mega-projects of Dubai, the most extravagant is the construction of four artificial archipelagos reclaimed from the sea through the accumulation of dredged sand used to build solid foundations. Of these, the most astounding is The World, a group of 300 small islands which form the silhouette of the five continents and which cover an area of 3 x 5 miles (6 x 9 km), some 3 miles (5 km) off the coast. Owing to the financial crisis which began in 2008, fewer islands have been built on than planned in the original project.

Palm Jumeirah

ATLANTIS

Another of the artificial archipelagos built along the Dubai coast is Palm Jumeirah. These islands form the shape of an enormous palm tree with roots connected to the land. Each of the fronds of the palm is a street, on both sides of which are shops and establishments dedicated to leisure and relaxation.

Atlantis Hotel
One of the best hotels in Dubai, it is located on Palm Jumeirah.

THE WORLD

DUBAI

Extended area

PALM JUMEIRAH

N

KEY FACTS ABOUT DUBAI

EMIRATE OF DUBAI
The city of Dubai is the center of the emirate namesake and one of the seven emirates which, since 1971, have formed the United Arab Emirates. Abu Dhabi is the capital.

LOCATION
Latitude 25° 15' 0" N
Longitude 55° 16' 0" E
Altitude
39 ft (12 m) above sea level

IN FIGURES
Surface area
1,588 mi² (4,114 km²)
Population
2,262,000
Population density
1,425/mi²
(550/km²)

FOUNDATION
Foundation date
Middle Ages
Pearls and commerce
The first settlements in this coastal region of the Arabian Peninsula appeared in the medieval period as a result of the pearl industry and the energetic commercial trade with India over the Strait of Hormuz. In the 19th century, it began to expand under the government of the Al Maktoum family who established a commercial port in the bay which soon became the most important port on the Persian Gulf.

Downtown

Designed in the style of North American cities, Downtown grew around the historic center of Dubai, with which it contrasts in height and modernity. It is the location of several of the tallest buildings in the city, the monumental fountain in the center of the lake and the Dubai Mall, the largest commercial center in the world.

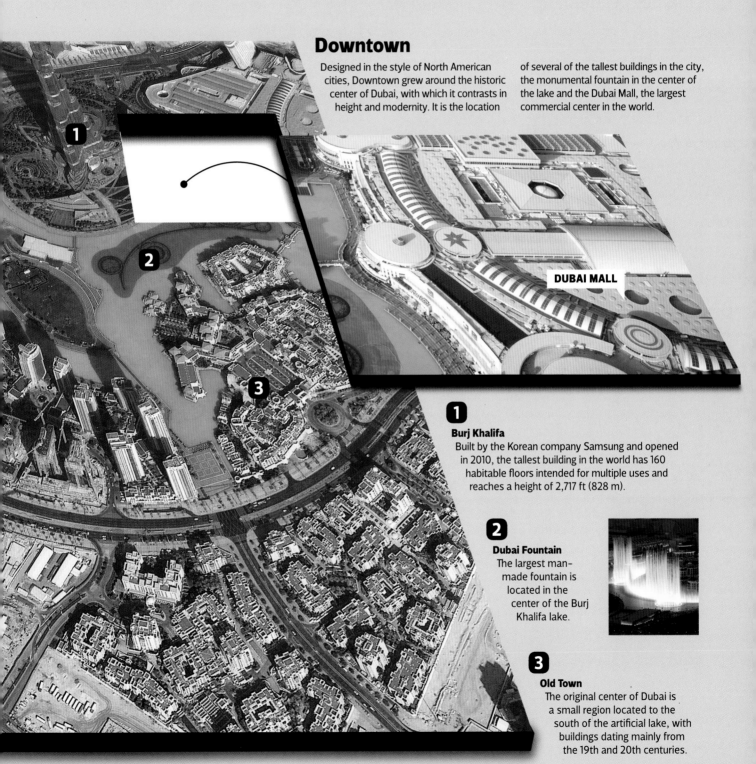

DUBAI MALL

1 Burj Khalifa
Built by the Korean company Samsung and opened in 2010, the tallest building in the world has 160 habitable floors intended for multiple uses and reaches a height of 2,717 ft (828 m).

2 Dubai Fountain
The largest man-made fountain is located in the center of the Burj Khalifa lake.

3 Old Town
The original center of Dubai is a small region located to the south of the artificial lake, with buildings dating mainly from the 19th and 20th centuries.

Oasis of luxury in Persia

Situated on a desert coast, Dubai's population has multiplied 75-fold and has become the city of Guinness World records.

Not London, during the Industrial Revolution. Not San Francisco during the Gold Rush. Not 19th-century New York. In the history of mankind, only Shenzhen, the Chinese city, subject of a bold socio-economic experiment, has experienced growth more rapid than Dubai. Born practically from nothing on a coastal area of the Arabian Desert, Dubai has gone from being a modest port of some 30,000 inhabitants after World War II to become a colossal focus of economic and dynamic immigration, with almost 2.3 million inhabitants in 2008.

Skyscraper fever

In any location in the world, the number of skyscrapers is a reliable indicator of the economic power of a city. Up until 1999, the date the Burj Al Arab—the famous hotel in the form of a sail—opened, the tallest building in Dubai was the Hyatt Regency, which today stands at number 150 in the list of tallest buildings in the city. At the peak of this construction fever in 2007, Dubai monopolized 20 percent of the world's cranes. The paradigm is the ostentatious Burj Khalifa, the only seven-star hotel in the world and the tallest building on the planet. Standing at 2,716 ft (828 m) high, it is double that of the Empire State Building in New York.

This property tide, largely concentrated along Sheik Zayed Road, parallel to the coast is an indication of Dubai's recent history. Eighty percent of its residents today are foreigners, the majority of which are low-skilled workers from southern Asia—particularly Filipinos, Iranians, Indians and Pakistanis—who, in exchange for plenty of work, endure working conditions akin to the 19th century. On entering the emirate they are obliged to hand over their passports to the police, accept low salaries, live in small, crowded apartments owing to the high property prices, and are prohibited from forming a union.

Westerners—mainly British—form the minority contingent of foreigners and occupy executive positions in emirate companies. In contrast to those from Asia, these qualified workers receive very high salaries which encourage them to sample the Arabian adventure, even accompanied by their families. These people and the 20 percent of native residents of the country—whose Muslim rhythms traditionally contrast with the frenetic nature of business and the prevailing consumerism—are the reason the streets of Dubai feature the largest concentration of luxury cars in the world.

Major financial center

In fact, the concept "best in the world" is a recurring theme in this city. A traditional stopover for Persian Gulf traders, Dubai is strategically located close to the Strait of Hormuz. Since the Middle Ages it has made its mark on the world, albeit a relatively small one, thanks to the export of pearls, and in the 1960s it began its first metamorphosis with the discovery of gas and oil deposits along the coast. However, the governments of the Al Maktoum dynasty, anticipating the end of crude oil reserves, transformed the city into a financial, commercial and tourist center, under the motto "Dubai, Do Buy."

With this idea in mind, in barely a decade Dubai had built the tallest building in the world, the largest commercial center in the world—in which, each year, the famous Dubai Shopping Festival is held, an orgy of fashion sales from the recently ended European season—

← ← **Dubai Fountain**
Inaugurated in 2009, the fountain is thought to be the largest in the world. It is 902 ft (275 m) long and shoots water 492 ft (150 m) into the air.

← **Sheik Zayed Road**
This road is the city's main artery. Giant skyscrapers of the financial district extend along each side of the street.

↙ **Emirates Mall**
This impressive commercial center contains one of the whims of the emirates: Ski Dubai, a spectacular covered ski slope.

the largest hotel in the world, the biggest port in the world, the largest gasoline station in the world, the first submarine hotel in the world, a covered ski slope in one of the hottest and driest regions in the world, the first rotating skyscraper in the world and even four archipelagos just off the coastline.

The big problem came with the spread of the financial crisis from Western economies. In 2009, in just six months, property and office prices in Dubai fell 40 percent. Some of the main sponsors of the emirates began to accumulate enormous debts which today raises doubts about an economic model that is unusual and difficult to sustain but which has survived thanks to the massive contribution of petroleum dollars from the United Arab Emirates government.

Burj Al Arab

Inspired by a sailing ship, the Burj Al Arab is considered to be the best hotel in the world. This 1,053-ft (321-m) tall building is built on an artificial island.

The atrium At 597 ft (182 m) high, it is actually the tallest lobby in the world and is decorated with marble, gold leaf, velvet, dancing fountains, light shows and aquariums.

Lights Strobe lights provide 150 color changes as the night progresses. The lights are projected onto the giant sail which covers the building.

The giant sail Composed of glass fiber, it is covered in Teflon to resist the wind, dirt and the heat of the desert. It covers 49,213 ft^2 (15,000 m^2) and is divided into a dozen panels.

The island Supported by 250 columns which penetrate some 148 ft (45 m) below sea level, this triangular-shaped island has sides measuring 492 ft (150 m).

Heliport This is 695 ft (212 m) high. In February 2005, Roger Federer and André Agassi played a game of tennis here as part of a publicity campaign.

Access The hotel is located 820 ft (250 m) off the coast and is connected by a bridge.

Skeleton The steel structure supports the rest of the building, built as two wings connected by a sail.

Main column The mast, measuring 196 ft (60 m), is the top of a reinforced concrete spine which supports the steel structure.

The restaurant Al Muntaha is located 656 ft (200 m) high on a platform which extends 88 ft (27m) each side of the mast. There are seven other restaurants.

The suites It has 202 luxury suites between 554 and 2,559 ft^2 (169 and 780 m^2), equipped with advanced technology and distributed over two wings supported by a large steel structure.

Design The island's edge has holes that break up the swell.

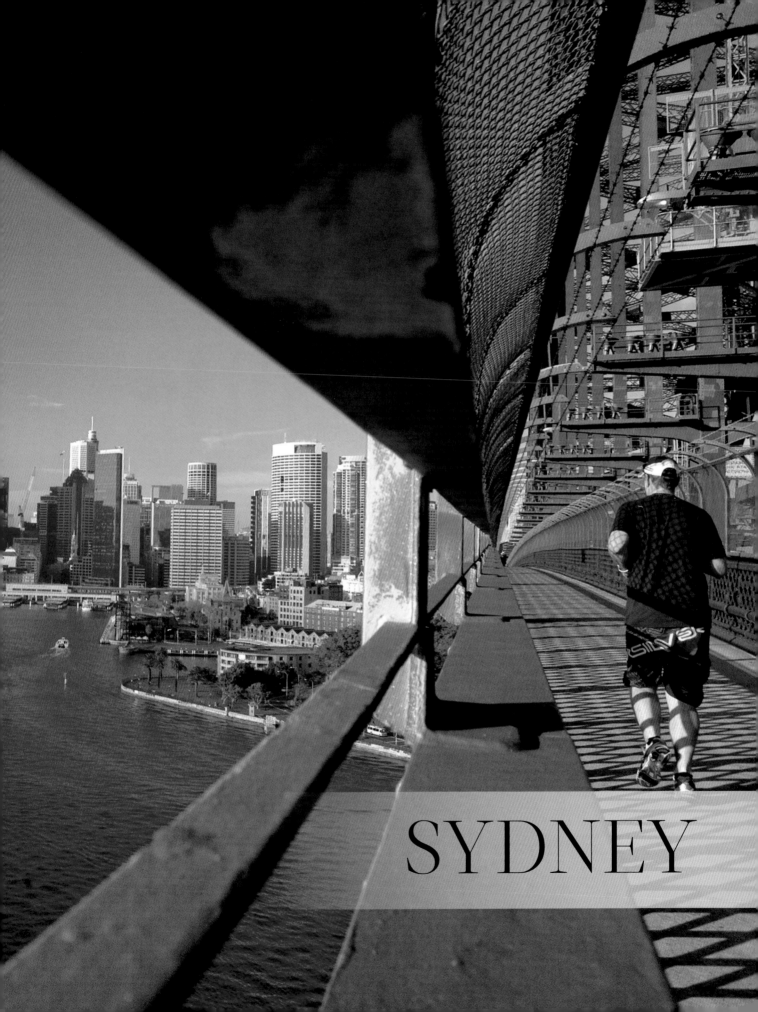

SYDNEY

The city of bays

The center of the city of Sydney is relatively small in relation to the vast expanse of its metropolitan area.

Australia

Sydney

The city center
Established to the south of Port Jackson, the historic center of Sydney has today become the Central Business District (CBD) and is crammed with skyscrapers of large multinationals and banking companies. Hyde Park is located to the south, the Royal Botanic Gardens to the east and The Rocks district, which has the oldest buildings in the city, to the west.

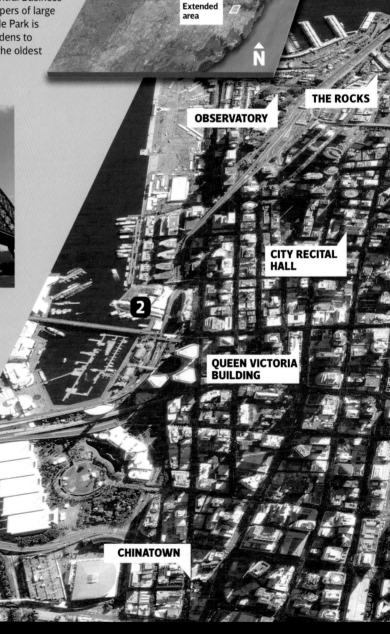

SYDNEY

Extended area

N

THE ROCKS

OBSERVATORY

CITY RECITAL HALL

QUEEN VICTORIA BUILDING

CHINATOWN

1

Sydney Harbour Bridge
Work began on Sydney Harbour Bridge in 1924 and it opened in 1932. It is the longest single-arc bridge in the world and measures 3,770 ft (1,149 m). It connects the center with the North Shore.

2

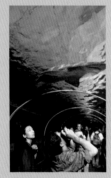

Aquarium
Located at Darling Harbour, one of the city's most popular areas for tourists, the Sydney Aquarium has more than 12,000 species of fish and other marine creatures from the Australian coast—particularly from the Great Barrier Reef— and the surrounding regions of the Pacific and Indian Oceans.

3

Hyde Park Barracks Museum
This former prison, now a museum, was designed in 1818 by convict architect Francis Greenway. It was built one year later by, and to house, prisoners deported from Great Britain. It functioned as a prison until 1848.

KEY FACTS ABOUT SYDNEY

CAPITAL OF NEW SOUTH WALES
Despite being the most populated and famous city in Australia, Sydney is not the country's capital. This privilege is reserved for Canberra. Sydney is the headquarters of the state government for New South Wales.
LOCATION
Latitude 33° 51' 0" S
Longitude 151° 12' 0" E

Altitude 10 ft (3 m) above sea level
IN FIGURES
Surface area 4,790 mi^2 (12,406 km^2)
Population 4,340,000
Population density 907/mi^2 (349.8/km^2)

FOUNDATION
Foundation date
January 26, 1788
Founder
Arthur Phillip
Penal colony
In 1788, a fleet led by British Captain Arthur

Phillip disembarked at Port Jackson, where, by order of the British authorities, he established a penal colony. This became the first Western settlement in Australia.

More than 30 bays

The deep estuary on which Sydney was settled comprises more than 30 bays and coves. The city has existed for over two centuries and these areas have been urbanized throughout this period without losing any of their natural beauty.

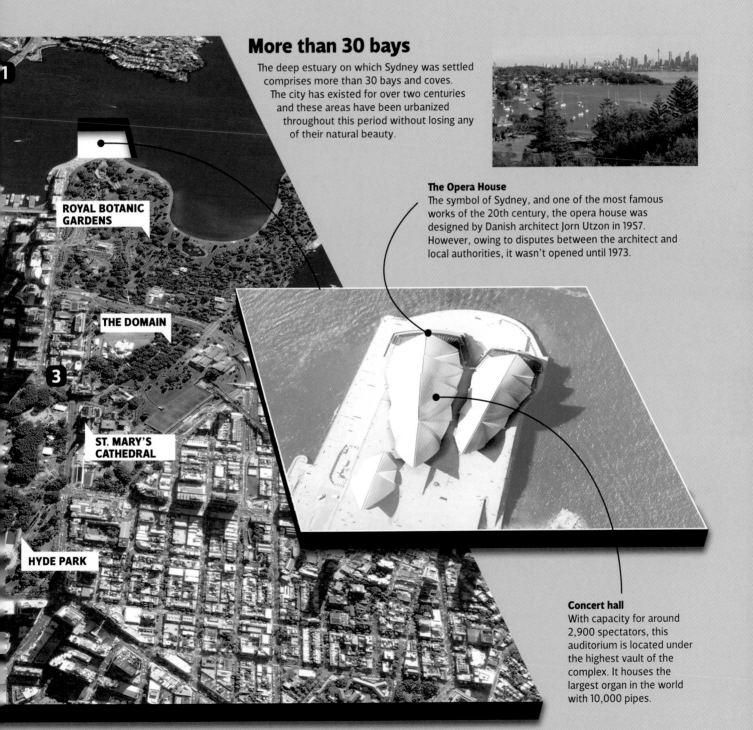

ROYAL BOTANIC GARDENS

THE DOMAIN

ST. MARY'S CATHEDRAL

HYDE PARK

The Opera House
The symbol of Sydney, and one of the most famous works of the 20th century, the opera house was designed by Danish architect Jorn Utzon in 1957. However, owing to disputes between the architect and local authorities, it wasn't opened until 1973.

Concert hall
With capacity for around 2,900 spectators, this auditorium is located under the highest vault of the complex. It houses the largest organ in the world with 10,000 pipes.

Prosperity and diversity

Existing for little more than two hundred years, Sydney is an open and tolerant city built by several generations of immigrants.

Although today it is a country with a bright future, Australia was underestimated by Westerners for more than two centuries. Portuguese, Spanish, and Dutch explorers discovered and superficially explored the region between the 16th and 17th centuries, but it was the British who colonized it at the end of the 18th century.

In 1770, English explorer Captain James Cook landed in Botany Bay to the south of the current metropolitan area of Sydney. He called this region New South Wales. On his return, London authorities found the solution to the problem of overcrowding in British prisons in the newly discovered land. In 1787, a fleet of 11 ships set sail for the New World under the command of Captain Arthur Phillip with 1,500 people—half of them convicts—and 800 cows on board. On January 18, 1788, they arrived in Botany Bay with the aim of establishing a prison for deported prisoners. After a few days, Captain Phillip decided to locate the prison some 12 miles (20 km) to the north, on an area of land—Port Jackson—situated on a deep natural estuary and an excellent site for a natural wharf. And so Sydney, the first European settlement in Australia, was born.

It is not surprising that Captain Phillip chose this place. Even today, with the entire bay built upon to make it one of the most expansive metropolitan areas in the world, the most captivating way of arriving in Sydney is, without doubt, by sea. The experience is unforgettable. Considered by many to be the best harbor in the world, Sydney has adapted to an unparalleled natural setting, between the Blue Mountains—in the last few years the scene of terrifying fires which threatened the residential areas on the outskirts—and a coast filled with bays, inlets, beaches,

and reefs. In addition, the spectacular Sydney panorama has, since 1973, enjoyed one of the great architectural icons of the 20th century: the Sydney Opera House. It was designed by Danish architect Jorn Utzon, whose concave vaults of concrete covered in ceramic tiles reflect the sun onto the tranquil waters of the bay.

A few decades after the arrival of the British, a large number of the almost 8,000 aborigines who lived in the region had either died as a result of the aggressive nature of the settlers, succumbed to diseases brought over from Europe, or were expelled into the outback. Therefore, there was, in the southeast of Australia, an extensive coastal region of practically virgin territory ripe for European colonization.

Multiculturalism

During the 19th century large waves of British and Irish settlers arrived in New South Wales. They monopolized immigration into Sydney until Australia's independence in 1901 and they were later followed by mainly Greek and Italian settlers in the 20th century. They crossed the globe in order to make a living in this land of opportunity, now recognized by three principal characteristics: the tough nature of the immigrants who have cultivated an

1. The Opera Bar
The bar terrace located on the ground floor of the Opera House offers splendid views of Sydney's city and harbour.

2. Queen Victoria Building
Built in 1898, this building with large glazed domes has, since 1984, housed a large commercial center.

3. ANZ Stadium
Built for the 2000 Olympic Games, the ANZ Stadium was the venue for the event's opening and closing ceremonies.

4. Darling Harbour
The Sydney monorail connects the commercial zone of Darling Harbour with the financial district and other tourist and commercial areas over 1.4 miles (3.6 km).

5. Bondi Beach
A group of swimmers train on one of the numerous beaches in the city.

6. The Rock district
The oldest buildings in the city, contrasting with the modern skyscrapers, are in The Rocks.

identity based on the motto "Work hard–play hard," which translates into a certain narcissism, as illustrated by the culture of body worship clearly visible on the city's beaches; by the combination of elegance and informality of dress; and by the ancestral English accent similar to London's East End cockney which, on occasion, visitors wrongly interpret as a lack of education.

This constant immigration provided the capital of New South Wales with a pronounced multicultural talent. Characterized by its good climate, its quality of life and high property prices, Sydney is the seventh city in the world ranked by most residents born abroad, exceeding that of large cities with great cosmopolitan traditions such as London and Paris. In addition, 15 percent of residents speak a language other than English at home, a proportion which increased in the last few decades owing to the arrival of large numbers of Asians –especially Chinese, Vietnamese, Lebanese, Indians and, Filipinos–who provide a rich complexity to local customs and gastronomy. Paradoxically, this diversity is one of the best bonds of unity between Sydneysiders and Australians who are, in general, proud to belong to an open, welcoming and radically free country that is respectful of difference.

The Sydney Opera House

Surprising and innovative, this building, which opened in 1973, is one of the architectural icons of the 20th century. It was designated a World Heritage Site in 2007.

Concert hall This is the largest of the five theaters of the Sydney Opera House. Symphonies, opera, ballet, and theater of great cultural significance are debuted here.

Utzon Room In 2004, the old hall was transformed into this room which takes the surname of the creator of the complex and which retains the design of the Danish architect who resigned in 1966 while the project was still unfinished.

Auditorium

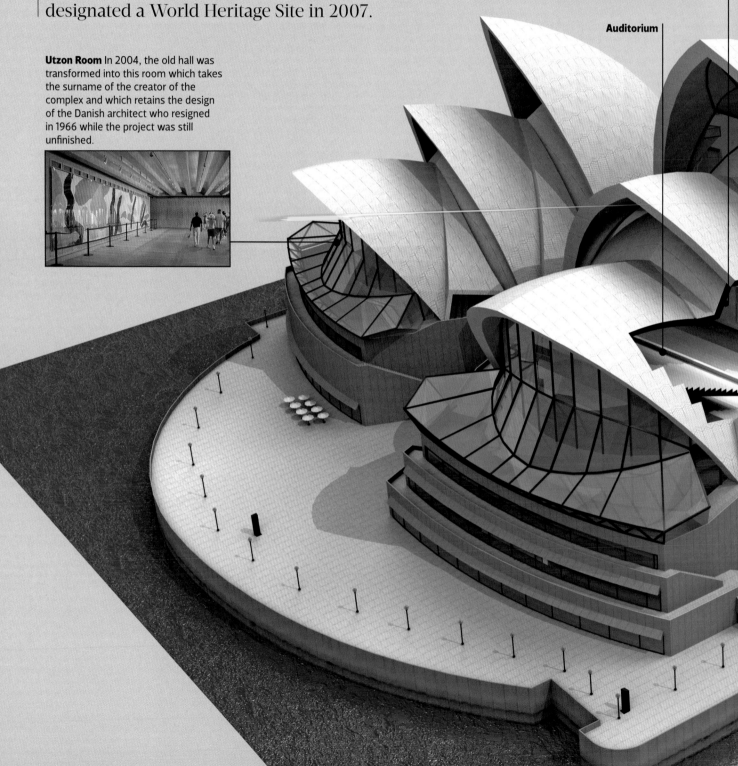

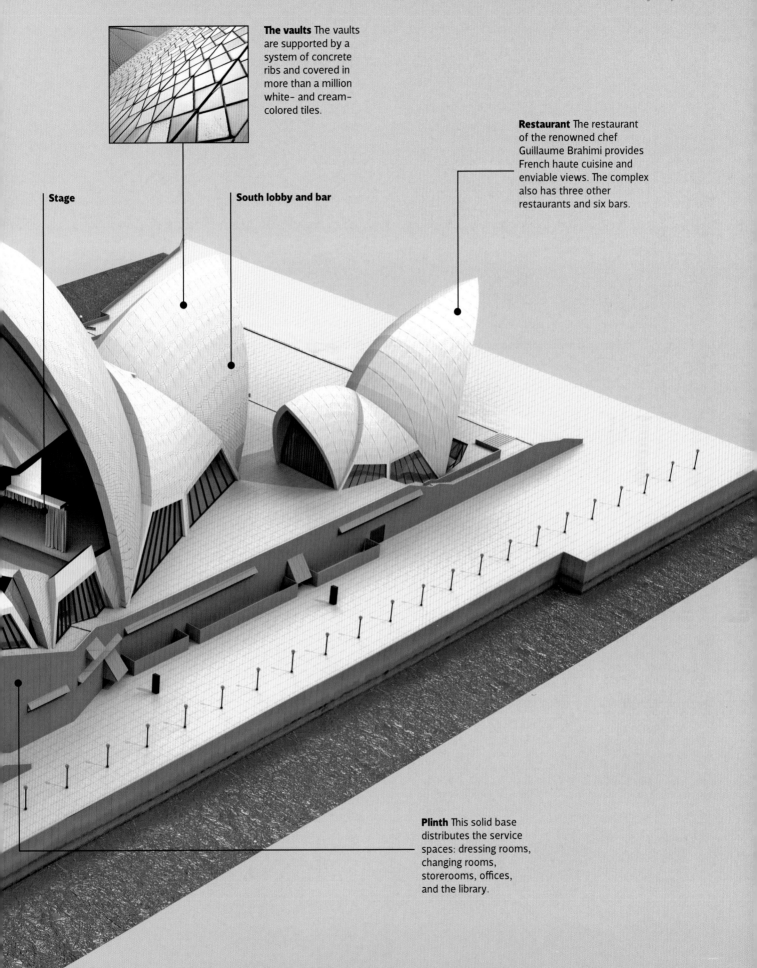

The vaults The vaults are supported by a system of concrete ribs and covered in more than a million white- and cream-colored tiles.

Restaurant The restaurant of the renowned chef Guillaume Brahimi provides French haute cuisine and enviable views. The complex also has three other restaurants and six bars.

Stage

South lobby and bar

Plinth This solid base distributes the service spaces: dressing rooms, changing rooms, storerooms, offices, and the library.

AUCKLAND

Maori land

The natural port of Waitemata determined the location of Auckland, whose city center developed during the second half of the 19th century.

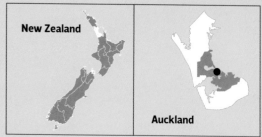

New Zealand

Auckland

The historical and economic heart of the city
The original city center in the 19th century, is today its economic heart. The center of Auckland runs along the docks of the main port, connecting it with the Pacific Ocean.

AUCKLAND

Extended area

N

VICTORIA PARK

1

Aotea Square
A recent addition to the city, Auckland's most central square was opened in 1979, near Queen Street, as a civic meeting place for entertainment, musical and cultural events and also political meetings; and then restored in 2010 to adapt it to its role as the center of city life.

2

Auckland Town Hall
The city's old Town Hall maintains some functions in local administration, in combination with its use as a concert hall. Inaugurated in 1911, the Town Hall was built in an Edwardian and neo-Renaissance style. It houses an organ built in the same period, which is considered the country's most important musical instrument.

3

Queen Street
Queen Street crosses the city center, descending from the residential districts in the hills down to the port. When the city was founded in 1840, the center was located in Shortland Street, but a great fire in 1858 started a progressive transfer of shops and local institutions to Queen Street.

4

Sky Tower
Located in the center of Auckland, at the corner of Federal Street and Victoria Street, the Sky Tower is the center of the city's telecommunications, and the most distinctive building of its skyline. Its height of 1,142 ft (348 m) makes it the highest tower in the Southern Hemisphere, (16 ft (5 m) higher than the Q1 Tower of the Gold Coast (Australia).

KEY FACTS ABOUT AUCKLAND

FIRST CAPITAL
Located near the end of North Island, Auckland is New Zealand's most populous city and its main economic center.

LOCATION
Latitude 36° 51' 0" S
Longitude 174° 47' 0" E
Altitude 85 ft (26 m) above sea level
IN FIGURES
Surface area 420 mi² (1,086 km²)

Population
1,290,000
Population density
3,071/mi² (1,188/km²)
FOUNDATION
Foundation date
1840
Colonial enclave

The first governor general of New Zealand, William Hobson, chose the enclave as the seat of what was to become the capital of the colony. To achieve this, first of all he had to sign the Treaty of Waitangi (1840) with the chiefs of the Maori tribes of North Island. Twenty years later, the government and parliament were transferred to the city of Wellington, in order to be in a more central location with regard to the entire country.

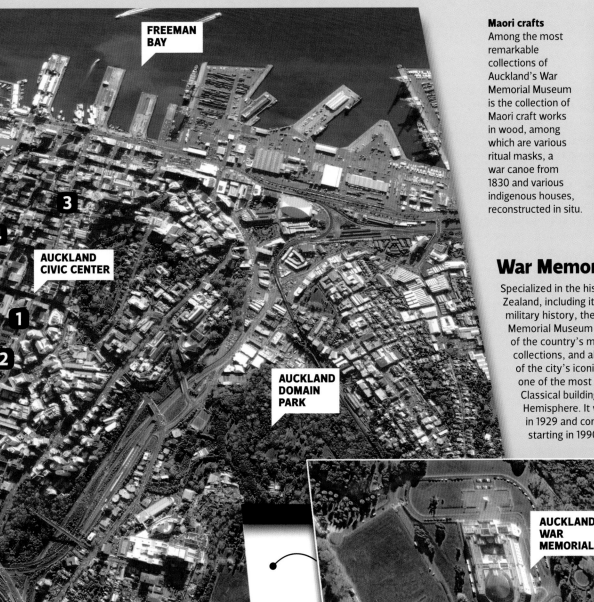

FREEMAN BAY

3

4

AUCKLAND CIVIC CENTER

1

2

AUCKLAND DOMAIN PARK

AUCKLAND WAR MEMORIAL

Maori crafts
Among the most remarkable collections of Auckland's War Memorial Museum is the collection of Maori craft works in wood, among which are various ritual masks, a war canoe from 1830 and various indigenous houses, reconstructed in situ.

War Memorial

Specialized in the history of New Zealand, including its natural and military history, the Auckland War Memorial Museum displays one of the country's most important collections, and also stands as one of the city's iconic buildings, and one of the most important neo-Classical buildings of the Southern Hemisphere. It was inaugurated in 1929 and completely restored starting in 1990.

Between two seas

Even though it stands on dangerous volcanic land, Auckland enjoys a privileged location.

The governor William Hobson, an Irishman in the service of the British Crown, had a good eye: searching for the ideal area to build the future capital of the colony of New Zealand, he settled on an unusual enclave located in the northern part of North Island, where the climate is temperate and the earth very productive. The location enjoyed an exceptional natural port, protected by a sheltered, deep bay, and surrounded by hills that gave it a rich and diverse relief. So it was here, from 1840, that the city of Auckland was built. Although it soon lost the status of capital to Wellington, it has maintained until today the status of the archipelago's primary economic and financial center.

The advantage created by Auckland's location is, in fact, almost unique in the world. Demographic growth throughout the 20th century meant that Auckland could become one of the very few cities on the planet with two ports in different seas. To the north, the port of Waitemata, around which the original city grew up, opens to the Pacific Ocean, while the southern port of Manukau, the region's principal industrial center, communicates with the Tasman Sea. Auckland occupies a very narrow isthmus, only 5 miles (7 km) wide, between these two ports.

The volcanic threat

No one is perfect. Hobson didn't know that this stretch of almost virgin and extremely fertile black earth was only 50,000 years old, next to nothing in geological terms. The hills that adorn the city and provide such beautiful panoramic views are of volcanic origin—there are as many as 48 craters in the metropolitan area—and Rangitoto Island, which stands so beautifully to the northwest of Auckland, with its distinctive almost

perfect cone shape, emerged from the sea only 600 years ago after an eruption. The earthquake risk for the population is thus relatively high, even in the context of an island where people are used to living surrounded by volcanic and tectonic phenomena.

The Maoris did not take much notice of this danger either. They had lived in the region long before the coming of the Europeans, and gave the geographical features that surrounded the city the exotic place names that are part of Auckland's identity. They were once very numerous, but diseases imported from Europe and contact with firearms—used in their own tribal wars—caused a sharp reduction in the Maori population in the few decades after British colonization. But even so, today about 11 percent of Auckland's population is made up of residents with Maori roots, adding to 56 percent of European descent—mostly from Great Britain and Ireland—14 percent of Polynesians (the largest colony of Polynesians anywhere) and 19 percent of Asians, chiefly Chinese.

Great economic and social activity

This mix has created an incredibly original ethnic and cultural fusion, unique in the world, which is

←Volcanic area
General view of
the city with Mount
Eden crater in the
foreground: one of
the city's five former
volcanoes.

↓Viaduct Basin
The remodeled
commercial port is
one of Auckland's
most luxurious
office and restaurant
areas.

↓↓Ponsonby
Aerial view of this
picturesque district,
with its peculiar
wooden houses
topped by iron roofs.

reflected in the city's customs and daily life; the latter
marked by heavy traffic, due to the scarcity of public
transportation. Relaxed, confident, and open to the sea,
the Jafas—as the Aucklanders are known in the rest of
New Zealand—enjoy a high standard of living thanks
largely to the considerable dynamism generated by the
multinationals based around Viaduct Basin, the old
commercial port, which today has become a district of
offices and luxury apartments for executives.

When they finish their working day, most of them go
to Queen Street, the main commercial street in the
city center, to go shopping. They then finish up with a
dinner washed down with the excellent white wine of
the Marlborough region, and a drink in the pedestrian
area of Karangahape Road, conveniently truncated to
K'Road by the locals. The wealthiest, however, don't
move out of the comfortable district of Ponsonby Road,
where the luxury restaurants are located.

Weekends are reserved for going to a rugby match—the
national sport—or maybe a trip to Devonport, on the
northern shore of the bay, where visitors can enjoy a
curious mixture of beaches, open-air barbecues, and
contemporary art galleries.

Sky Tower

With its balconies, restaurants, and attractions, this large telecommunications tower which opened in 1997, is one of the city's main tourist attractions.

Elevators It has three glass-walled elevators (one of which has a transparent floor) that can carry some 225 people to the Main Observation Level every 15 minutes.

SkyJump It is possible to jump from a height of 629 ft (192 m) thanks to this attraction, in which adrenaline junkies reach speeds of 46 mph (75 km/h) in 16 seconds.

Telecommunications aerial Reaching a height of 1,246 ft (380 m) it transmits 17 radio and several television stations.

Sky Deck The highest observation deck of the tower is 722 ft (220 m) high and has views stretching some 32 miles (82 km).

Orbit Restaurant Located on the floor immediately below The Observatory restaurant, it makes one complete revolution every hour.

Main Observation Level 610 ft (186 m) high, it has glass floors and modern informative displays with touch screens.

Sky Lounge It claims to be the highest café (597 ft or 182 m) in the Southern Hemisphere.

Foundations The main structure is a concrete frame 39 ft (12 m) in diameter, reinforced at the base with eight "legs" also of concrete which are connected by a concrete collar.

CAIRO

Growing around the Nile

The modern city of Cairo extends to the north of the old Muslim city, located between the fortress of the citadel and the Nile.

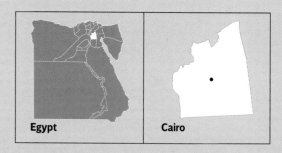

Egypt | Cairo

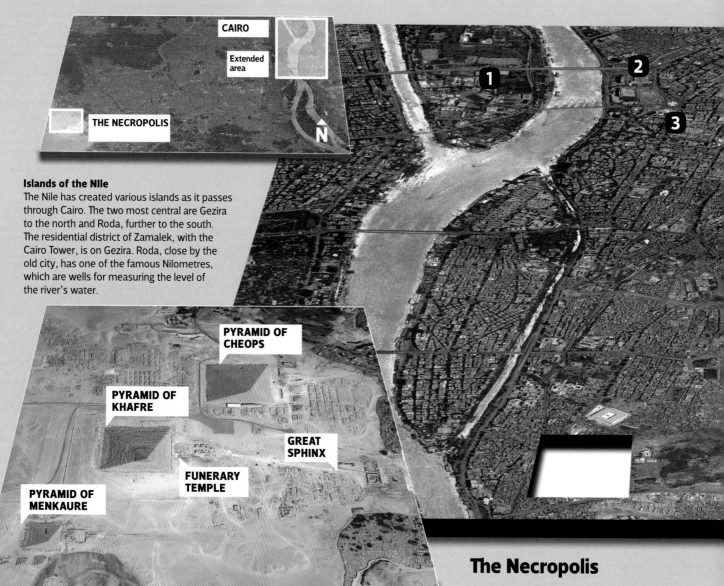

CAIRO

Extended area

THE NECROPOLIS

N

Islands of the Nile

The Nile has created various islands as it passes through Cairo. The two most central are Gezira to the north and Roda, further to the south. The residential district of Zamalek, with the Cairo Tower, is on Gezira. Roda, close by the old city, has one of the famous Nilometres, which are wells for measuring the level of the river's water.

PYRAMID OF CHEOPS

PYRAMID OF KHAFRE

GREAT SPHINX

FUNERARY TEMPLE

PYRAMID OF MENKAURE

The Great Sphinx and the Pyramid of Cheops

The Great Sphinx of Giza is a sculpture that was cut in the 26th century BC, probably as part of the funerary complex of the Pharaoh Khafre, who was buried in the central pyramid of the necropolis. Behind it is the Great Pyramid of Cheops, built around 2570 BC.

The Necropolis

Located on the outskirts of the city of the same name, some 12 miles (20 km) to the south of Cairo, this Necropolis holds the pyramids of the pharaohs Cheops, Khafre, and Menkaure—the only one of the Seven Wonders of the ancient World still standing. This enclave was first used as the necropolis of Memphis, the capital of Ancient Egypt from the Second dynasty, between 2850 and 2700 BC. The three pyramids were raised as a funerary monument for the aforementioned pharaohs from the Fourth dynasty.

⊕ KEY FACTS ABOUT CAIRO

CAPITAL OF EGYPT
Cairo is the capital of Egypt, has one-fifth of its population, and is the biggest city in Africa and the Arab world.

LOCATION
Latitude
31° 02' 0" N
Longitude
31° 21' 0" E
Altitude
381 ft (116 m) above sea level

IN FIGURES
Surface area
175 mi² (453 km²)
Population
15,500,000
Population density
88,619/mi²
(34,216/km²)

FOUNDATION
Foundation date
AD 969
The Victorious
The area on the east bank of the Nile, several miles further on from the beginning of the delta, was an inhabited strategic enclave for more than 5,000 years. However, the name of al-Qahirah, meaning "the Victorious" was given to it by the caliph of the Fatimid dynasty, Jawhar al-Sigilli, in 969. He is considered to be the founder of the city, which became the capital of Egypt.

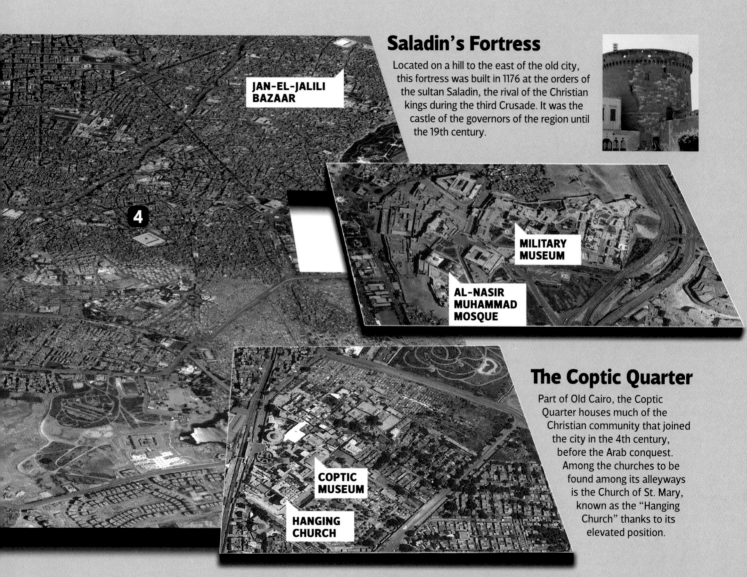

JAN-EL-JALILI BAZAAR

4

Saladin's Fortress

Located on a hill to the east of the old city, this fortress was built in 1176 at the orders of the sultan Saladin, the rival of the Christian kings during the third Crusade. It was the castle of the governors of the region until the 19th century.

MILITARY MUSEUM

AL-NASIR MUHAMMAD MOSQUE

The Coptic Quarter

Part of Old Cairo, the Coptic Quarter houses much of the Christian community that joined the city in the 4th century, before the Arab conquest. Among the churches to be found among its alleyways is the Church of St. Mary, known as the "Hanging Church" thanks to its elevated position.

COPTIC MUSEUM

HANGING CHURCH

❶ Egyptian Museum
Located in modern Cairo and designed in 1900 by Marcel Dourgnon in neoclassical style, this museum holds the largest collection of objects and works of art from ancient Egypt.

❷ Cairo Tower
This television tower, 141 ft (43 m) high, was built between 1950 and 1960 on the island of Gezira, with the same granite stone from which the monuments of ancient Egypt were built.

❸ Tahrir Square
The Liberation Square (*tahrir* in Arabic) is the largest civic space in the modern center. It gained world fame in 2011 with the public protests of the Arab Spring.

❹ Mosque of ibn Tulun
Built in the 9th century by the Abbasid governor Ahmad ibn Tulun, this great Islamic temple is the oldest mosque in the city still standing in its original form.

Five thousand years of history

From ancient Memphis to Tahrir Square, Cairo, the city of the Nile, Africa's greatest city, has an incredibly rich history.

The Nile is the longest river on Earth. It captures the waters from the rain on the equatorial forests and on the Ethiopian high plains and transports them to the Mediterranean across the Sahara, the largest and most arid desert in the world. Along its majestic course through the northern third of the African continent, the flow of the Nile creates a wide strip of fertile vegetation which gives life to a region which would otherwise be uninhabitable. In the past, the river gave life to ancient Egypt, one of the most extraordinary civilizations in history. Today, 98 percent of the inhabitants of modern Egypt, the most populous Arab state, are concentrated on the banks of the Nile, and especially in Cairo, its capital, the greatest city of Africa, the Arab world, and the Middle East.

A strategic location

Located some 186 miles (300 km) from the Mediterranean coast, Cairo is only 9 miles (15 km) south of the place where the Nile divides into two branches, creating its legendary delta. This strategic location has given the area a prominence and importance for more than 5,000 years, when the first pharaoh established his court at Memphis, a city whose royal necropolis was the Pyramids of Giza, to the south of today's Cairo. Another great city of ancient Egypt was Heliopolis, nowadays included as one more district of the extensive urban structure of the capital.

After the fall of the pharaohs and the subsequent domination of Persians, Greeks, Romans, and Byzantines, in AD 641 the Arab conquest reached Cairo, just nine years after the death of the Prophet Muhammad. Various settlements on the eastern bank of the Nile (Al–Fustat, Al–Askar, and Al–Qatta'i) precede the foundation of Cairo in 969. The new city absorbed all these older sites and became the indisputable capital of Egypt, making the district that is known today as Historical Cairo. Its skyline, full of minarets, takes in the Coptic District–the Christian community, which was established before the Islamization of the country; the Citadel–built in the 12th century during the fruitful reign of Saladin; the immense souk of Jan–el–Khalili– the city's oldest bazaar, as bustling now as when it was created in the 14th century; and, at the foot of the Citadel, the impressive City of the Dead, where tens of thousands of people live among the tombs of an enormous cemetery that has shops, workshops, cafes, and markets, and in which even the most unfortunate can set up an old pantheon as a home.

Modernization

Just before the British Protectorate, 140 years ago, after a long period of prosperity during the Low Middle Ages, the rhythm of Old Cairo–whose oldest building still standing today is the 9th–century Mosque of ibn Tulun–radically changed, when local authorities undertook a profound planning reform, and built an ambitious new area toward the north. This led to a massive movement of the wealthier classes to the new residential areas, leaving the Old City as an extremely impoverished district.

The creation of the modern city also made it possible for Cairo to absorb massive immigration from rural areas along the Nile Valley, which meant an increase of 250 percent in the city's population over 60 years, between 1880 and 1940. With this extraordinary growth, the center of the metropolis moved toward Tahrir Square (Liberation Square), close to the Nile and near the prestigious Egyptian Museum and the seat of the Arab League. This area was the main focus of the many citizens' protests that, during the Arab Spring, forced the resignation of President Hosni Mubarak after almost 30 years in power.

Nearly 150 years after the great planning reform, the city is putting the brakes on the tourist industry that its colossal heritage has attracted, due to serious environmental problems – terrible noise and high pollution levels – derived from the dry climate, which brings suffocating heat, frequent sandstorms, and bad planning, giving rise to hellish traffic and over-stretched public services.

↖Jan el-Jalili Bazaar
This souk, founded in the 14th century, is the oldest in the city.

↑Hassan Mosque
Built in the 14th century, this mosque is one of the largest Islamic places of worship in the world.

↖The City of the Dead
In this cemetery to the east of Cairo, thousands of people live among the tombs and mausoleums of the Mamlukes.

←The Nile
Feluccas, traditional Arab boats, sailing on the Nile.

The Pyramid of Cheops

Built between 2551 and 2528 BC, the Great Pyramid is the largest of the pyramids in the Giza Necropolis, on the outskirts of Cairo.

Ventilation conduits In September 2002, a robot demonstrated that the ventilation conduits, sometimes thought to be channels for the pharaoh's spirit, led to doors and chambers that were previously unknown.

Discharge chambers There are five of these, and their function was to discharge the pressure that the blocks of stone exerted on the King's Chamber from higher up the pyramid.

The King's Chamber This funerary chamber covers some 164 ft^2 (50m^2) and after having been robbed several times, holds just one empty red granite sarcophagus. The body of the Pharaoh Cheops has never been found.

The funeral barge of Cheops Found in 1954 in a ditch next to the pyramid, it was disassembled into more than 2,000 pieces. It took 14 years to put it back together. Now it is exhibited in the museum set up on the same site where it was found.

Queen's chamber Despite its name, this chamber contains a statue of Cheops, while his wife was buried in an adjacent pyramid.

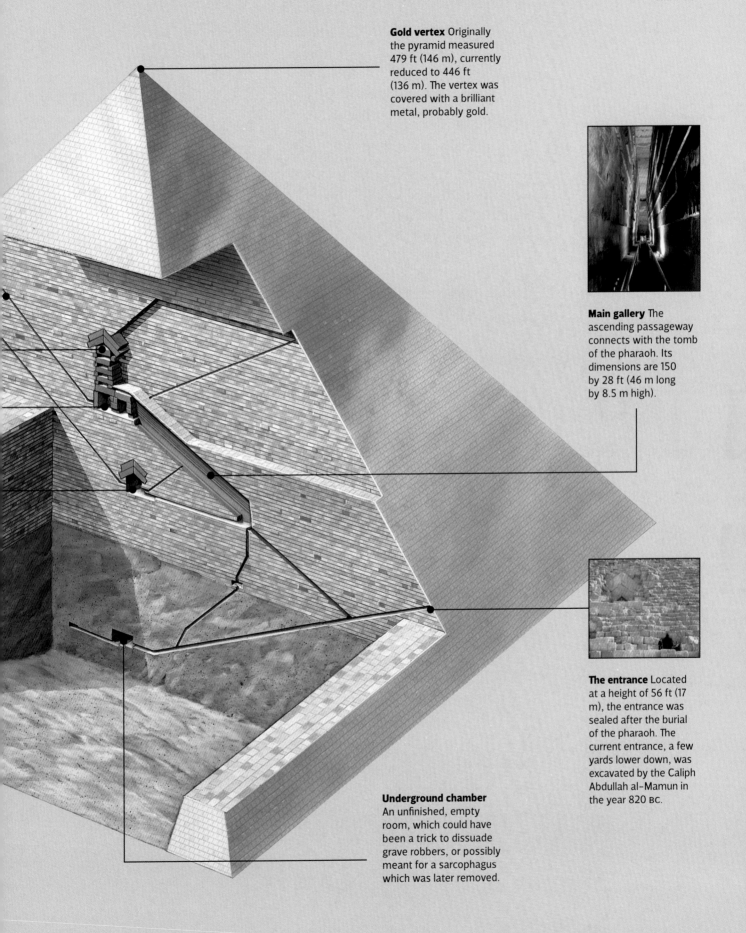

Gold vertex Originally the pyramid measured 479 ft (146 m), currently reduced to 446 ft (136 m). The vertex was covered with a brilliant metal, probably gold.

Main gallery The ascending passageway connects with the tomb of the pharaoh. Its dimensions are 150 by 28 ft (46 m long by 8.5 m high).

The entrance Located at a height of 56 ft (17 m), the entrance was sealed after the burial of the pharaoh. The current entrance, a few yards lower down, was excavated by the Caliph Abdullah al-Mamun in the year 820 BC.

Underground chamber An unfinished, empty room, which could have been a trick to dissuade grave robbers, or possibly meant for a sarcophagus which was later removed.

JOHANNESBURG

Queen of the South

The metropolitan area of Johannesburg is a collection of large districts and suburbs, from which Soweto stands out due to its size and its history.

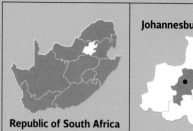

Republic of South Africa

Johannesburg

Soweto

Founded by the racist government of South Africa in 1948 to house the native people who until then had been living in areas subsequently assigned as residential districts for white people, the South Western Township, abbreviated to Soweto, occupies a large part of the metropolitan area of Johannesburg. In 1976 it was the scene of the biggest wave of protests in the history of apartheid (the South African system of racial segregation), when 575 students were killed by the police. Today, the enormous district is divided into various subdistricts, some of which are upper-middle class, and have some tourist attractions, such as the Nelson Mandela Museum.

1

Nelson Mandela Museum
The Orlando West area in Soweto contains the house where Nelson Mandela, architect of the end of apartheid, lived until he was incarcerated in 1962. Today, the house is a museum dedicated to the South African leader.

SOWETO DISTRICT

2

Soccer City
The site of the first match and then the final of the soccer World Cup in 2010, this stadium was built in 1987 and then rebuilt for the World Cup championship to hold 94,700 spectators, a figure that makes it the largest stadium on the African continent.

3

Apartheid Museum
From the same entrance, where visitors are separated according to the color of their skin, the Apartheid Museum, founded at the suggestion of Nelson Mandela, shows the full cruelty of the atrocities of the apartheid system that the country experienced for decades.

GOLD REEF CITY

Memory of racism
The apartheid system ruled in South Africa from 1947 to 1990.

KEY FACTS ABOUT JOHANNESBURG

CAPITAL OF THE PROVINCE OF GAUTENG
Although it is the biggest city in South Africa and its economic and financial center,

Johannesburg is not the capital of the country, but the seat of the provincial government of Gauteng.
LOCATION
Latitude 26° 12' 0" S

Longitude
28° 02' 0" E
Altitude 5,751 ft (1,753 m) above sea level
IN FIGURES
Surface area
635 mi² (1,645 km²)

Population
3,888,000 (7 million in the metropolitan area)
Population density
6,120/mi² (2,363/km²)
FOUNDATION
Foundation date
1886

Founders
European colonists
Gold Rush
Even though the area has been inhabited by hominids for millions of years and by

bushmen for several hundred thousand years, the foundation of Johannesburg was in 1886, in the middle of the Gold Rush.

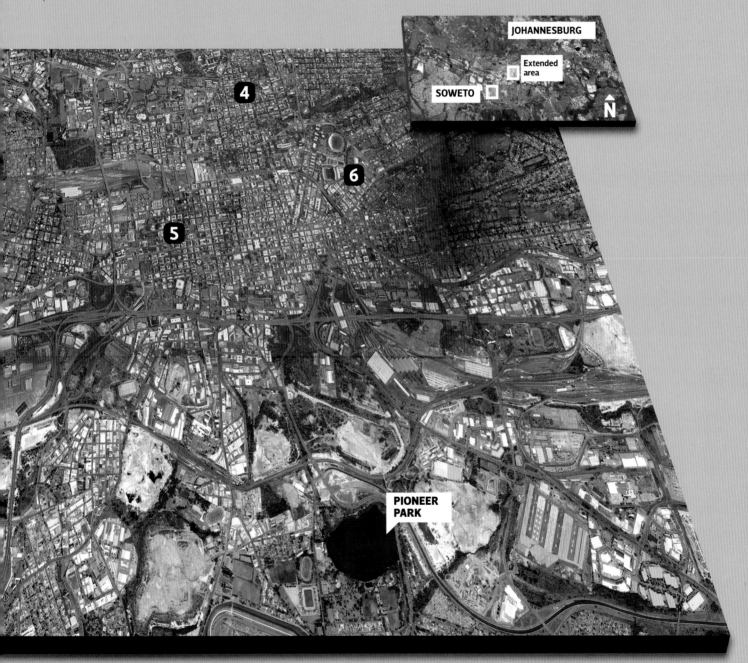

JOHANNESBURG

Extended area

SOWETO

N

PIONEER PARK

Hillbrow Tower
Completed in 1971 and located in the center of Johannesburg, the Hillbrow Tower at 883 ft (269 m) high was the highest structure in Africa for 40 years.

Turbine Hall
This old electric power station, built between 1927 and 1934, is today a center for conferences and conventions in the heart of Johannesburg.

Ellis Park
Inaugurated in 1928, this is the stadium of South Africa's extremely strong rugby team, the Springboks, champions of the world in 1995 and 2007.

History in black and white

The Gold Rush at the end of the 19th century and apartheid, abolished 100 years later, have marked Johannesburg's entire existence.

It does not stand out for the beauty of its streets, buildings, and monuments. It pales in comparison with the extraordinary natural scenery around Cape Town, its counterpart on the South African coast. And it still suffers harshly from the social consequences of apartheid, which created enormous black suburbs –such as Soweto–around the residential white districts. Despite all this, Johannesburg is one of the most dynamic cities in Africa, and has a history which is short but very intense.

Jo'burg or Jozi, as the South Africans call it, is one of many cities that have arisen around the world as a result of gold fever, which explains the name of the city for the Zulus: EGoli (the gold place). Many of these places over time turned into ghost towns. Johannesburg, on the other hand, survived, succeeded, and today is the financial capital of South Africa, although three other cities house the main institutions of state power: Pretoria (executive), Cape Town (legislative) and Bloemfontein (judicial).

Times of gold and racism

Located on a high plain at 5,577 ft (1,700 m), Johannesburg stands in the middle of a mountain range–the Witwatersrand–which has been the source of 40 percent of the gold extracted during the entire history of the Earth. The city was born in 1886 following the discovery of this extraordinary deposit and just ten years later there were 100,000 inhabitants. But the gold not only created great fortunes: the disputes over the huge development led to the Second Boer War, in which the British Army defeated the Dutch colonists and took control of the city and the region.

In a few years, however, the two white minorities came to an agreement to subject the black native majority to one of the most discriminatory racist systems that has ever existed. The lure of the mines, plus rapid industrialization, caused a huge wave of immigration from rural areas. The dominant European groups felt that their political and economic authority was threatened by this situation and created the so-called "townships," districts built to rehouse blacks expelled from areas reserved for whites. Soweto (an abbreviation of South Western Township), like the neighboring district of Meadowlands, was the product of this segregationist project.

After decades of injustice, in which Soweto was converted into one of the symbols of the antiapartheid struggle, the racist system was dismantled in 1990 and the townships began to be administered like any other district of the city and its metropolitan area. Cultural activity resurfaced, concentrated mainly in the district of Newtown, and led by a revolutionary music scene that vibrates every year with the Arts Alive Festival.

The good things in the city–whose streets and parks have more than six million trees, one per inhabitant–in the end succeed in turning your head away from its sombre past. The excellent cooking, with a special mention for the Afro–Asiatic fusion inherited from the large number of Hindu immigrants; the street vendors with delicious roasted meat and corn on the cob; the markets of Faraday, dedicated to traditional medicine, and of Rosebank Rooftop, specialized in handicrafts, as well as the passion for rugby and, more recently, for soccer, all raise local self–esteem in this period of liberation.

📷

← ← Apartheid Museum
The face of the anti-racist activist and first black president of South Africa, Nelson Mandela, in the Apartheid Museum: a visit is obligatory if you want to understand the city today.

← The business area
The skyscrapers are proof of the economic clout of the South African financial capital.

↓ Soweto
A daily scene in the historic district of Soweto, where between three and four million people live.

However, more than 20 years after the end of apartheid, there are still profound inequalities between the white population of the northern districts and the black suburbs. Also, the commercial and business activities, traditionally based in the Central Business District, the most dense concentration of skyscrapers in Africa, has been moving steadily north. This is because of the enormous problems with traffic and the high crime rates, a consequence of the extraordinary differences of standard of living between areas that are very close, as for instance between Sandton, today the principal residential and business district of the city, known as the "richest square mile of Africa," and the extremely poor black suburb of Alexandra, which are separated only by a highway.

Soccer City Stadium

Built in 1987, Soccer City Stadium was remodeled for the soccer World Cup of 2010, when it was converted into the biggest soccer stadium in Africa.

Illumination
The stadium is illuminated by 540 lights distributed around the roof.

Screens There are two screens of 926 ft² (86 m²) with the latest LED technology, located above each of the goals, in the middle level of the stands.

Opening roof It is made of semitransparent polycarbonate (PTFE) on a steel structure imported from Europe.

Ten bands Both the inside and the outside of the stadium have ten gray bands representing the other nine sites of the 2010 World Cup plus Berlin, site of the 2006 Cup final.

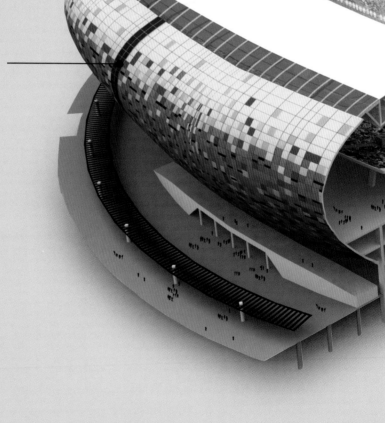

Nelson Mandela Soccer City passed into history in 1990 when it hosted the first speech of the South African leader after liberation from apartheid.

Parking It has private underground parking with 4,000 places, plus 15,000 public parking spaces in the surrounding area.

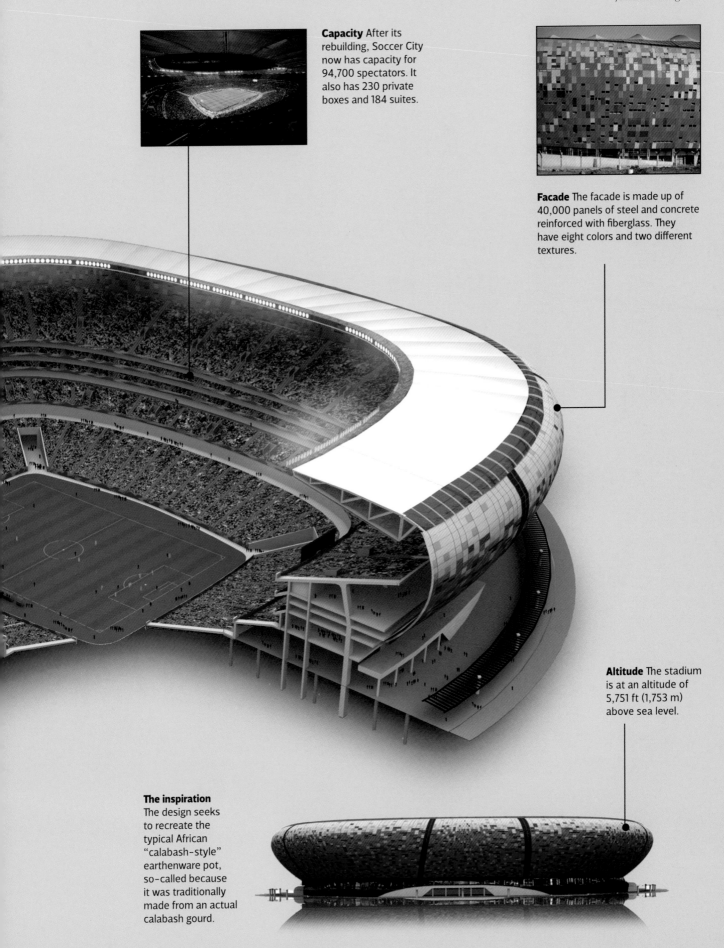

Capacity After its rebuilding, Soccer City now has capacity for 94,700 spectators. It also has 230 private boxes and 184 suites.

Facade The facade is made up of 40,000 panels of steel and concrete reinforced with fiberglass. They have eight colors and two different textures.

Altitude The stadium is at an altitude of 5,751 ft (1,753 m) above sea level.

The inspiration The design seeks to recreate the typical African "calabash-style" earthenware pot, so-called because it was traditionally made from an actual calabash gourd.

MUMBAI

Colonial India

The historic Victorian buildings with touches of local architecture stand out in the urban complex of Mumbai.

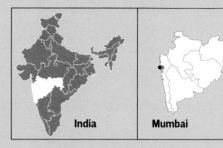

India   Mumbai

The island
Originally seven islands, today Mumbai is one single island separated from the mainland by narrow maritime canals which enclose a large bay and a natural deepwater port.

Extended area
ELEPHANTA ISLAND
MUMBAI
MALABAR HILL
N

Towers of Silence

The Parsi community leave their dead out in the open in these special circular buildings located on the Malabar hill, to the west of Mumbai, so that the vultures can eat their flesh. The Parsi religion, based on the doctrines of Zarathustra, says that corpses are impure elements that should not contaminate the earth, and they do not bury them until there is nothing left but bones.

TOWERS OF SILENCE

MUMBAI HIGH COURT

UNIVERSITY OF BOMBAY

4

1

Taj Mahal Palace Hotel
Located near the Gateway of India, this hotel occupies a luxurious building constructed in a blend of Moorish and European design, and inaugurated in 1903.

2

Gateway of India
Built in 1924 in honor of King George V, this basalt triumphal arch in Indo-Gothic style welcomes visitors who arrive in Mumbai by boat.

3

Prince of Wales Museum
The Chhatrapati Shivaji Museum, previously known as the Prince of Wales Museum, exhibits a large collection of Indian art from all epochs.

⊕ KEY FACTS ABOUT MUMBAI

CAPITAL OF THE STATE OF MAHARASHTRA
Located in western India, on the shore of the Arabian Sea, Mumbai (formerly known as Bombay) is the capital of the Indian state of Maharashtra.

LOCATION
Latitude
18° 57' 0" N
Longitude
72° 49' 0" E

Altitude
36 ft (11 m) above sea level

IN FIGURES
Surface area
175 mi² (603 km²)
Population
12,500,000
(20.51 million in the metropolitan area)
Population density
71,429/mi²
(20,694/km²)

FOUNDATION
Foundation date
1626

Founders
British colonists

A British commercial colony
Inhabited since prehistoric times, the seven islands of the region of Mumbai were occupied by the Portuguese in the 16th century, then conquered by the British in 1626, who established their first commercial port here.

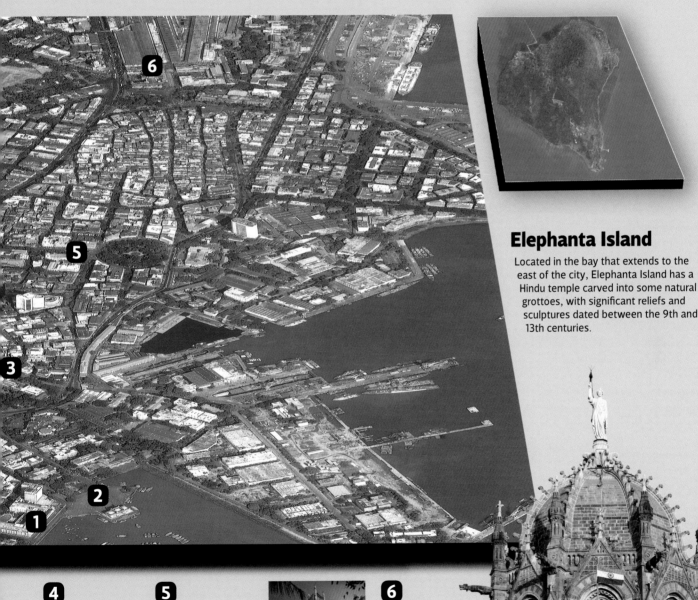

Elephanta Island

Located in the bay that extends to the east of the city, Elephanta Island has a Hindu temple carved into some natural grottoes, with significant reliefs and sculptures dated between the 9th and 13th centuries.

4
Hutatma Chowk Square
Located in the Fort area, the original location of the British colonial fortress, this square contains the 1869 monumental Flora Fountain.

5
St. Thomas Cathedral
Consecrated in 1718, this Anglican church is the city's oldest colonial building. It combines Gothic and neoclassical styles and has a tower added in 1838.

6
Victoria Terminus
Built between 1878 and 1888, the station of Chhatrapati Shivaji is one of the most representative buildings of Mumbai.

The union of two cultures

A city of contrasts, and a direct heir of the British Empire, today Mumbai is the cultural and economic capital of India.

It was the jewel of British colonization and at the same time the home of Gandhi, father of Indian independence, for more than 30 years. It is the home of the richest businesses in the country, but at the same time one-third of the inhabitants live in miserable shacks, or even actually in the street. It is the most European capital of the subcontinent, but at the same time one of its hills is the location for ancient funeral rites that remain shocking for Europeans. Mumbai is without a doubt a city of great contrasts.

Covered by the sea

Looking at its size and its population (with more than 20 million inhabitants, it is the second most populous city in India and the ninth most populous on the planet) it seems miraculous that up until less than 200 years ago most of the territory of today's city was covered by the sea. When the British disembarked for the first time in the 17th century, the area was made up of seven small islands located off a swampy coast in the Arabian Sea. The colonists were looking for a natural deepwater harbor which could serve as a port for trade entry and exit between the metropolitan power and the colony, and they found it there, thus starting a long process of uniting the islands with artificial isthmuses, then draining the interior lagoon.

The excellent conditions of the port (which currently has 40 percent of India's foreign commercial traffic) allowed the city to grow exponentially, from the 10,000 inhabitants of 1661 to 100,000 in 1764. The opening of the Suez Canal in 1869 accented Mumbai's strategic importance, which initiated a long period of magnificence, whose fruits we can admire today: the impressive historicist buildings from that period, like the enormous railroad terminal of Chhatrapati Shivaji, the Prince of Wales Museum, and the University of Mumbai.

The city of Gandhi

Despite being the official capital of British rule in Asia and undisputed jewel of the empire, Mumbai paved the way at the beginning of the 20th century with the first movements of independence for India. After his return from his long exile in South Africa, Mahatma Gandhi settled in Mumbai in 1915, where he lived for the next 30 years. It was from the Gowalia Tank Maidan of Mumbai on August 8, 1942 where he launched his message of civil disobedience based on passive resistance, which culminated five years later in independence.

The departure of the British, which paradoxically ended on February 28, 1948 with the embarkation of the last troops from the Gateway of India—the monument that they themselves had built and baptized a quarter of a century previously to receive newcomers from the ruling power—could not remove the colonial stamp from the city. Even today you can see the double-decker buses inherited from London in the streets, and St. Thomas Cathedral, the oldest colonial building

1. Dhobi Ghat
Some 200 people work in these open-air laundries, washing clothes for hospitals, hotels, and companies.

2. Dabbawala
In Mumbai there are thousands of these delivery men who take food to their customers at their workplace.

3. Juhu Beach
This is one of the city's most popular and crowded beaches, with many bars and restaurants.

4. Caves on Elephanta Island
The temple carved into this island occupies an area of 60,278 ft^2 (5,600 m^2) with three chambers, patios, and secondary sanctuaries.

5. Bollywood
Movie posters are everywhere in Mumbai, which produces more than 800 movies per year.

6. Prince of Wales Museum
Victorian architecture is found everywhere in Mumbai, and this museum is one of the most beautiful examples.

surviving in Mumbai, continues to serve the Christian community, which with a share of 4 percent forms part of the city's complex religious universe (which has been the origin of numerous conflicts and terrorist attacks over recent decades) together with: Hindus (68 percent), Muslims (19 percent) and significant minorities of Jains, Buddhists, Jews, Sikhs, and Parsis. The Parsees, followers of the prophet Zarathustra, are the builders of the horrifying Tower of Silence, which stands on Malabar Hill, to the west of the city, where cadavers are eaten by vultures in order for the souls to be liberated from their impure bodies.

This extraordinary search for eternity contrasts with the happy and rather superficial beat from the Bollywood movies, with their popular musical numbers. Surpassing its famous Californian predecessor in numbers, the huge film industry of Mumbai (the birthplace of Rudyard Kipling and Salman Rushdie) is one of the foundations of the area's economic and cultural boom, confirmed in recent years by the rise of a large local company, Tata Motors, whose successful international expansion has allowed it to take a kind of revenge against the old colonial power by acquiring two such powerful British symbols as Jaguar and Land Rover.

Victoria Terminus

This railroad station, completed in 1888, is one of the best examples of British colonial architecture in India.

Dome It has eight decorated ribs and is crowned by a 12-ft (4-m) high statue symbolizing progress.

Synthesis of two cultures The building was designed by English architect Frederick William Stevens, though local craftsmen also worked on its construction. This makes Chhatrapati Shivaji Terminus, as it was renamed in 1996, an example of the synthesis of the two cultures.

Sculptures The moldings of the windows, the trellises, and the friezes have reliefs and stone sculptures that are intricately worked. They represent figures of animals.

Interior It is covered by a vault with wooden beams, decorated by colored tiles, iron grilles, and stained-glass windows with images copied from nature.

Ornamentation The building, made of stone, granite, and marble, is in Victorian neo-Gothic style, with elements of traditional Indian architecture.

Entrance A lion and a tiger sculpted in stone, symbols respectively of Great Britain and India, decorate the pillars of the main entrance of the station.

Transit This railroad station handles more passengers than any other station in India. Some three million people a day pass through the station. It also houses the offices of the Indian Railways.

BEIJING

From the empire to Mao

The historic center of Beijing grew around Tiananmen Square, the heart of the Chinese capital, and the Forbidden City.

China | Historic center of Beijing

Dongcheng district

Located at the heart of historical Beijing, Dongcheng is an attractive neighborhood with bustling streets, such as Wangfujing, and is home to many tourist attractions, such as the Forbidden City and Tiananmen Square. East of Dongcheng is Guomao, the central business district which has become the city's new financial hub.

The Forbidden City

Built between 1406 and 1420 at the orders of the Yongle emperor, the third emperor of the Ming dynasty, the Forbidden City was the imperial Chinese palace for 500 years. Today, it is visited for its uniqueness and the museum that houses objects and works of art from the entire period.

Hall of Supreme Harmony

Bridges of the Five Virtues

There are five bridges that cross the moat which surrounds the palace; each one symbolizes one of the virtues of Confucianism.

Noon Gate

From his balcony, the emperor would survey his army and observe the gates.

BEIJING

Extended area

PACIFIC OCEAN

BEIHAI

1

2

3

KEY FACTS ABOUT BEIJING

CAPITAL OF CHINA
Beijing is the historic and current capital of China, serving as such during both the Imperial and Republic periods, although it lost the privilege to Nanjing on a number of occasions.

LOCATION
Latitude 39° 54' 0" N
Longitude 16° 23' 0" E
Altitude
171 ft (52 m) above sea level

IN FIGURES
Surface area 6,487 mi² (16,801 km²)
Population
17,400,000
Population density
2,682/mi²
(1,035/km²)

FOUNDATION
Foundation date 1272
Founder
Kublai Khan
Origins
There is evidence of urban settlements around Beijing that date back over 3,000 years. In 1215, the emperor Genghis Khan conquered the area which then became part of the Mongol Empire. In 1272, his grandson, Kublai Khan consolidated the city, naming it Khanbaliq ("city of the Khan"), consolidating it with the intention of converting it into the capital of the Chinese Empire.

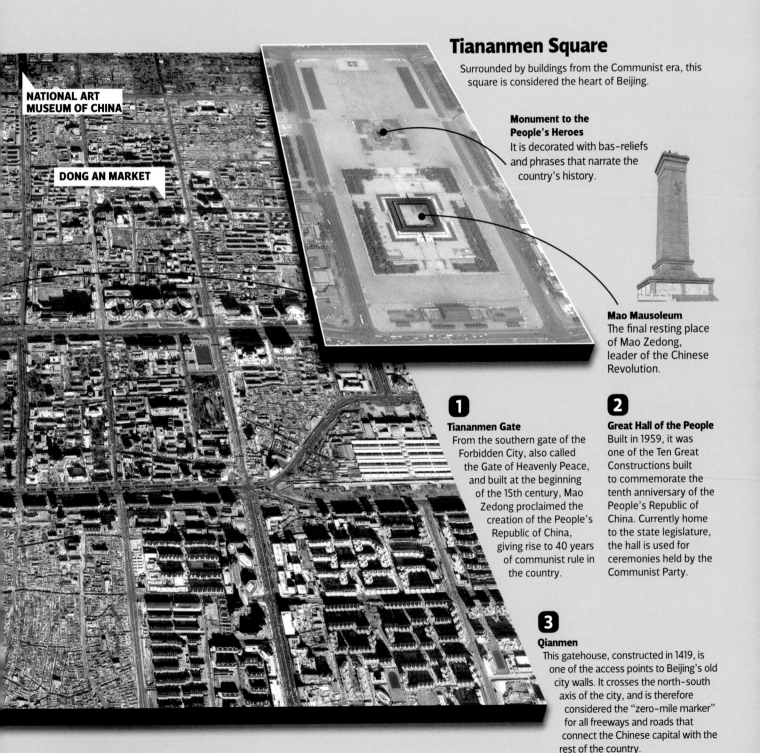

NATIONAL ART MUSEUM OF CHINA

DONG AN MARKET

Tiananmen Square

Surrounded by buildings from the Communist era, this square is considered the heart of Beijing.

Monument to the People's Heroes
It is decorated with bas-reliefs and phrases that narrate the country's history.

Mao Mausoleum
The final resting place of Mao Zedong, leader of the Chinese Revolution.

1 Tiananmen Gate
From the southern gate of the Forbidden City, also called the Gate of Heavenly Peace, and built at the beginning of the 15th century, Mao Zedong proclaimed the creation of the People's Republic of China, giving rise to 40 years of communist rule in the country.

2 Great Hall of the People
Built in 1959, it was one of the Ten Great Constructions built to commemorate the tenth anniversary of the People's Republic of China. Currently home to the state legislature, the hall is used for ceremonies held by the Communist Party.

3 Qianmen
This gatehouse, constructed in 1419, is one of the access points to Beijing's old city walls. It crosses the north-south axis of the city, and is therefore considered the "zero-mile marker" for all freeways and roads that connect the Chinese capital with the rest of the country.

Among temples and skyscrapers

Despite the breathtaking urban development of recent years, it is still possible to find tributes to Beijing's past.

Beijing, the historic capital of China since the start of the 15th century, boasts a unique urban and architectural heritage which has been preserved throughout the centuries, despite the significant political changes that the country has undergone. In recent years this heritage is being updated by skyscrapers and wide avenues that are writing a new chapter in the city's history.

Beijing is, without a doubt, one of the great metropolises of human history. The city owes its existence to Kublai Khan, who ordered construction of the city in 1272, having been conquered 60 years before by his grandfather Genghis Khan. The idea was to convert the area into the capital of the Chinese Empire, given its northern location, a position that allowed the emperor to be close to his homeland, Mongolia, as well as being at the center of the empire that expanded from the Pacific coast of Asia to the shores of the Danube in Europe. The city was originally given the name Khanbaliq ("city of the Khan"); however, its current name, given by the third emperor of the Ming dynasty at the beginning of the 15th century, transmits the dichotomy between Beijing ("city of the North") and Nanjing ("city of the South"), which has served as the alternative capital of China on various occasions throughout history.

The splendor of the Ming dynasty

It was actually under the Ming dynasty empire, during the 15th century, that Beijing experienced its period of greatest splendor, and during which time the Forbidden City was built; the complex served as the palace of the emperors from 1420 until 1912. Located in the Dongcheng district, at the heart of Beijing, the Forbidden City is the

📷 **←Central Business District (CBD)**
The business hub located in the Chaoyang district, to the east of the city, is home to most foreign companies and embassies.

↙Temple of Heaven
Built in 1420, this complex was a center of prayer where locals would give thanks following the harvest.

↓Tiananmen Square
A monument that represents the farmers, workmen, and soldiers, located across from the Mao Mausoleum, in Tiananmen Square.

largest palace on earth. It occupies an area equivalent to almost 100 football fields, on which there are almost 1,000 buildings, mostly constructed using wood in the traditional Chinese style. Its name derives from the fact that nobody was allowed to pass through its four gates without the emperor's permission.

Despite Puyi, the final emperor, having been removed from power over a century ago, the imperial palace – which was converted into a museum in 1925 – continues to occupy an important place, both physically and spiritually, at the heart of Beijing. Thus, not even the Communist revolution that resulted in the creation of the People's Republic of China in 1949 was able to touch this remnant of Oriental feudalism.

Modernization

With a view to building a financial district from scratch that was befitting of the major multinationals they aimed to attract, Communist Party leaders promoted the use of street planning involving wide avenues flanked by

skyscrapers to house luxury offices and accommodation. The economic boom allowed many families to replace their bicycle, a symbol of private transportation in China for decades, with a car. The designers of the new Beijing publicized these neighborhoods as the culmination of traditional architecture, promising that they had been constructed following the rules of "feng shui," the local science which is based on placing everything in line with the cosmic order.

Despite the massive influx of migrants from rural areas in search of urban prosperity, the city's population is still homogeneous for the large part; the vast majority are of Han origin and speak Mandarin. Traditionally, Beijing locals consider themselves more discreet, austere, and hospitable than their Shanghai or Hong Kong counterparts. The increasing amount of traffic has burdened them with high pollution levels; however, their entrepreneurial and optimistic nature pushes them to value the positives of progress, while they ignore the setbacks that they face in their new-life circumstances.

📷
→ Summer Palace
Located in a spacious park 5 miles (12 km) from the center of Beijing, this palatial complex built in 1750 was named as a World Heritage site in 1998.

1. From the emperor to Mao
A portrait of Mao Zedong, father of the People's Republic, presides over the entrance to the Forbidden City.

2. Beijing Opera
The most famous of the 300 different varieties of Chinese opera.

3. The hutong
These areas of narrow streets and low-built houses are the strongholds of traditional Beijing.

4. Pedal power
Although the increase in the use of cars is threatening the traditional mode of transportation in Beijing, bicycles are still very popular.

5. National Center for the Performing Arts
Built from titanium and glass, this huge opera house was finished in 2007.

6. Incense burning
It is common to see incense burners at temples to accompany prayer.

The Forbidden City

Constructed between 1406 and 1421 by the Yongle emperor, this palatial complex was the pride of the Ming dynasty and the site of the imperial residence until 1912.

Supreme Harmony In this hall, the emperor held court to discuss matters of the utmost importance. Built on a marble base, and standing 113 ft (37.44 m) tall, it was the highest building in China for a number of centuries.

Figures The roofs are decorated with porcelain figures which served to drive away evil spirits.

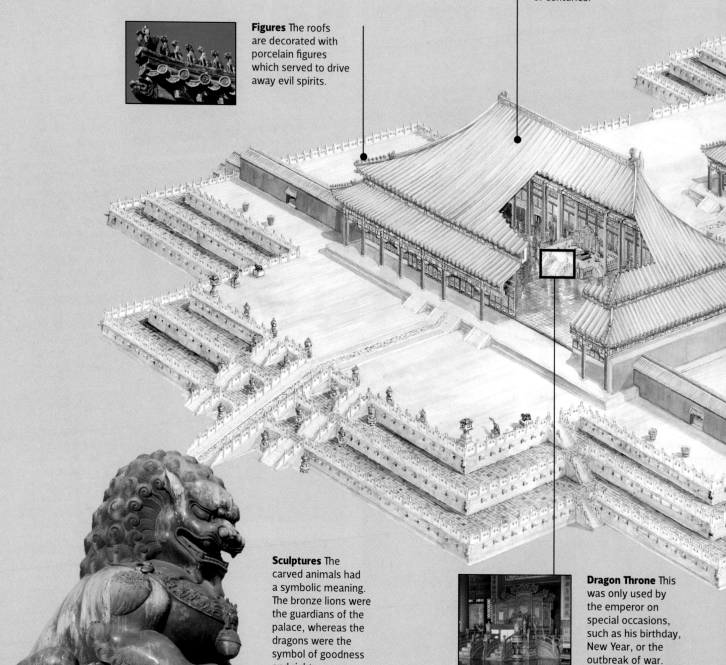

Sculptures The carved animals had a symbolic meaning. The bronze lions were the guardians of the palace, whereas the dragons were the symbol of goodness and righteousness.

Dragon Throne This was only used by the emperor on special occasions, such as his birthday, New Year, or the outbreak of war.

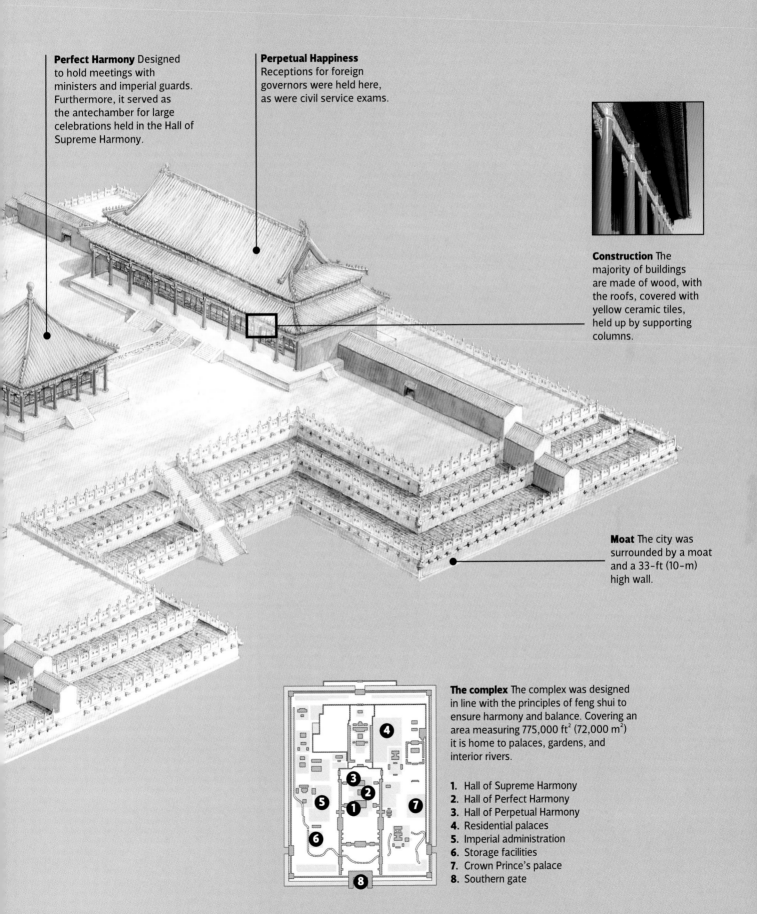

Perfect Harmony Designed to hold meetings with ministers and imperial guards. Furthermore, it served as the antechamber for large celebrations held in the Hall of Supreme Harmony.

Perpetual Happiness Receptions for foreign governors were held here, as were civil service exams.

Construction The majority of buildings are made of wood, with the roofs, covered with yellow ceramic tiles, held up by supporting columns.

Moat The city was surrounded by a moat and a 33-ft (10-m) high wall.

The complex The complex was designed in line with the principles of feng shui to ensure harmony and balance. Covering an area measuring 775,000 ft² (72,000 m²) it is home to palaces, gardens, and interior rivers.

1. Hall of Supreme Harmony
2. Hall of Perfect Harmony
3. Hall of Perpetual Harmony
4. Residential palaces
5. Imperial administration
6. Storage facilities
7. Crown Prince's palace
8. Southern gate

SEOUL

The Korean giant

The city center is located on the spot where the original settlement was created by the first emperors of the Joseon dynasty in the 14th century.

Gyeongbokgung Palace

This vast palatial complex was the main residence of the Joseon dynasty, which governed Korea from 1395 until 1910, over 600 years in total. It measures 0.2 mile^2 (0.5 km^2) over several buildings, among which are the Geunjeongjeon, the main hall used for official receptions, the palaces of the Queen and the Queen Mother, and the lotus-flower pool.

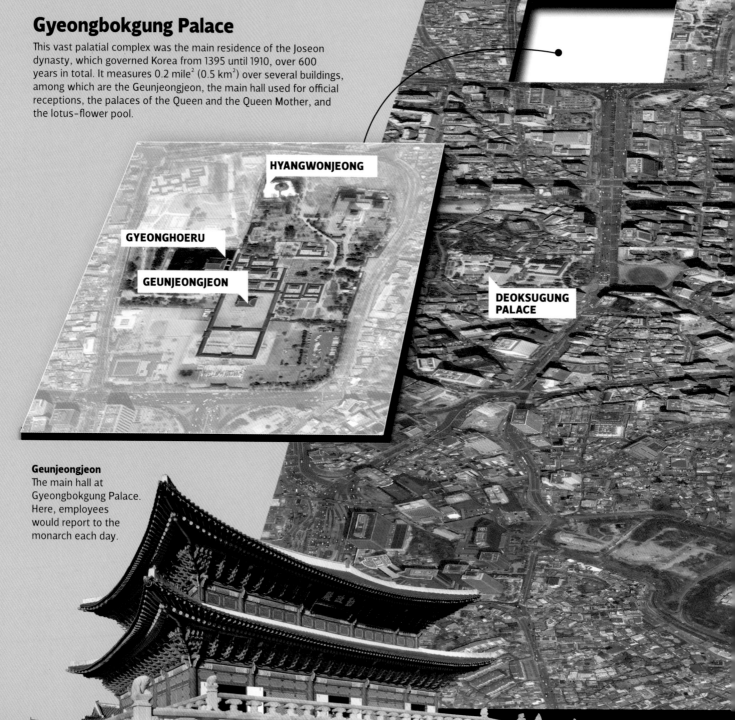

South Korea

Seoul

HYANGWONJEONG

GYEONGHOERU

GEUNJEONGJEON

DEOKSUGUNG PALACE

Geunjeongjeon
The main hall at Gyeongbokgung Palace. Here, employees would report to the monarch each day.

⊕ KEY FACTS ABOUT SEOUL

CAPITAL OF KOREA
Seoul has been the
capital of Korea
for more than six
centuries, and is
currently the political
center of the Republic
of South Korea.

LOCATION
Latitude
34° 37' 0" N
Longitude
126° 58' 0" E
Altitude
285 ft (87 m) above
sea level

IN FIGURES
Surface area
234 mi² (605 km²)
Population
10,900,000
(24.5 million
in the metropolitan
area)

Population density
46,581/ mi²
(17,219/km²)
FOUNDATION
Foundation date
18 BC
Founder
Baekje Kingdom

Historic capital
During the year 18 BC,
the Baekje Kingdom
constructed its capital
in the area currently
occupied by Seoul.
Almost 14 centuries later,
in 1394, the first emperor

of the Joseon dynasty
installed his court in
Seoul, baptizing it
Gyeongseong; the
name that is still
used by the Chinese
to refer to the 14th-
century city.

Extended
area

SEOUL

Insa-dong neighborhood

Located in the central district
of Jongno-gu, the Insa-dong
neighborhood features a street
of the same name which is full
of local restaurants, tea-
houses, and antique shops
and is closed off to traffic on
Sundays.

1 Unhyeongung

Built in the 14th century, this royal palace was home to the prince
regent Daewongun, father of emperor Gojong in the 19th century.
Some original buildings have been preserved, and the palace has
been restored following its acquisition by the government.

2 Jogyesa

Chief temple of the Jogye
order, this Buddhist temple
was originally built in 1395,
at the same time as the
establishment of the
Joseon dynasty; however,
the current building was
built in 1910.

3 Jongno Tower

Opened in 1999,
this skyscraper
stands 433 ft (132
m) high, and
was designed
by Uruguayan
architect
Rafael Viñoly.

4 Bosingak

Built in 1396 and rebuilt in 1895,
this bell pavilion—which served to
mark the time at which the city's
walls opened and closed—gave
the neighborhood its name,
Jongno, as in ancient Korean
this translates to "bell street."

SEOUL TOWER

Past meets future

Seoul treads a line between the deep-rooted ancestral customs of the Korean people and the futurist modernity of its large-scale technology companies.

Its heart remains loyal to the comfortable security of tradition, whereas its head is permanently looking toward the future. There is no other city on earth in which such a radical contrast between the past and the future can be seen. The transformation of South Korea into a major economic power in recent decades has seen its capital become one of the greatest megacities on earth, but the veneration of the ancestral customs of this nation, able to survive among the giants, forced leaders and local businesses to respect the past while taking this great step.

South Korea's GDP is among the 15th highest in the world. And Seoul is the third largest city on earth, surpassed only by Tokyo and Mexico City, and economically speaking, the sixth most powerful. The Korean capital is home to major multinational electronics companies, such as LG and Samsung—the world leader of the competitive cell-phone industry—and internationally renowned car manufacturers, such as the Hyundai group, which in addition to its commendable performance in the automotive sector, is also a world leader in the shipping industry.

This great economic push stems from the good use of the considerable external support received from the U.S. and Japan at the end of the bloody Korean War (1950–53), a conflict which has left an impression on the contemporary Korean mentality and which can be recalled by visiting Seodaemun Prison or the National War Museum. This economic push was underpinned by first rate education—occasionally rated by the international community as being too harsh on children —and South Korea's laborious efforts to emerge from the 1970s, in just a short number of years, from being

an agrarian economy to the industrial powerhouse it has become today. This radical transformation resulted in a mass influx of migrants from rural areas to Seoul; consequently, the historic center of the city was quickly enveloped by vast residential districts.

Today, the relatively old and ethnically homogeneous population—there are very few foreigners involved in the production system currently in place in South Korea— despite its workaholic ethic, maintains a philosophy inherited from various generations of rural existence. Seoul's residents preserve certain attitudes that would be considered chauvinistic by the West and pay a great deal of attention to their status and that of their relatives. Disrepute, regardless of the motive, is the scourge most feared by Koreans, who grant strangers the utmost respect and reverence. They make a significant effort to be friendly and pleasant in all social relationships, even during infrequent periods of exhaustion or bad humor.

Historic palaces and skyscrapers

The historic capital of South Korea since the kings of the Joseon dynasty made it the seat of governement in 1394. Seoul emerged on the northern shore of the Han

⬅⬅Royal Guard
The changing of the guard ceremony at Deoksugung Palace takes place three times a day, and is one of the most popular tourist attractions.
⬅Namdaemun Market
Founded in 1964 and located in the center of the city, this is the largest traditional market in the country.
⬇Changdeokgung Palace
Ancient palaces and modern skyscrapers live side by side in the South Korean capital.

River, which meanders between various hills on which the majority of the city's historic palaces are located, before ending in the Yellow Sea, a number of miles downstream, across from the shores of China, Korea's giant and influential neighbor. The original heart of the city, where the modern-day district of Jung-gu stands, is where many tourist attractions, the offices of major companies, the best hotels, and traditional markets are located. Dongdaemun Market, at which the excellent Korean gastronomy and traditional ginseng tea can be sampled, is worth a special mention.

Between Jung-gu (literally meaning Central District) and the river is the popular neighborhood of Itaewon, the largest shopping and leisure area in the city. Facing it, separated by a narrow canal, is Yeouido Island which houses the National Assembly and the country's main financial institutions. Outside the city's main district are the more residential areas and traveling farther north, just 24 miles (40 km) away is the 38th Parallel, a demilitarized area separating North and South Korea. It is one of the most closely guarded borders in the world that, paradoxically, divides the two irreconcilable halves of the peninsula that until 1948 formed just one country.

Bulguksa Temple

This surprising Buddhist temple located in Gyeongju, the ancient capital of the Silla Kingdom 143 miles (370 km) southeast of Seoul, has stood here for over three centuries.

Seokgatap stone pagoda This features basic shapes, representing masculinity, reflection, and isolation. Also known as the "shadowless pagoda," it measures 27 ft (8.2 m) in height.

Geuknakjeon or Hall of Supreme Bliss One of the most impressive parts of the temple, which houses the gilt-bronze Buddha, a national treasure.

Lotus Flower Bridge and Seven Treasures Bridge Leading to the Peace Enhancing Gate.

Main entrance The complex is accessed by a staircase with balustrades, called bridges, that leads to the Mauve Mist Gate (Jahamun), flanked by sculptures of colorful guardians.

Daeungjeon or Hall of no words The main building. It dates back to 681 and is dedicated to Shakyamuni Buddha.

Museoljeon or No-word Hall Symbolizes the teachings of Buddha that cannot be expressed in words. It is the oldest construction in the complex.

Dabotap stone pagoda Richly decorated, it represents femininity and the complexity of the world. Known as the "pagoda of many treasures," it measures 34 ft (10.4 m) in height.

TOKYO

Oriental might

Technology capital of the world, Tokyo also boasts real treasures of ancient Japanese culture.

Japan

Tokyo

Built on the sea

Few know that 40 percent of Tokyo's surface area is built on land reclaimed from the sea, and that the foundations of the area are blocks of pressed garbage, called "gomi" by the Japanese. With a view to limiting the effect of pollution in a metropolis that is home to 36 million people, the city has imposed strict recycling regulations.

PACIFIC OCEAN

TOKYO

Extended area

1

The Imperial Palace

The first shogun of the Tokugawa dynasty built his castle in 1590. His successors converted it into one of greatest palaces on earth and, since the mid-19th century, it has been the residence of the imperial family.

HIBIYA PARK

2

International Forum

Designed in 1966 by Uruguayan architect Rafael Viñoly, the International Forum is an emblematic cultural center in Tokyo. It comprises a curved glass-covered atrium in the shape of a boat, and a white-colored cubic building that houses four auditoriums, the largest of which has the capacity to hold up to 5,000 attendees.

3

Tsukiji Market

Fish is the star ingredient in Japanese gastronomy. Tsukiji Market is the largest fish market in the world, selling products by the traditional method of auctioning. Auctions are held every day between 5 and 10 am. The surrounding area is full of restaurants serving freshly prepared sushi.

NHK MUSEUM OF BROADCASTING

⊕ KEY FACTS ABOUT TOKYO

CAPITAL OF JAPAN
The city of Tokyo, the capital of Japan, consists of 23 wards and occupies a third of the total surface area of the metropolitan area.

LOCATION
Latitude
35° 42' 0" N
Longitude
139° 42' 0" E
Altitude
20 ft (6 m) above sea level

IN FIGURES
Surface area
845 mi² (2,187 km²).
5,234 mi² (13,556 km²) in the metropolitan area
Population
13,160,000

(36 million in the metropolitan area)
Population density
15,574/mi²
(6,016/km²)
FOUNDATION
Foundation date
1457

A Castle, the city's origin
It was in the year 1457 that Ota Dokan built Edo castle (Japanese for "estuary"), around which the city grew, becoming the capital

of Japan by 1603. In 1868, the emperor transferred his residence from Kyoto, at which time Edo became known as Tokyo (translating to "capital of the East").

Ginza district

The old silver coin factory ("ginza," in Japanese) that gave its name to this neighborhood was destroyed by fire in 1872. The reconstruction project was awarded to British architect Thomas Waters; only a few remains of his buildings are still visible. Today, it is one of the best theater, shopping, and restaurant districts in Tokyo.

Mitsukoshi department store
This classic and prestigious shopping center in the Ginza neighborhood maintains a distinguished atmosphere in which customers still to this day dress in their finest to visit. It houses a lavish kimono department.

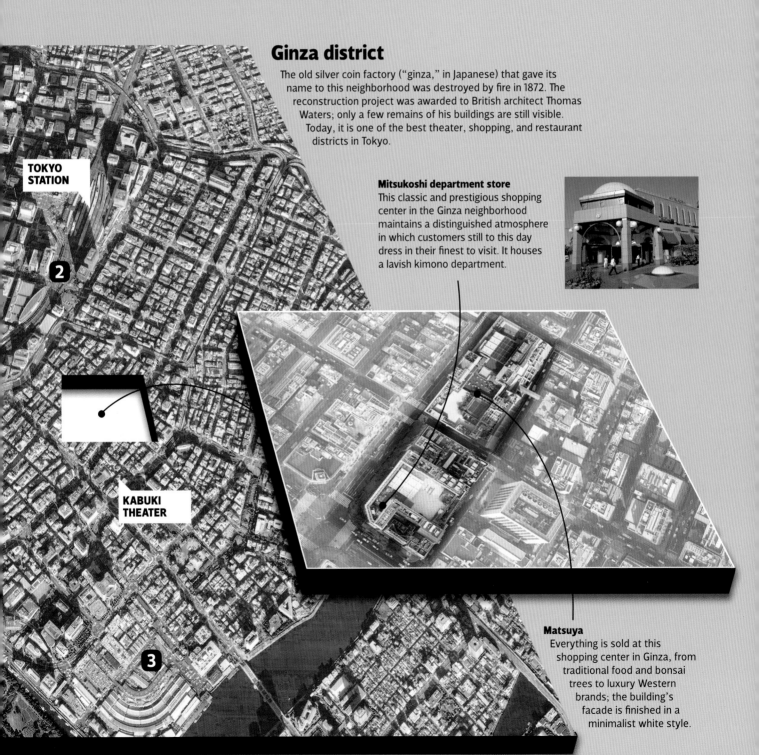

TOKYO STATION

2

KABUKI THEATER

3

Matsuya
Everything is sold at this shopping center in Ginza, from traditional food and bonsai trees to luxury Western brands; the building's facade is finished in a minimalist white style.

The Japanese miracle

Built on the dangerous Pacific Ring of Fire, the largest city on earth is an extremely powerful economic center.

At first glance, you wouldn't expect to find many similarities between Tokyo and Canada. Located on opposite sides of the Pacific Ocean, both enjoy a high standard of living and high development indices. Yet that's not all: Tokyo, the most populous metropolitan area on earth, has 36 million inhabitants... exactly the same number as the whole of Canada, the second largest country on earth, with a surface area 740 times greater than the Japanese capital. And the similarities don't end there: Canada—a major mining, agricultural and industrial power occupies 13th place in the ranking of countries by GDP, the same spot that Tokyo would occupy were it an independent country.

These simple pieces of information are enough to demonstrate the economic and social magnitude of the Japanese capital, which has become, thanks to its dynamism and modernity, a genuine laboratory for land planning, environmental, and transportation policies. Furthermore, it is a melting pot for interesting social phenomena that are really typical of the city; take the endless number of urban groups that can be seen on the traffic-filled streets, from decor or oshare kei youths (who dress childishly), and cosplay fanatics (who dress to represent a specific character, especially from the manga comics), to those who wave the flag of sexual abstinence and say "no" to marriage in an ethnically homogeneous society. The locals here tread a fine line between Western lifestyles during the week and sacred Japanese traditions on public holidays.

Historic capital

Founded in 1457 following the construction of Edo castle on a bay to the east of Honshu island, Tokyo has been the capital of Japan since 1603. However, the emperor maintained his residence in Kyoto until the mid-19th century, when the imperial palace was transferred to the central neighborhood of Chiyoda, in Tokyo.

The city's location, on the Pacific Ring of Fire, has contributed to its turbulent history. In 1657, 100,000 residents died as a result of a deadly fire that swept through an area of wooden houses. In 1707, Tokyo suffered at the hand of Mount Fuji, which rises 12,388 ft (3,776 m) above the southeast of the city, just 39 miles (63 km) away. Then, in 1855 and 1923, earthquakes resulted in widespread panic and the destruction of the Japanese capital. In addition, in 1942 and 1945, bombs dropped by the Allied forces wreaked havoc on the city. Therefore, it is understandable that Tokyo is a city undergoing constant reconstruction and that its center, which was left relatively unscathed by the 2011 tsunami, preserves very little evidence of older, traditional architecture, other than the palaces and temples for which there are always funds to support their restoration.

Equally, it is not so strange that the city's residents have learned to understand precisely what to do when the earth shakes. The obvious dangers of the active geological formations in the region, unite the well-

←The monorail
The city is covered by more than 70 subway and railroad lines. The overhead monorail that connects the airport to the Minato district was inaugurated in 1964.

↓Meiji Shrine
This Shinto sanctuary dedicated to Emperor Meiji was finalized in 1920 and is home to a large forest, used as an area for both rest and recreation.

↓↓Tsukiji Market
The largest fish market on earth is home to 1,700 fish and seafood stalls.

known discipline of the locals; an extremely useful quality for such difficult circumstances. Accustomed to sharing small spaces, Tokyoites always put the community before themselves and rarely dare to express personal opinions that are at odds with widely accepted views... unless a little sake has helped them to loosen up. The traditional Japanese rice liquor is even capable of making locals spend the night singing off-key karaoke in one of the nightclubs in the Roppongi district.

The great Asian metropolis
The aforementioned discipline was a decisive factor in Tokyo becoming the launchpad for the so-called Japanese miracle between 1950 and 1980: an economy destroyed by the War of the Pacific which rose from the ashes to become the second largest world power. The enormous wave of immigration generated by prosperity gave Tokyo – home to major electronics and automotive multinationals such as Sony, Toshiba, Hitachi, Honda, Nissan, Mitsubishi, Canon, Nikon, Ricoh, and TDK – the status of the most populous city on earth before, at the end of the 1980s, the financial and property bubble burst, and left the country falling into what is known by locals as "the lost decade," a crisis from which they had barely managed to escape by the turn of the century.

Senso-ji Temple

The origins of this Buddhist temple dedicated to Kannon, the goddess of mercy, date back to AD 645. It enjoyed its greatest period of splendor during the Edo period.

Okoro In front of the main building there is a large incense burner. It is said that the smoke strengthens the weak and cures the sick.

Pagoda With five floors and standing at 210 ft (64 m) high, the pagoda was built in 942 and then rebuilt in 1648, in the same style as the Treasury Gate and the main temple.

Hozomon Built in 912, the Treasury Gate houses Buddhist objects and a large red lantern. It was rebuilt after its destruction during the bombing raids of World War II.

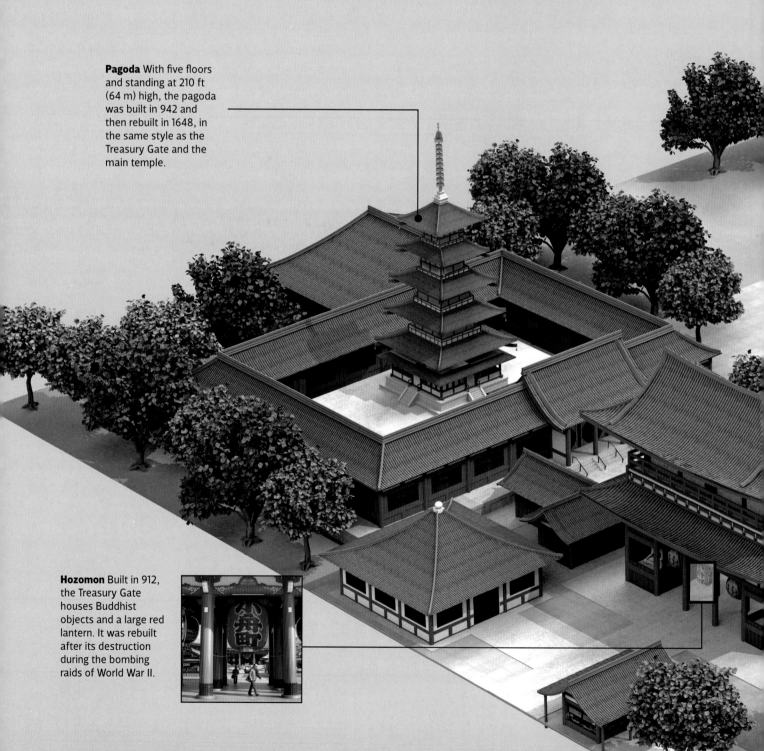

Kannondo The current appearance of the main building follows a 1958 reconstruction of the 17th-century temple built during the Edo period. It is divided into an external shrine (gejin) and an internal shrine (naijin).

Kannon Bodhisattva In the middle of the internal shrine is a statue of Kannon Bodhisattva which, according to legend, was found in the 7th century by three fishermen who kept it a secret. A replica is displayed to the public every December 13.

Kaminarimon The Thunder Gate is the first entrance to the site and dates from the Edo period. It then opens out onto a 820-ft (250-m) long passageway, Nakamise-dori, filled with shops and food stalls, which leads to Hozomon, the main door to the complex.

Index of photographs

Photography AGE Fotostock: 8-9, 21 (r), 26-27, 31 (up), 31 (d), 34-35, 39 (up), 39 (3), 42-43, 46, 47 (d), 50-51, 54-55, 55 (m), 55 (d), 64, 65 (3 y 6), 68-69, 73 (m), 80-81 (d), 80-81 (up), 81 (up/m), 81 (up/r), 82, 82-83, 86-87, 90-91, 91 (all), 99 (4), 102-103, 110-111, 114-115, 115 (2, 4, 5, 6), 122, 123 (3, 5, 6), 126-127, 138 (d), 139 (up), 139 (m), 139 (d), 142-143, 146-147, 147 (d), 150-151, 154 (d), 155 (d), 158-159, 162-163, 163 (d), 166-167, 170-171, 171 (m), 174-175, 178-179, 179 (up), 179 (m), 179 (r), 182-183, 186, 187 (up), 187 (d), 190-191, 195 (2, 3, 5, 6), 198-199, 202-203, 203 (m), 211 (m), 214-215, 222-223, 227 (2, 5), 234-235 (up), 234-235 (d), 235 (r), 236, 237 (2, 5), 240-241, 245 (up), 248-249, 252-253, 253 (m), 253 (d); Getty Images: 47 (up), 62-63 (d), 76-77, 83 (r), 123 (4), 130, 211 (d), 218, 219 (abajo), 226-227; Thinkstock: 12-13, 13 (m), 47 (m), 65 (5), 98-99, 99 (2, 3), 107 (d), 115 (3), 147 (m), 154 (up), 237 (3); Cordon Press/Cubo Images: 16-17, 23 (d), 73 (up), 134-135, 203 (d), 227 (6), 230-231, 237 (l), 237 (4), 244; Cordon Press/Corbis: 6-7, 13 (d), 20-21 (up), 20-21 (d), 22, 23 (up), 23 (2), 23 (3), 30, 38-39, 39 (4), 39 (5), 39 (d), 58-59, 62-63 (up), 63 (r), 65 (1, 2, 4), 72, 73 (d), 94-95, 106-107, 107 (up), 107 (m), 118-119, 123 (l), 131 (up), 131 (d), 138 (up), 155 (up), 163 (m), 171 (d), 194-195, 195 (4), 206-207, 210, 211 (up), 219 (up), 227 (3, 4), 237 (6), 245 (d).